Giving is a Blessing

D. H. Stamatis, Ph.D.

Giving is a Blessing
It is more blessed to give than to receive (Acts 20:35)

D. H. Stamatis, Ph.D.
**Protopsaltis at the Annunciation Cathedral,
Metropolis of Detroit, MI
Professor of Management and Statistics at ANHUI Economics and
Finance University, Bengbu China; International Consultant in
Quality and Reliability**

XULON PRESS

Xulon Press
2301 Lucien Way #415
Maitland, FL 32751
407.339.4217

www.xulonpress.com

© 2021 by D. H. Stamatis, Ph.D.

All rights reserved solely by the author. The author guarantees all contents are original and do not infringe upon the legal rights of any other person or work. No part of this book may be reproduced in any form without the permission of the author. The views expressed in this book are not necessarily those of the publisher.

Unless otherwise indicated, Scripture quotations taken from the Amplified Bible (AMP). Copyright © 1954, 1958, 1962, 1964, 1965, 1987 by The Lockman Foundation. Used by permission. All rights reserved.

Scripture quotations taken from the English Standard Version (ESV). Copyright © 2001 by Crossway, a publishing ministry of Good News Publishers. Used by permission. All rights reserved.

Scripture quotations taken from the Holy Bible, New International Version (NIV). Copyright © 1973, 1978, 1984, 2011 by Biblica, Inc.™. Used by permission. All rights reserved.

Scripture quotations taken from the New King James Version (NKJV). Copyright © 1982 by Thomas Nelson, Inc. Used by permission. All rights reserved.

Scripture quotations taken from New Life Version (NLV). Copyright © 1969 by Christian Literature International.

NT New Testament (The Greek New Testament is the authorized 1904 text of the Ecumenical Patriarchate of Constantinople. It was retrieved from: http://onlinechapel.goarch.org/biblegreek/?id=0&book=Matt
OT Old Testament LXX (Elpenor's Bilingual (Greek / English) Old Testament, by L.C.L. Brenton from: https://www.ellopos.net/elpenor/greek-texts/septuagint/

Printed in the United States of America

Paperback ISBN-13: 978-1-6628-0559-2
Hard Cover ISBN-13: 978-1-6628-0560-8
Ebook ISBN-13: 978-1-6628-0577-6

Table of Contents

Dedication 5
Icons/Pictures/Sketches 6
Acknowledgments 7
Acronyms 8
Special explanations 9
Preface 11
    What the Bible says about selfishness 20
    Bible verses about helping others 21
    What Jesus taught us about generosity 22
    What it means to be generous in everyday life 23
Introduction 28
    Giving is important 28
    Principles of Giving from the Parable of the Talents 31
    Conclusion 37

Chapter 1: Stewards versus owners 41
    Stewards are grateful and content 41
    Stewards give willingly 41
    Stewards can enjoy blessings 42
    Stewards realize work is a gift 42

Chapter 2: Connecting to God through giving 52
    Never enough 65

Chapter 3: Tithing in a historical context 76
    Where do we stand 87
    Orthodox Christian stewardship 87

Chapter 4: How giving makes one joyful 90
    10 Essential Truths about Christian Giving 98

Chapter 5: God's giving promises 103

Chapter 6: Stewardship of the money we do not give 118
    How to live below our means 122

Chapter 7: Learning and teaching stewardship 127

Chapter 8: First Fruits 141
    A short guide to understanding First Fruits Offering 146
    Understanding the full significance of God's "First Fruits" command 149
    First fruits and best fruits 163

Chapter 9: What does the Scripture say about Giving? 172
    An overview of giving as found in the Scriptures 172
    Specific Old Testament scriptures on tithing 176
    Specific New Testament scriptures on tithing? 181
    Living a generous life 186

Chapter 10: Offering versus Tithing ....…...188
    Membership 191

Appendix A: Melchizedek………………………………...193

Appendix B: A Classic example of giving:
The Samaritan Story ………………………………………197

Appendix C: Closing the loop on Tithes,
Festivals and Alms ………………………………………….215

Epilog ……………………………………………………….240

References ……………………….....………………………243
Selected Bibliography ……………………………………..249
About the author ……………………………………………250
Books by the same author ………………………………....251

Dedication

To all those who are concerned with giving and tithing.
God Bless you all

Icons/Photographs/sketches

Front cover: The High Priest and King of Salem – Melchizedeck
Inside cover: The Oblation (Prothesis) – The preparation Table. This is where our gifts of bread and wine are prepared for the consecration into the Body and Blood of Jesus Christ. This transformation takes place during the Great Anaphora of the Holy Liturgy.
P.1 Ruth meeting Boaz
Figure 1.1. The Maslow's pyramid of needs
Icon 2.1 The widow giving an offering
P.2.1 Three different examples of public recognition for giving: a) name on bricks; b) name on tree branches and c) name on a plaque (the most common)
Icon 2.2 The icon of St. Nectarios with a string of Tamata
Figure 6.1. A typical purse (πουγκί)
Back Cover: The contribution of the widow (Painting by: *William Teulon Blandford Fletcher*)

Special Note:

The following items are blurred on purpose to show anonymity and more importantly humbleness, compunction, giving with enthusiasm and without hesitation.

Icon 2.1 The widow giving an offering
P.2.1 Three different examples of public recognition for giving: a) name on bricks; b) name on tree branches and c) name on a plaque (the most common)
Icon 2.2 The icon of St. Nectarios with a string of Tamata. Notice the different colors. They are made from: Tin, aluminum, or silver and gold (plating) – No names are engraved. They are ALL placed in anonymity!
Back Cover: The contribution of the widow

Acknowledgements

No book has ever been written without any help or consultation from others. This book is no different. Many individuals have helped over the last two years and it will be impossible for me to give individual credit to everyone. However, some deserve a special thank you for their advice but also their enthusiasm for tackling such a sensitive subject.

I want to thank my Father Confessor John, who was both an inspirational coach but also a guide for my research to the Fathers of the Church.
I want to thank Mr. T. Mills for sowing the seed of the topic on giving. His perseverance to address the issue with sources from the Scriptures and Fathers was worth the effort.
I want to thank Fr. A. Boyd for giving me permission to use the material on Melchizedek found in the site: https://www.stbasil.com/news/2019/5/22/the-old-testament-melchizedek-showing-us-Jesus.
I want to thank Mr. J. Wisnewski for giving me permission to use some of his material on the "short guide to understand first fruits offering in https://get.tithe.ly/blog/first-fruit.
I want to thank Mr. M. Kerns for giving me permission to use some of his material on Tithes, Festivals and Alms being kind to the ungrateful" (October 4, 2015 in the site: https://www.stathanasius.org/services/.
I want to express my thank you and gratitude to A. Kalozoumi who every week would ask me how my project was coming along and what could he do to make things easier for me. His prayers, suggestions and enthusiasm were appreciated.
I also want to recognize Mr. C. X. for his editorial comments and suggestion for the layout of the book. Thanks Chris.
Finally, I want to thank my wife Carla, who passionately put up with me over the long hours in my library. Her suggestions and comments were greatly appreciated and became part of this book. She has proved to be a real trooper and support for this entire project.

Thanks to all of you, and may God bless you all.

Acronyms

AB	Amplified Bible. Sometimes is known as AMB
A.D.	Anno Domini, Latin for "in the year of the lord." After Christ
ANF	Ante-Nicene Fathers
ASV	American Standard Version
B.C.	Before Christ
c. or c.a.	It means circa. That is: around in the sense of "more or less" or "approximately"
cf	Abbreviation for the Latin word *confer*. It means compare or bring together
CUA	Catholic University of America Press. Quite often reported as CUP
CUP	Catholic University Press
ESV	English Standard Version
ff	Following pages
KJV	King James Version
LXX	The Official OT text of the Orthodox Church. It is called the Septuagint after the 72 scholars that Ptolemy assigned to translate the Jewish Scriptures
MIT	Multiple International Translation. It is related to NIV
NAF	Ante Nicene Fathers
NIV	New International Version
NKJV	New King James Version
NLT	New Living Translation
NPNF	Nicene and Post-Nicene Fathers
NPNF1	Nicene and Post-Nicene Fathers, 1st Series;
NPNF2	Nicene and Post-Nicene Fathers, 2nd Series
NT	New Testament
OT	Old Testament

Special explanations

Out of the 450 Scriptural translations, I have used primarily the NIV translation for most of the verses for its simplicity. However, where I have deviated from that translation, I have made a note of it. Two special comments here. My notation of the Psalms is in the form: 15(16). That means the Psalm is the 15th in the LXX Scripture but the 16th in the Masoretic text. Also: Kings I, Kings II, Kings III and Kings IV is in the LXX version. [Please notice that in III Kings chapters 20 and 21 are reversed. In the Septuagint chapter 20 is 21 in the Masoretic text. Chapter 21 in the Septuagint is 20 in the Masoretic. The fundamental difference is the emphasis. Septuagint emphasizes the Jezebel story in ch.20 and the story of Ahab in ch. 21]. The notation is also given in the Masoretic version which is Samuel I, Samuel II, Kings I and Kings II. When there is no separation the text is based on the Masoretic version.

I have used the text as presented in Elpenor's Bilingual (Greek / English) Old Testament English translation by L.C.L. Brenton which is the Septuagint (LXX) text and may be found in: https://www.ellopos.net/elpenor/greek-texts/septuagint/Default.asp.

Notice that the order of the Proverbs is different: Thus, we find the a) Masoretic 30:1–14 is after Septuagint Proverbs 24:22, b) Masoretic 30:15–31:9 is after Septuagint Proverbs 24:34 and c) Masoretic 31:10–31 is after Septuagint Proverbs 29:27.

Also, the numbering system of the Psalms is different and is shown here as:

Septuagint Numbering	Masoretic Numbering
1-8	1-8
9	9 and 10
10-112	11-113
113	114 and 115
114	116:1-9
115	116:10-19
116-145	117-146
146	147: 1-11
147	147: 12-20
148-150	148-150

All the NT verses are based on: *The Greek New Testament as authorized in 1904 by the Ecumenical Patriarchate of Constantinople.* It may be found in: http://onlinechapel.goarch.org/biblegreek/?id=16&book=Titus. The English translation is primarily the NIV version with other translations as noted in the text.

Preface

To appreciate the concept of giving, one must understand the POWER of God. That understanding is fundamentally based on at least 28 characteristics which are:

1. **Aseity** (The aseity of God means "God is so independent that He does not need us." It is based on Acts 17:25);
2. **Eternity** (The eternity of God concerns his existence beyond time. Drawing on verses such as Psalm 89(90):2. See also Rev. 1:8 (Alfa and omega));
3. **Goodness** (The goodness of God means that "God is the final standard of good, and all that God is and does is worthy of approval." Romans 11:22 in the King James Version says "Behold therefore the goodness and severity of God." Many theologians consider the goodness of God as an overarching attribute as including kindness, love, grace, mercy and longsuffering. The idea that God is "all good" is called his *omnibenevolence*);
4. **Graciousness** (The graciousness of God is a key tenet of Christianity. In Exodus 34:5-6, it is part of the Name of God, "Yahweh, Yahweh, the compassionate and gracious God);
5. **Holiness** (The holiness of God is that he is separate from sin and incorruptible. Noting the refrain of "Holy, holy, holy" in Isaiah 6:3 – here, is the ONLY place in scripture that a single attribute of God (Holy) is elevated to the point where it is mentioned three times. For example: God has never said that He is Love, Love, Love. See also Revelation 4:8);
6. **Immanence** (The immanence of God refers to him being in the world. It is thus contrasted with his transcendence, but Christian theologians usually emphasize that the two attributes are not contradictory. To hold to transcendence but not immanence is deism, while to hold to immanence but not transcendence is pantheism. Let us remember that the God of the Bible is no abstract deity removed from, and uninterested in his creation. Rather, the whole Bible "is the story of God's involvement with his creation." This is based on Acts 17:28, "in him we live and move and have our being);

7. **Immutability** (Immutability means God cannot change. There is constancy. James 1:17 refers to the "Father of the heavenly lights, who does not change like shifting shadows");
8. **Impeccability** (The impeccability of God is closely related to his holiness. It means that God is unable to sin, which is a stronger statement than merely saying that God does not sin. Hebrews 6:18 says that "it is impossible for God to lie");
9. **Incomprehensibility** (The incomprehensibility of God means that he is not able to be fully known. Isaiah 40:28 says "his understanding no one can fathom");
10. **Incorporeality** (The incorporeality or spirituality of God refers to him being a Spirit. This is derived from Jesus' statement in John 4:24, "God is Spirit);
11. **Infinity** (The infinity of God includes both his eternity and his immensity. Isaiah 40:28 says that "Yahweh is the everlasting God," while Solomon acknowledges in III Kings LXX (1 Kings) 8:27 that "the heavens, even the highest heaven, cannot contain you." Infinity permeates all other attributes of God: his goodness, love, power, *etc.* are all considered to be infinite);
12. **Jealousy** (Exodus 20:5-6, of the Decalogue says, "You shall not bow down to them or worship them; for I, the LORD your God, am a jealous God, punishing the children for the sin of the parents to the third and fourth generation of those who hate me, but showing love to a thousand generations of those who love me and keep my commandments" (NIV);
13. **Love** (1 John 4:8, 16 says "God is Love");
14. **Mission**; Mission is the divine activity of sending intermediaries, whether supernatural or human, to speak or do God's will so that his purposes for judgment or redemption are furthered. The biblical concept is expressed by the use of verbs meaning "to send," normally with God as the expressed subject. The Hebrew verb is salah (סָלַח) and the Greek is apostello [αποστελλω]. These terms emphasize the authoritative, commissioning relationship involved. The Scriptures also employ the cognates Apostolos [αποστολος] ("apostle," the one sent) and apostole [αποστολη] ("apostleship," the function of being sent), referring to the one sent and his function.

The biblical concept of "mission" comprehends the authority of the one who sends; the obedience of the one sent; a task to be accomplished; the power to accomplish the task; and a purpose within the moral framework of God's covenantal working of judgment or redemption.

- *Mission in the Old Testament.* The first records in biblical history of God's sending is his banishment of Adam and Eve from the garden and the angelic mission to destroy Sodom and Gomorrah (Gen 3:23; 19:13). The redemption from Egypt and the conquest of the land has its dark side: judgment on the idolatrous nations Israel escapes from or displaces. The emphasis, however, in the Pentateuchal accounts on mission centers on God's positive action. In securing a bride for Isaac and thus keeping the hope of the covenant promise alive for another generation, God sends his angel before Abraham's chief household servant to give him success on his journey (Genesis 24:7, 40). And in the fourth generation it is Joseph, as he says to his brothers, whom "God sent ahead of you to preserve for you a remnant on earth and to save your lives by a great deliverance" (45:7; cf. vv. 5, 8; Psalm 104(105):17). In Joseph's case, aside from prescient dreams in his youth (Gen 37:5-11), there was no specific call to mission. But he could look back on harmful circumstances and discern God's sending of him to Egypt to preserve the nation.
- *Mission in the Ministry of Jesus.* So significant is the redemptive mission of the Messiah, the Son of God, that God sends an angel not only to announce his birth (Luke 1:26), but to announce the birth of John the Baptist, the messenger who will be sent to prepare his way and introduce him (1:19; Matt 11:10; cf. Mark 1:2; Luke 7:27; John 1:6 John 1:33).

    Jesus had much to say about his own understanding of his mission. He saw his purpose as being sent by God his Father to proclaim and accomplish spiritual deliverance for humankind (Luke 4:43; John 3:34; 8:42; 10:36). He consciously appropriates Isaiah 61:1-2 as the Old Testament passage his ministry fulfills (Luke 4:18-19).

Jesus characterizes his mission as authenticated and sustained by the Father who sent him (John 5:37; 6:57; John 8:18 John 8:29). More than that - Jesus comes with the full authorization of God, so that he fully, even interchangeably, represents him (John 12:44-45). So, he can say to his disciples when he sends them on mission: "He who receives you receives me, and he who receives me receives the one who sent me" (Matt 10:40; cf. Mark 9:37). At the same time, Jesus carries out his mission in full obedience to the will of the one who sent him (John 4:34; 5:30; 6:38-39; 7:18). He speaks his words and does his works (7:16; 8:26; 9:4; 12:49; 14:24).

To believe that God has sent his Son Jesus on this saving mission is critically decisive for an individual's eternal destiny. "Now this is eternal life: that they may know you the only true God, and Jesus Christ, whom you have sent" (17:3; cf. 5:24; 6:29; 11:42; 17:21). To reject divinely sent messengers and their message will mean, even for the sons of Israel, receiving the retributive justice and forfeiting kingdom blessings at the last judgment (Matt 22:1-14; Luke 14:17).

Jesus recognized his place in the midst of a long train of divinely sent, yet humanly rejected, messengers both past and future. There were the prophets, wise men, scribes, and apostles, whom Israel had and would reject, even kill (Matt 23:33-36; Luke 11:47-51; 13:34; cf. Matt 22:3-4; Luke 14:17). Through parables Jesus let them know that he, the Son, was among that number (Matt 21:34-37; Mark 12:2-6; Luke 20:10-13).

So, ***the mission of God and the church is our salvation***. This is accomplished by believing in Christ, His Apostles and those who followed (Holy Fathers) His commandments and Laws. In the Orthodox Church we call it *Holy Tradition* and it has been uninterrupted since Christianity was formed on the Day of the Pentecost 33 A.D. [Luke 2:30-32 tells us directly that Jesus is our salvation with the words of the High-Priest Simeon (Simeon in Hebrew means *hear*) in the presentation of the Lord in the

Temple. As Orthodox we recite the words of Simeon's words towards the end of every Vesper service. The words are: "··· For mine eyes have seen thy salvation, which thou hast prepared before the face of all people; A light to lighten the Gentiles, and the glory of thy people Israel (KJV) - ὅτι εἶδον οἱ ὀφθαλμοί μου τὸ σωτήριόν σου, ὃ ἡτοίμασας κατὰ πρόσωπον πάντων τῶν λαῶν, φῶς εἰς ἀποκάλυψιν ἐθνῶν καὶ δόξαν λαοῦ σου 'Ισραήλ..."

15. **Mystery** (mystery as God's primary attribute because he only reveals certain knowledge to the human race);
16. **Omnipotence** (The omnipotence of God refers to Him being "all powerful." This is often conveyed with the phrase "Almighty," as in the Old Testament title "God Almighty" (the conventional translation of the Hebrew title *El Shaddai*) and the title "God the Father Almighty" in *the Symbol of Faith* (I [We] believe) Jesus says in Matthew 19:26, "with God all things are possible);
17. **Omnipresence** (The omnipresence of God refers to him being present everywhere. In Psalm 138(139), David says, "If I go up to the heavens, you are there; if I make my bed in the depths, you are there" (Psalm 138(139):8, NIV);
18. **Omniscience** (The omniscience of God refers to him being "all knowing." Romans 16:27 speaks about the "only wise God.");
19. **Oneness** (The oneness, or unity of God refers to his being one and only. This means that Christianity is monotheistic, although the doctrine of the Trinity says that God is three persons: Father, Son, and Holy Spirit. The *Athanasian Creed* says "we worship one God in Trinity, and Trinity in Unity." The most notable biblical affirmation of the unity of God is found in Deuteronomy 6:4. The statement, known as the *Shema Yisrael*, after its first two words in Hebrew, says "Hear, O Israel: Yahweh our God, Yahweh is one." In the New Testament, Jesus upholds the oneness of God by quoting these words in Mark 12:29. The Apostle Paul also affirms the oneness of God in verses like Ephesians 4:6. The oneness of God is also related to his simplicity);
20. **Trinity** (Trinitarian traditions of Christianity propose the Trinity of God - three persons in one: Father, Son, and the Holy Spirit. Support for the doctrine of the Trinity comes from several verses in the Bible and the New Testament's

trinitarian formulae, such as the Great Commission of Matthew 28:19, "Therefore go and make disciples of all nations, baptizing them in the name of the Father and of the Son and of the Holy Spirit". Also, 1 John 5:7 (of the KJV) reads "...there are three that bear record in heaven, the Father, the Word (Logos; the Son), and the Holy Spirit, and these three are one," but this *Comma Johanneum* is almost universally rejected as a Latin corruption); See also Genesis 1:26 the word "us" is used to reflect the H. Trinity.

21. **Providence** (While the providence of God usually refers to his activity in the world, it also implies his care for the universe, and is thus an attribute. Although the word is not used in the Bible to refer to God, the concept is found in verses such as Acts 17:25, which says that God "gives all men life and breath and everything else" (NIV);

22. **Righteousness** (The righteousness of God may refer to his holiness, to his justice, or to his saving activity. A notable occurrence of the word is in Romans 1:17 - "for in the gospel the righteousness of God is revealed" (NIV);

23. **Simplicity** (The simplicity of God means he is not partly this and partly that, but that whatever he is, he is so entirely);

24. **Sovereignty** (The sovereignty of God is related to his omnipotence, providence, and kingship, yet it also encompasses his freedom, and is in keeping with his goodness, righteousness, holiness, and impeccability. It refers to God being in complete control as he directs all things - no person, organization, government or any other force can stop God from executing his purpose – see Isaiah 46:10);

25. **Transcendence** (God's transcendence means that he is outside *space and time*, and therefore eternal and unable to be changed by forces within the universe. It is thus closely related to God's immutability, and is contrasted with his immanence. A significant verse which balances God's transcendence and his immanence is Isaiah 57:15); Compare this with the two examples of demolishing the boundaries of *time and space* in two specific examples, *NOT PARABLES*. The first one is the miracle at the wedding in Cana when he transformed the water in wine (John 2: 1-11). He destroyed the time constrains of wine making. It usually takes about 40 days to make wine but Jesus made it instantly. Time had no

bearing on the transformation. The second example is when he smashes space parameters. So, we see Jesus and His disciples in the middle of the lake in a very bad weather and suddenly He moved His disciples about 13 ½ miles on the shore of Capernaum. The Apostle John (6: 16-21) describes it in his Gospel as "And when even was now come, his disciples went down unto the sea, and entered into a ship, and went over the sea toward Capernaum. And it was now dark, and Jesus was not come to them. And the sea arose by reason of a great wind that blew. So, when they had rowed about five and twenty or thirty furlongs, they see Jesus walking on the sea, and drawing nigh unto the ship: and they were afraid. But he saith unto them, It is I; be not afraid. Then, they willingly received him into the ship: and immediately the ship was at the land whither they went (KJV) - Ὡς δὲ ὀψία ἐγένετο, κατέβησαν οἱ μαθηταὶ αὐτοῦ ἐπὶ τὴν θάλασσαν, καὶ ἐμβάντες εἰς τὸ πλοῖον ἤρχοντο πέραν τῆς θαλάσσης εἰς Καπερναούμ. καὶ σκοτία ἤδη ἐγεγόνει καὶ οὐκ ἐληλύθει πρὸς αὐτοὺς ὁ Ἰησοῦς, ἥ τε θάλασσα ἀνέμου μεγάλου πνέοντος διηγείρετο. ἐληλακότες οὖν ὡς σταδίους εἴκοσι πέντε ἢ τριάκοντα θεωροῦσι τὸν Ἰησοῦν περιπατοῦντα ἐπὶ τῆς θαλάσσης καὶ ἐγγὺς τοῦ πλοίου γινόμενον, καὶ ἐφοβήθησαν. ὁ δὲ λέγει αὐτοῖς· ἐγώ εἰμι· μὴ φοβεῖσθε. ἤθελον οὖν λαβεῖν αὐτὸν εἰς τὸ πλοῖον, καὶ εὐθέως τὸ πλοῖον ἐγένετο ἐπὶ τῆς γῆς εἰς ἣν ὑπῆγον.

26. **Veracity** (The veracity of God means his truth-telling. Titus 1:2 refers to "God, who does not lie");
27. **Wrath** (Moses praises the wrath of God in Exodus 15:7. In Deuteronomy 9, after the incident of The Golden Calf, Moses describes how: "I feared the furious anger of the LORD, which turned him against you, would drive him to destroy you. But again, he listened to me." (9:19). In Psalm 68(69):24, the psalmist begs God to "consume" his enemies "with your burning anger." In the New Testament, Jesus says in John 3:36, "Whoever believes in the Son has eternal life; whoever does not obey the Son shall not see life, but the wrath of God remains on him");
28. **High Priesthood** (Hebr. 4: 14-16). The high priest was the supreme religious leader of the Israelites. The office of the high priest was hereditary and was traced from Aaron, the

brother of Moses, of the Levite tribe (Exodus 28:1; Numbers 18:7). The high priest had to be "whole" physically (without any physical defects) and holy in his conduct (Leviticus 21:6-8).

Because the high priest held the leadership position, one of his roles was overseeing the responsibilities of all the subordinate priests (2 Chronicles 19:11). Though the high priest could participate in ordinary priestly ministries, only certain functions were given to him. Only the high priest could wear the *Urim* and the *Thummin* (engraved dice-like stones used to determine truth or falsity). For this reason, the Hebrew people would go to the high priest in order to know the will of God (Numbers 27:21). An example of this is when Joshua was commissioned by Eleazar, the high priest, to assume some of Moses' responsibilities (Numbers 27:21). In the New Testament, we find a reference to the high priest having the gift of prophecy (John 11:49-52).

The high priest had to offer a sin offering not only for the sins of the whole congregation, but also for himself (Leviticus 4:3-21). When a high priest died, all those confined to the cities of refuge for accidently causing the death of another person were granted freedom (Numbers 35:28).

The most important duty of the high priest was to conduct the service on the *Day of Atonement*, the tenth day of the seventh month of every year. Only he was allowed to enter the Most Holy Place behind the veil to stand before God. Having made a sacrifice for himself and for the people, he then brought the blood into the Holy of Holies and sprinkled it on the mercy seat, God's "throne" (Leviticus 16:14-15). He did this to make atonement for himself and the people for all their sins committed during the year just ended (Exodus 30:10). It is this particular service that is compared to the ministry of Jesus as our High Priest (Hebrews 9:1-28).

In understanding the role of the high priest, we can better comprehend the significance *of Christ offering Himself for our sins once for all* (Hebrews 9:26; 10:10, 12). Through

Christ's sacrifice for us, we are sanctified and set apart for Him. By entering God's presence on our behalf, Christ has secured for us an "eternal redemption" (Hebrews 9:12). As Paul has written, "For there is one God, and there is one mediator between God and men, the man Christ Jesus" (1 Timothy 2:5).

The high Priest is associated with *Melchizedek*, (also spelled *Melchisedech*), in the Old Testament, a figure of importance in biblical tradition because *he was both king and priest,* was connected with Jerusalem, and was revered by Abraham, **who paid a tithe to him.** (See Appendix A for more information). He appears as a person only in an interpolated vignette (Gen. 14:18–20) of the story of Abraham rescuing his kidnapped nephew, Lot, by defeating a coalition of Mesopotamian kings under Chedorlaomer (also spelled as: Chodollogomor).

Now that we have a fundamental understanding of the power of God, let us examine some verses of the Holy Bible and see how this "power" relates to "giving" and our expected behavior.

1. **Leviticus**: *Giving to those in need.* Be generous and merciful. "And if thy brother who is with thee become poor, and he fail in resources with thee, thou shalt help him as a stranger and a sojourner, and thy brother shall live with thee. Thou shalt not receive from him interest, nor increase: and thou shalt fear thy God: I [am] the Lord: and thy brother shall live with thee. Thou shalt not lend thy money to him at interest, and thou shalt not lend thy meat to him to be returned with increase" (25:35–37 LXX). See note 1.
2. **Deuteronomy**: *Giving sufficiently.* "And if there shall be in the midst of thee a poor [man] of thy brethren in one of thy cities in the land, which the Lord thy God gives thee, thou shalt not harden thine heart, neither shalt thou by any means close up thine hand from thy brother who is in want. Thou shalt surely open thine hands to him, and shalt lend to him as much as he wants according to his need" (15: 7-8 LXX). See appendix B.
3. **Psalm**: *God's Promise to the generous.* David acknowledges the covenant that exists between God and the generous. God responds to the kindness and generosity of his people with protection,

health, and abundance. "Blessed [is the man] who thinks on the poor and needy: The Lord shall deliver him in an evil day. May the Lord preserve him and keep him alive, and bless him on the earth, and not deliver him into the hands of his enemy. May the Lord help him upon the bed of his pain; thou hast made all his bed in his sickness" (Ps. 40(41): 2-4 LXX).
4. **Luke**: *Having a generous spirit.* To withhold judgment, condemnation, and unforgiveness is to act generously, and, in God's economy, it is rewarded with the same kind of benevolence - pressed down, shaken together, and running over. "Judge not, and you will not be judged; condemn not, and you will not be condemned; forgive, and you will be forgiven; give, and it will be given to you. Good measure, pressed down, shaken together, running over, will be put into your lap. For with the measure you use it will be measured back to you" (6:37-38).
5. **Galatians**: *Fulfilling the law of Christ*, which is: "Love the Lord with all our heart, soul, mind, and strength, and to love our neighbor as ourselves" (Luk. 10:27). It is fulfilled by bearing one another's burdens. *"Bear one another's burdens, and so fulfill the law of Christ."* (6:2).

What the bible says about selfishness

6. **Psalm**: *Eschewing selfishness.* "Incline mine heart to thy testimonies, and not to covetousness" (118(119):36, LXX). The key to living a life of generosity is in having a heart that delights in the Lord.
7. **Proverbs:** *Maintaining generous ears.* "He that stops his ears from hearing the poor, himself also shall cry, and there shall be none to hear [him]. A secret gift calms anger: but he that forbears to give stirs up strong wrath" (21:13-14, LXX). It's interesting that God attaches intention to not responding to the needs of the poor. No matter what justification we might fabricate to excuse ourselves, the Lord calls it a willful "closing of our ears." In the same way that we lend to the Lord by giving to the poor, we withhold from the Lord when we respond selfishly to need—that gets repaid as well.
8. **Matthew:** *Investing in future treasure.* "Do not lay up for yourselves treasures on earth, where moth and rust destroy and where thieves break in and steal, but lay up for yourselves treasures in heaven, where neither moth nor rust destroys and

where thieves do not break in and steal. For where your treasure is, there your heart will be also" (6: 19-21). Jesus challenges us with a choice: accumulate *stuff* (material wealth) here (which ultimately has no value), or use it in such a generous way that we're investing it in the coming Kingdom. When we are generous with the things that come through our life, we are actually sending it ahead, and we'll be compensated by God. The beauty in this passage is found in Jesus' promise that as we invest our resources in God's Kingdom, our heart will also be pulled in that direction. See Appendix C.

9. **Proverbs:** *Our generosity defines our experience.* There are [some] who scatter their own, and make it more: and there are [some] also who gather, [yet] have less. Every sincere soul is blessed: but a passionate man is not graceful (οὐκ εὐσχήμων) (11:24-25, LXX). This passage communicates a principle sewn into the fabric of God's world. The more you grasp and hoard, the more you need. Those who give freely and generously find that they're happier, healthier, and experience more blessings.

Bible verses about helping others

10. **Proverbs:** *Lending to the Lord.* He that has pity on the poor lends to the Lord; and he will recompense to him according to his gift. (19:17). The more one ponders this verse, the more one becomes overwhelmed with the concept that God has you in mind and a payment of your generosity is coming your way. Obviously, for one to think this way, it requires a certain amount of faith.

11. **Proverbs**: *Expecting the lord's generosity.* He that has pity on the poor shall himself be maintained; for he has given of his own bread to the poor. He that gives liberally secures victory and honor; but he takes away the life of them that possess [them] (22:9). Many people live from deficit, believing that there's only so much to go around—and if you don't get yours, someone else will. It is nearly impossible to see the world that way and be a generous person. However, if you live with a "bountiful eye" that sees the world ruled by a magnanimous God who owns everything "For all the wild beasts of the thicket are mine, the cattle on the mountains, and oxen" (Psalm 49(50):10, LXX), you're more apt to be open-handed with the resources you have, because you know that God will repay you.

12. **Matthew:** *God keeps track of our giving.* "And whoever gives one of these little ones even a cup of cold water because he is a disciple, truly, I say to you, he will by no means lose his reward" (10:42). Again, we see a relationship between how we treat the needy and vulnerable around us and our future reward. The Lord is keeping pretty intricate accounts and doesn't even neglect to record water given in his name.

What Jesus taught us about generosity
13. **Luke:** *Jesus' enthusiasm about generosity.* "Jesus looked up and saw the rich putting their gifts into the offering box, and he saw a poor widow put in two small copper coins. And he said, "Truly, I tell you, this poor widow has put in more than all of them. For they all contributed out of their abundance, but she out of her poverty put in all she had to live on" (Luk. 21:1-4). True generosity doesn't come from our excess; it comes from sacrificial hearts. The beauty of this passage is in Jesus' enthusiasm to point out this woman's magnanimity out to the disciples. To think that God gets this excited when we're openhanded is pretty inspiring.
14. **John:** *Love gives. Period.* "for God so loved the world, that he gave his only son, that whoever believes in him should not perish but have eternal life" (3:16). Is it any wonder that the Bible verse that most explicitly expresses the beauty of the gift we have received in Christ Jesus would also communicate something about God's gracious generosity? Because God loved the world, he gave. *Love blossoms into generosity - always.*
15. **1 John:** *Giving like Christ.* "By this we know love, that he laid down his life for us, and we ought to lay down our lives for the brothers. But if anyone has the world's goods and sees his brother in need, yet closes his heart against him, how does God's love abide in him? Little children, let us not love in word or talk but indeed and in truth" (3:16-18). Our generosity should model our savior's selflessness. *He gave his life for us, so we are called to be willing to do the same.* It isn't enough to talk about our love; it needs to be expressed in concrete examples of generous sacrifice.
16. **1 John:** *Following Christ's example.* "By this we may know that we are in him: whoever says he abides in him ought to walk in the same way in which he walked" (2: 5-6). Quite a powerful statement for all of us to digest. However, as strong as this verse

is, Apostle Paul goes even further by encouraging us to examine ourselves to see whether we're in the faith (2 Cor. 13:5). One important way we do that is by taking stock in whether our lives are beginning to take on the self-sacrificial and cruciform nature of Jesus. We'll give of ourselves and our resources.

What it means to be generous in everyday life
17. **Acts:** *Set a generous example.* "And now I commit you to God and to the message of His grace, which is able to build you up and to give you an inheritance among all who are sanctified. I have not coveted anyone's silver or gold or clothing. You yourselves know that these hands have provided for my needs and for those who were with me. In every way I've shown you that by laboring like this, it is necessary to help the weak and to keep in mind the words of the Lord Jesus, for He said, *it is more blessed to give than to receive*" (20:32-35). Paul's visit with the Ephesians ends with these words. He wants to leave them an example to follow. The pattern he wants to impart is one of hard work and sacrifice because he wants them to understand the virtue of generous living.
18. **2 Corinthians:** *Giving shouldn't be a burden.* "For if the readiness is there, it is acceptable according to what a person has, not according to what he does not have. For I do not mean that others should be eased and you burdened, but that as a matter of fairness your abundance at the present time should supply their need, so that their abundance may supply your need, that there may be fairness. As it is written, "Whoever gathered much had nothing left over, and whoever gathered little had no lack." (8:12-15). The generosity that we're called to isn't intended to be a burden. It's intended to create a culture of equitability.
19. **2 Corinthians:** *God doesn't want to coerce generosity.* "The point is this: whoever sows sparingly will also reap sparingly, and whoever sows bountifully will also reap bountifully. Each one must give as he has decided in his heart, not reluctantly or under compulsion, for God loves a cheerful giver. And God is able to make all grace abound to you, so that having all sufficiency in all things at all times, you may abound in every good work" (9:6-8). God's ultimate desire is that we would give happily. He doesn't want us to have to give out of obligation or coercion. He wants to bless his children. Not so that we can live in complete comfort

and luxury, but so that we can be even more generous – abounding in every good work.
20. **1 Timothy:** *Being rich in good works and generosity*. "As for the rich in this present age, charge them not to be haughty, nor to set their hopes on the uncertainty of riches, but on God, who richly provides us with everything to enjoy. They are to do good, to be rich in good works, to be generous and ready to share, thus storing up treasure for themselves as a good foundation for the future, so that they may take hold of that which is truly life" (6:17-19). God richly provides everything for our enjoyment. It isn't his desire to withhold or diminish our pleasure. In fact, he wants us to experience true pleasure. (See John 10:10 "I came that they may have life, and may have *it* abundantly - ASV." He wants us to experience the joy of being rich in goodness and generosity. Once again, Paul echoes the sentiment so prevalent throughout the scriptures: our benevolence now is an investment in eternity.

Obviously, our return on investment (ROI) is infinity. In other words: we have everything to gain (eternity) and nothing to lose, if we keep "the" generosity of giving in the front of all our behaviors. To hold fast on this notion, we ALL must be conformed to the image of Christ and that means emulating his sacrificial, *giving nature*. Therefore, to gauge our spiritual health we must be concerned with our generosity. That gauging can be measured by asking ourselves two questions: 1) How open are we to giving? 2) How sacrificially are we willing to participate? The answer to these questions must be framed against the beauty of Christ's promise "Look, I am coming soon, bringing my reward with me to repay all people according to their deeds" (Rev. 20:12). As Scripture reminds us constantly, this will include checking his meticulous accounts of our generous giving.

So, when it comes down to it, ***practicing generosity requires faith***. In fact, it might be the best way to gauge how strong our faith is. Do I believe enough to make sacrifices because I believe that I'm not really losing anything? Our generous God does not want to motivate us through guilt and fear. He's inviting us to put our faith in Him, to test Him. Giving is such a test.

Furthermore, I hope the reader has realized by reading this preliminary information that our GOD does not need anything. Therefore, we are the ones who need HIS love, guidance and protection. As such, through our giving, we hope to create a relationship with Him. When that relationship is active and mutual, then *out of gratitude we offer* what is already HIS.

Note 1: The notion of helping the poor is an old tradition. Perhaps one of the most moving stories in the Bible is the story of Ruth – in the Book of Ruth. So, let us review it. In the time of the judges, the neighboring pagan peoples were constant enemies of the Israelites. There were occasions though when several pagans from these people accepted faith in the true God, and then the Israelites considered them as their fellow-tribesmen. Such a person was the Moabite Ruth. This is her story.

In Bethlehem, Judah, lived a man, whose name was Elimelech, with his wife Naomi. They had two sons, Mahlon and Chilian. During the famine Elimelech was obliged to move with his family to the land of Moab. There Elimelech soon died. His sons married the Moabites Orpah and Ruth, and after living with them not more than ten years, they both died. The widow Naomi remained with her daughters-in-law. When Naomi heard that the Lord had sent a rich harvest to the Israelite land, she decided to return to her homeland. She and both her daughters-in-law went.

On the way Naomi began to urge them to return home, saying to them, "Go, return each of you to your mother's house. May the Lord grant you mercy for the way you dealt with the dead and with me," and she kissed them. The daughters-in-law sobbed and cried and did not want to leave her, but one of them, Orpah, with tears, obeyed Naomi and returned home. But Ruth said: *"Whither thou goest, I will go, and where thou lodgest, I will lodge; thy people shall be my people and thy God my God. Where thou diest, will I die and there will I be buried"* (Ruth 1:16).

Naomi and Ruth, coming to the land of the Israelites, settled in the town of Bethlehem and lived on the wheat which Ruth picked up from the harvested fields. This was enough for sustenance, since it is written in the Law of God, *"And when ye reap the harvest of your land, thou shalt not wholly reap the corners of thy field, neither shalt thou gather the gleanings of thy harvest; thou shalt leave them for the poor and the stranger"* (Lev. 19:9-10 KJV).

The Lord God rewarded Ruth for her attachment and respectfulness towards her mother-in-law. The Israelites had a law: if one of them died, not leaving children, then the nearest relative had to marry the widow of the person who died, and the children from this marriage were considered the dead man's children. This law was called the Levynite Law.

At this time in Bethlehem there lived a rich man, Boaz, a relative of Ruth's dead husband. According to Levynite Law, Boaz married the poor Moabite Ruth. When a son was born to them, Obed, women said to Naomi, "Blessed be the Lord, Who hath not left thee this day without a kinsmen, that his name may be famous in Israel." Naomi rejoiced and was Obed's nurse. In fact, Obed's name was glorified in Israel, for he was the father of Jesse, the father of King David.

P.1.Lithograph by Julius Schnorr von Carolsfeld,
1860 - Ruth meeting Boaz

A personal story about the poor gleaning the fields: As of 1963, in my village of Thisvi – Thivon (Greece) the tradition was that during the June harvest of wheat, barley, chick peas and lentils the owner of the field would leave the corners unharvested for the gleaning (σταχυολόγημα) of the poor.

In addition, in September and mid-November they would leave small amounts of grapes and olives on the vines and olive trees respectively for the gleaning (κοκολοη) of the poor. Both practices were in line with Lev.19:9-10 LXX: And when ye reap the harvest of your land, ye shall not complete the reaping of your field with exactness, and thou shalt not gather that which falls from thy reaping. And thou shalt not go over the gathering of thy vineyard, neither shalt thou gather the remaining grapes of thy vineyard: thou shalt leave them for the poor and the stranger: I am the Lord your God - Καὶ ἐκθεριζόντων ὑμῶν τὸν θερισμὸν τῆς γῆς ὑμῶν, οὐ συντελέσετε τὸν θερισμὸν ὑμῶν τοῦ ἀγροῦ σου ἐκθερίσαι, καὶ τὰ ἀποπίπτοντα τοῦ θερισμοῦ σου οὐ συλλέξεις. καὶ τὸν ἀμπελῶνά σου οὐκ ἐπανατρυγήσεις, οὐδὲ τὰς ῥῶγας τοῦ ἀμπελῶνός σου συλλέξεις· τῷ πτωχῷ καὶ τῷ προσηλύτῳ καταλείψεις αὐτά· ἐγώ εἰμι Κύριος ὁ Θεὸς ὑμῶν."

Introduction

I closed the preface with the statement of: "out of gratitude we give to God what is already His." That is a powerful statement. However, sublimely it tells us: for that "gratitude" to come about in our life, we MUST enter into a "relationship," a contract of sorts. The contract of course, is between God (He offers us salvation) and us (we offer our life to His rules). [Here, I want to be unequivocally clear. Salvation is not a transactional task. It is given free to those who recognize the Trinitarian God (Father, Son and Holy Spirit) as the Lord and follow His commandments and rules. The usage of the "contract" here, is used as an analogy and nothing more].

We often think our relationship with God is a contract and we put a name to it, that is: tithing and offerings. Sometimes we have the idea that God expects a percentage of what we produce, sort of like a tax. The truth is that giving is an important part of who we are if we are a Christ-follower, but the reason behind our giving is just as important as the fact of our giving. The basis for this, is the parable of talents (Mat. 25: 14-30). We give a tithing and an offering for many reasons. However, the greatest of them all, is *gratitude* for HIS love for us.

Of course, there are contracts for the short, and long term. Some in fact, are renewable. Some may be broken if the content of the contract (by us) is not met. The contract that we enter with God is all of the stated situations with one major difference. That difference is that even if we break the contract, through contrition, repentance, confession and forgiveness we can reenter the contract at any time without penalty.

Giving Is Important:

All Christians, want to be saved, healed and certainly want to go to "heaven" rather than to hell when they die. We want to become like Christ (become partakers in Christ –1 Peter 4:13 and 2 Peter 1-4). Tithing doesn't purchase all that for us, but tithing is a powerful way that we give of ourselves, that we turn over what we have to God so that we are opened to receiving His healing and blessing.

It is a basic principle for all Christians that want to have a spiritual life, that we cannot receive God's blessing if we are holding back on Him. Why? We can't be filled with God if we remain full of ourselves. Tithing helps us to empty ourselves and become self-less. The reason for this, is that money generally is the hardest to let go of. Jesus predicted that discomfort with the words: "Where your treasure is, there will your heart be also" (Matt. 6:21, Luke 12:34). Where we put our money proves where our hearts are.

Obviously, God's blessings are not ONLY dependent on giving money but giving what we have. The important thing about giving is our attitude, enthusiasm and being serious about it.

1. **Tithing shows that we're serious.** When I speak of tithing here, I am referring most obviously to giving 10% of income, but here we can define tithing as **serious giving**. 10% is serious for most of us. For some of us who are more affluent, 10% is not that serious, and we should do more because we can. And for some of us, 10% is unaffordable, so we need to be serious with another percentage. But the point is to be serious. So, if you're not serious, get serious.

   How do you know if you're serious? Well, to start with, if you're spending more on cable TV or other forms of entertainment every month than you're giving to the Church, it's a safe guess that you're not being serious about giving. I love the phrase "put your money where your mouth is." It's definitely true. Where is *your* heart?

2. **Tithing is absolutely orthodox.** Some people say that tithing is not Orthodox. This is nonsense. Giving is Orthodox. Asceticism is Orthodox. Generosity is Orthodox. Ministry is Orthodox. Discipline is Orthodox. Hospitality is Orthodox, *etc.* The purpose in tithing is not because it is an "absolute requirement" in order to be saved. It is not. But how can we be saved if we do not nurture a truly generous heart? And how can we nurture that generous heart without becoming disciplined about giving all that we have? The Orthodox Church understands how to become disciplined. We understand asceticism, *etc.* Tithing is one of the best ways to do it.

Tithing was a *minimum* set up in the Old Covenant (and there were multiple tithes, equaling about 23%), 100% is the standard in the New Covenant (Acts 4:32-37), and when the Fathers talk about tithing, they say that because the New is superior to the Old, we give *more* than the Old Covenant people did. However, in the Orthodox Tradition, *there is no specific percentage for giving*. The rule generally is: Give all you can afford.

So perhaps it's true that "tithing is not Orthodox." But that's not because we give *less* than 10%, but because we give *more* than 10%. God is merciful, of course, and if we're not ready to meet that standard, we can work toward it. But are we working toward it? If not, let's get on it.

There are many reasons why giving is of paramount importance. However, here we will address some key ones that most Christians can internalize.

1. **Giving makes us MORE LIKE GOD.** "God so *loved* the world that *He gave* His only Son ..." John 3:16 ESV. God is a Giver! He gave us life. He gave us this world to enjoy. He even gave us His only Son so that we might have a relationship with Him. That most famous of verses, John 3:16, shows us the connection between loving and giving. *You can give without loving, but you cannot love without giving!*
2. **Giving draws us CLOSER TO GOD.** "For where your treasure is, there your heart will be also" (Matthew 6:21 NIV). Where I put my money, my time, my efforts, my thinking, my life... that's where my heart will be! So where do I want my heart? If I want to be more like God, then I'll also want to be closer to God. When I give out of a heart of love and compassion, I'll find that I'm also next to God's heart.
3. **Giving strengthens us in our FAITH.** Trust in God with all thine heart; and be not exalted in thine own wisdom…; Honor the Lord with thy just labors, and give him the first of thy fruits of righteousness (Proverbs 3:5, 9 LXX). Nothing strengthens our faith more than giving when we don't understand how in the world we possibly can do so. Giving the way God gives - and the way He wants us to give - goes beyond our budgeting. It requires faith. The more we give, the stronger our faith will become. This is so because we discover that *we cannot out give God*. The more we give, the more He provides us the ability to give. This notion is expressed very eloquently and strongly with the words "Give, and it will be given to you... For with the measure you use it will be measured back to you" (Luke 6:38 NIV). Giving of our money and material possessions is the only place in the Bible where God

literally says, "I dare you." Here is another way of understanding what Luke is saying: "Give with a cup and you will be measured back by the cup standard. Give with a basket and you will be measured back with a basket standard!"

4. **Giving is an investment FOR ETERNITY.** "They are to do good, to be rich in good works, to be generous and ready to share, thus storing up treasure for themselves as a good foundation for the future, so that they may take hold of that which is truly life" (1 Timothy 6:18-19 ESV). It is a realistic check point for all of us. We cannot take it with us – no matter what it is or how large it is, but we can send it forward.

5. **Giving reveals our SPIRITUAL MATURITY.** "But just as you excel in everything - in faith, in speech, in knowledge, in complete earnestness... - see that you also excel in this grace of giving" (2 Corinthians 8:7 NIV). Ultimately giving is more about our spiritual maturity than it is about the actual gift. Our finances are the last part of our personal life that we will release in trust to God. We hold on to our money and our wealth as a form of security. We cannot trust in God AND trust in our money at the same time. Giving is the discipline of learning to trust God. And it reveals to us the truth of our spiritual maturity.

The principles behind giving were important to Jesus - the master teacher. Both the gospel of Matthew and Luke tell us the parable of the talents, and both are recorded in the final week of Jesus' life. Many of us, are familiar with the parable. However, not too many of us contemplate the underlining message of a *giving lifestyle* that comes from its content. So, let us examine it a little deeper.

Principles of Giving from the Parable of the Talents

1. **It all belongs to the Master.** "Again, it will be like a man going on a journey, who called his servants and entrusted his property to them" (Matthew 25:14 NIV). Our whole sense of perspective is off base when it comes to our possessions and our wealth. We may think that we are the owner and that we give - or not give (our choice) - out of what belongs to us. Any sense of such ownership is an illusion. We are not the owner. God is! Everything was created by God and returns to God.

Jesus - as God's Son - knew that he only had days left in his earthly life, when He shared this parable. He is the "man going on a journey." We are "his servants." He (God) has "entrusted his property" to us. We are caretakers; stewards; managers. (The Greek word used here is οικονομος, oikonomos – a specialist for allocation of resources). Everything belongs to the Master. We have been given the opportunity to manage his property here on Earth for the short period of our lifetime. Will we manage it in a way that reflects the values and priorities of our Master Jesus? Will we manage it in way that demonstrates His love, His compassion, and His selflessness?

2. **We receive equal to OUR ABILITIES not equal to ONE ANOTHER.** "To one he gave five talents of money, to another two talents, and to another one talent, each according to his ability" (Matthew 25:15 NIV). No where do we find anything about *fairness* or *equality* in this parable. The fact is that different people receive different talents - one 5, one 2, and the third only 1. What is a talent? In those days one talent = *6,000 denarii;* and one denarii = *one day's wage for a common laborer. Therefore,* each talent would be worth *20 years of labor!* Quite a substantial amount. The difference of the money was explained by Jesus by saying that each received an amount *according to his ability!* We shouldn't worry if anyone else has received more than us. Instead we should be focused on what we are doing with our money!

3. **What am I doing with what I've been given?** "The man who had received the five talents went at once and put his money to work and gained five more. So also, the one with the two talents gained two more" (Matthew 25:16-17 NIV). The different actions taken indicate three perpetual issues for humanity – all of us. They are:

    a. Do I have a sense of **URGENCY?** The servant went *at once* and put his money to work. He didn't know when the master would return. It could be any day. Do we have the false sense that we have a long time before we need to worry about this? Or do we make the most of every day and every opportunity?

    b. Do I have an ethic of **WORK?** Don't gloss over this idea of putting "His money to work." There is work involved in the kingdom of God! The principle here is that not only do we work in the kingdom - our labor - but

      that even our money labors for the kingdom too, if we have the right attitude of being a steward and not of owner.
   c. Do I have the objective of **GROWTH?** The five gained five more. The two gained two more. Even though different servants received different amounts, *the same growth happened with both!* In God's kingdom it is normal and expected that growth happens. Why? Because healthy things grow! God's first instructions to mankind were to "fill the Earth and multiply!" (Gen. 1:28).

Think of it this way - are you growing in your desire to give to God's kingdom? Are you growing in seeing the opportunities? Our financial *abilities* will not be the same - from time to time or from person to person. But growth should be present in whatever it is that we are doing for God and with His help!

4. **STEWARDSHIP - managing during the Master's absence.** "After a long time, the master of those servants returned..." (Matthew 25:19a). Money is a bad master, but a good servant! Remembering that will help me to determine whether I am God's servant - His steward – *oikonomos* - of all He has entrusted to me, or whether I have the attitude of an owner.

Being a good steward reflects the truth that none of what we have is ours because of our efforts alone. Our strength, our health, our opportunities, even our next breath comes from God's goodness and mercy to us.

When we hear something like that, we all WANT to be a steward - God's servant to allocate His gifts to us. The way we handle our money, though, tells us whether our actions equal our desires. That's why tithing is so important. It's not the money given as much as the attitude with which it is given. Not a tax (I must do it), and not a tip (I give a leftover amount). It's a tithe - the first tenth given to say to God: "I know this is all yours. You have entrusted it to me. I am managing it for you and for your kingdom. Here is the first fruit of my labor. Without You, none of this would be possible."

Therefore ultimately, we are caretakers of what Christ has entrusted to us for this brief time that we are on Earth. He will return some day and everything will be restored to Him as Creator and as Owner. As Orthodox Christians we are reminded of this during the prayers of the Holy Anaphora at every Holy Liturgy with the words: "We offer to You these gifts from Your own gifts in all and for all."

5. **ACCOUNTABILITY- when I report the results of how I've done.** "After a long time, the master ... returned and settled accounts with them" (Matthew 25:19b). There will come a time when Christ will return and *he will settle accounts* with us! How have we done? Have we managed the resources he has entrusted to us as if they belonged to Him for His benefit and His kingdom? Or selfishly for ourselves? Have we managed (allocated) with a sense of urgency, an ethic of work, and the objective of growth?

In the parable of *the Workers in the Vineyard*, Jesus addresses the resentment of the workers who claimed unfairness in their payment for their labor. The accountability however, was marked with the mercy and not injustice of God in paying everyone the same, something that the early labors objected (see Mat. 20: 1-16). Have we done that? The last servant in this parable of the talents *returned the talent* back to the master. At the very least he knew the talent belonged to the Master. How about us? Are we guilty not only of not managing the talent well, but of outright stealing the talent and using it for ourselves? Jesus is clear that there will be a day of accounting. Let's manage each day with that in mind!

6. **PROBATION - the reward of being entrusted with more based on my faithfulness.** "His master replied, 'Well done, good and faithful servant! You have been faithful with a few things; I will put you in charge of many things. Come and share your master's happiness!'" (Matthew 25:21 and 23). Sometimes we have the misguided idea of our eternal life in Heaven as if it will be eternal floating on clouds playing harps. In other words, doing nothing. Just being BORING! God has work for us to do; Exciting, wonderful, fulfilling, God-designed work! It will be work you will long to do, that will give you an eternal purpose. Jesus tells us that our assignment in Heaven will be based on how well we do with what we've been given here on Earth. Notice that

even though one servant received 5 talents and another only 2 talents, that their reward in Heaven was *exactly the same! Verses 21 and 23 are identical!* In Luke's version of this story, both are given multiple cities to manage! Imagine being entrusted with the leadership of heavenly cities! Are we handling our resources now as if we are on probation? Do we understand that how we handle our affairs here on Earth will play an eternal role in what we are entrusted with for eternity?

7. **RISK - the understanding that safety and growth are incompatible.** "So, I was afraid and went out and hid your talent in the ground. See, here is what belongs to you" (Matthew 25:25). We really don't understand this at all! We believe that safety is the most important thing. We pray that God would keep us safe. But Jesus teaches that *safety and growth are incompatible!* Growth requires risk - always! Why don't we want to take risks? Because we are afraid. The third servant admits his fear: "So I was afraid and hid your talent..." Here's something you need to know about risk. When you take real risks, you will be afraid. Risk and fear go hand in hand. The issue is not our fear but ***our response to fear.*** This is why giving in a *sacrificial way*, when we don't see how we can make it, is such a faith-building exercise. When we give selflessly instead of selfishly holding back, we learn to place our faith in God and not in ourselves or our own resources. This is what grows our faith. The more we act - in spite of our fear - the more faith we have. Our goal should always be to exchange our faith in ourselves and our possessions for faith in God. Because that's the only Person (Jesus) who is worthy of our faith anyway. Everything else will disappear. Everything else will let us down. Only God is worthy of our trust.

When Jesus taught this parable, he taught both sides of the equation - not only the two faithful servants, but also the unfaithful one, the one who hid the talent in the ground. Here Jesus shows us how important this lesson really is. Jesus shows us what's at stake! There are four items to consider. They are:

   a. **Loss of my REPUTATION.** "You wicked, lazy servant!" (Matthew 25:26). Jesus does not mince words. He describes the third servant as wicked. As lazy. Sometimes we think of being lazy as just the absence of work. But

Jesus says the heart's motivation of the lazy person is evil, wicked. Why? Because the servant presumes that he has the choice of working or not working. That, however, is the choice of the master - not the servant. What is the reputation you are after? The one of faithful servant entering into your Master's happiness someday? Or the one of wicked, lazy servant because you thought caution was the way to go.

"The master was furious. 'That's a terrible way to live! It is criminal to live cautiously like that! If you knew I was after the best, why did you do less than the least?'" (Matthew 25:26). The Message: Let's risk everything now to live faithfully for the LORD; Let's risk everything on this side of eternity so that we might hear those words, "Good and faithful servant" on the other side of eternity. That is why, one should always ask the question in his heart and mind: Am I keeping now what I cannot keep in order to gain what I can never lose?

b. **Loss of my ORIGINAL GIFT.** "Take the talent from him and give it to the one who has the ten talents... Whoever does not have, even what he has will be taken from him" (Matthew 25:28 - 29b). Jesus takes the story even one step farther. The only talent given to the third servant is taken away from him and given to the first servant! One of the things that is at stake is the very gift I was given in the first place. What is it that you are good at doing? What do you see as "yours" as "your ability" as "what makes you special?" If you use it for God's kingdom, unselfishly sharing it with others, then God will give you even more. But if you keep it to yourself, even what you have will be taken!

c. **Loss of my GREATER RESPONSIBILITIES.** Sometimes we learn as much from the Bible from what is not written as from what is written. Recall that the first two servants were given even greater responsibilities - put in charge of many things. Of course, nothing is said about the third servant. He lost *not only his original gift - he also lost the opportunity to do even more!* There is an *opportunity cost* to this probationary life we are living.

What are we risking losing in eternity some day *because we are afraid to risk today?*

d. **Loss of my FELLOWSHIP WITH THE MASTER.** "And throw that worthless servant outside, into the darkness, where there will be weeping and gnashing of teeth" (Matthew 25:30). This is the greatest tragedy of Jesus' entire parable - and must be included. In addition to the three risks mentioned, there is a fourth one which by far is the worst one. It is the LOSS OF FELLOWSHIP with God. This is what "outside - into the darkness - weeping and gnashing of teeth" mean. This is what it will be like for those who are deprived of the fellowship with Almighty Father God. This is a very serious point, so let me explain. Some may claim that one cannot lose their salvation, in which case what I just stated in the previous sentence may be a contrary statement. However, I do not think there is an inconsistency, if you are a true Christ believer, there is nothing that can take you away from Him. Why am I saying this? Because an authentic Christ follower has the ability to change their heart from self-serving person to a Jesus-serving person. An authentic Christ-follower is a giving person, who knows that everything belongs to the Master, and that he or she is a steward of the Master's resources. Period!

As Christians we all know that God does not force this issue with anyone. You do not have to name Christ as the Lord and Master of your life. One can - if they choose - remain to themselves and serve their own self. But one *cannot serve self and God at the same time.* One will be Master. And it is that Master with whom one will share fellowship.

Conclusion

The parable of the talents shows us the character of God which is basically His grace, His mercy and His love - that is, the way He gives. No one gives like God gives. If I (you) want to be like God, then I (you) will want to be a giver like God. The parable is a great one because it doesn't take much imagination to understand what Jesus was trying to say. No one needs to go to seminary to "get it." Our problem has never been one of understanding *how* to be a giver. Our problem has always been our decision - our act of the will - to be a giver.

The act of the will to be a giver is demonstrated with a story I heard some years ago – I do not know the source. Imagine that you are a solitary traveler in a desert. After hours of traveling, you become very thirsty. Just ahead you see a rusty old pump at the edge of an oasis. Attached to the pump is a note that reads, "I have buried a bottle of water to prime the pump. Do not drink any of it. Pour 1/2 to wet the leather. Wait and then pour the rest to prime the pump. When you have drawn your fill of water, refill the bottle and bury it in the sand for the next traveler." The question now is: Will you drink the water from the bottle or follow the instructions? Will you only worry about your own thirst and drink the bottle dry? Or will you pour every drop of the water into the pump? The dilemma is this: do you trust the note and take the risk or do you take care of your own needs?

Jesus gave us the note that will take care of us and others too. That's what this Parable of the Talents really is all about. We give everything we have to God and His kingdom because it all belongs to Him. And we trust God to take care of us and our needs along the way.

And now a personal story demonstrating the value of our possessions. My father was a professional violinist and he used to tell me a story about a famous violinist. In fact, he used to tell me he was the greatest violinist who ever lived. His name was Niccolo Paganini, who lived in the mid-1800s and was a heavy gambler. At the end of one of his performances he went to a tavern and started to drink and gamble. He lost his own violin in a gambling wager. At this point my father would stop, bend his knees and lean forward and with a soft voice he would ask me: Son, if you have a nice gift from your godfather, would you gamble it away? As I recall, my dad never gave me a chance to answer, instead, he continued the story.

The owner of the tavern, just happened to have a violin as he was also an amateur violinist. The owner lent the violin to Paganini who played it so masterfully that the owner refused to take it back. The owner showed he was a steward. My father again, at this point would stop and ask me: Son, that gift from your godfather is nice and I see you like it very much. Right? Would you let me give it to your cousin so that he will keep it for you? He will enjoy it. You know he likes it very much and his family cannot afford to buy him that gift even though it will be put to good use? Are you unselfish with your gift and use it for others? Again, he never allowed me the time to answer him, but continued with the story.

Paganini played on this gift for the rest of his life. When he died, he willed it to the city of Genoa, on the condition that it must never be played upon. Paganini forgot he was a steward. At this point my father would stop and ask me a question. Son, if you give your gift from your godfather would you expect something in return? As I started to answer him, he cut me off with another question which was: would you share it freely if you had a choice or told by your mother to do so? After all it was given to you? No opportunity for me to answer and by now I was getting angry even though I had heard that story with the same questions so many times and I knew the ending. In any case my father continued the story.

But the Genoa elders allow it to be taken out of the case once a year and it was played upon by a young musician, who has won a contest. Genoa knows it is a steward of this great musical instrument. Son, do you know that that gift from your godfather is so special that it will be an heirloom for your future family?

It took me about six years to finally get the opportunity to answer his questions. At this point of course it did not matter. What matter, and I still remember, was the time my father took to explain why he told me the story and why the questions - so many times. What he was trying to do was to instill in me – at an early age the principles of giving. Even though he knew, that I had memorized the entire story he kept telling it to me. Why? Because according to my father the two parables of the vineyard and the talents are very important to understand compassion, expectations and fairness in this world of ours. He elaborated by bringing the analogy of the gift from my godfather, with the following points which now are focused on God's gifts to us. He said:

- Before you gamble consider the value of the item you are willing to lose
- Have you considered the possibility that your gift may be more useful with someone else or where it is needed more?
- Are you unselfish enough to part with your gift for God and or others?

- Are you willing to share your gifts with others only with conditions that favor you? Or, do you share them freely, since they were given to you with no effort or cost to you?
- Son, Never, forget that you and all of us are stewards of all that God has given to all of us.

Chapter 1
Stewards versus owners

Stewards (care-takers – *oikonomoi*) think different than owners. Here are four specific areas about which stewards think differently than those who think they own possessions.

1. **Stewards are grateful and content**: I can be content with what I have if I accept that God picked it out for me (Philippians 4:12, 18). If I resent what others have, or demean what I have, I'm not a faithful steward.

   Sometimes we complain about our material things by calling them "junk or stuff." But if God owns everything, then what we call "junk or stuff" is actually His junk or stuff. He gave it to us. That means that everything we have; we have been given by God and therefore we must show *gratitude*. Gratitude is an attitude stewardship issue. There is always an upgrade. Stewardship means we are at peace with the fact that I'm not someone else. I'm me and God lovingly has given me the skills and the job and the money I need for right now. God assigns everything in life. It's really submission to God when we are content with our job, our income and all our material things.

2. **Stewards give willingly**: God asks for a "tithe" so we can express that He owns it all and that we trust Him to provide for our needs (Malachi 3:10-11). Only when we come to grips with the fact that we are stewards, not owners, does giving come willingly.

   If I really believe that God is the owner and I am a steward of my money, then that's how I should feel about my giving also. He determines my flow of income and what I should be "paid." I only have to be faithful to allocate it the way He wants. And if He wants a 10th or any other percentage, that's not a problem. He's the owner. See appendix B.

   Giving God a percentage is the foundational way we express that we accept the fact that we are the stewards and He's the owner. While we sacrifice emotionally – letting go of ownership – at the

same time we enter a new emotional freedom called trust. We can rest knowing that God will supply the rest that we need.
3. **Stewards can enjoy blessings**: God allows stewards to have many good things to enjoy. I don't have to "bless" myself. Paul told wealthy Christians to not "put their hope in wealth, which is so uncertain, but to put their hope in God, who richly provides us with everything for our enjoyment" (1 Timothy 6:17).

Thinking like stewards does not mean we give up good things. It means that we give up control. And a stewardship mindset does not mean that we don't enjoy good things. It actually means that we enjoy things more.

Enjoyment does not have a price tag. Many who are wealthier find it hard to enjoy what they have, because true enjoyment comes only from God (Ecclesiastes 2:24-25; 4:8). If we earn our money selfishly, we will spend it selfishly, and selfish people don't enjoy much. Selfish people complain the most – no matter what their station in life is.

4. **Stewards realize work is a gift**: Stewards realize that God enables us to earn any money we have. We didn't make ourselves so smart or good at what we do. Because we work so hard, it's pretty natural to think that the money we earn is really ours. We know the training we went through, the hours we go in early, the little techniques we have developed to do a good job and be successful at what we do. We are probably very good at something we do in our jobs. So, when our paycheck is in our hand, we don't go away feeling guilty. We earned it!

So, it's a little hard to swallow the thought that it all belongs to God! This self-righteous thought was anticipated by God in Deuteronomy (8:17-18 LXX) with the words: "Lest thou shouldest say in thine heart, my strength, and the power of mine hand have wrought for me this great wealth. But thou shalt remember the Lord thy God, that He gives thee strength to get wealth; even that he may establish his covenant, which the Lord swore to thy fathers, as at this day." In essence, Moses tries to teach us contentment with what we have.

But is it possible as humans to find contentment? Is it realistic that we can watch someone pass us on the freeway driving our dream car – and be grateful for our own? Is it possible to be at peace with the fact that less qualified people have better jobs and bigger incomes than we do? Can we stop looking at the nicer homes, better furniture and more fashionable clothes of others without envy gripping our heart? Is it possible to win the war over jealousy and just enjoy what we have with a contented heart?

The answer is yes, it's a winnable war, but it's a war. And the answer is found in God's stewardship principle. The key to contentment is the fact that it's not our *stuff*. We are not owners. The money or possessions we use are God's property and God's business. We are stewards given the task of managing something God owns.

Stewards think differently than owners. When we begin to think like God's stewards about the money and possessions we have, we will learn contentment. Whether the possessions we "use" is old or new, shiny or not, really doesn't matter because it all belongs to God.

Our goal in our lives is to begin to think like stewards. Believe it or not, "the" how much we have and "the" how nice it is really, is not our business. Thinking like stewards instead of owners is the key to contentment. And likewise, our contentment level is maybe the crucial measuring stick of whether God considers us good and faithful stewards.

A bad example that we can learn from is the story of King Ahab in, III Kings (LXX) - 1 Kings 21, who is really evil and has been dead for about 3000 years. Ahab embarrasses himself for posterity by his bad example of greed and discontentment. Ahab became king of Israel (in 874 B.C.), 55 years after Solomon's death. He is registered in the Bible as the 9th of the 19 bad kings of the Northern 10 tribes after the kingdom of the N. Israel was divided. [These 10 tribes are called the "10 lost tribes of Israel" after the conquest of the Assyrians].

We are introduced to Ahab in III Kings (LXX) - 1 Kings 16:30. "Ahab son of Omri did more evil In the eyes of the LORD than any of those before him." What a wonderful way to be known! We have a clear picture of what God thought about this man, and Ahab's greed was Exhibit A in making the case for God's condemnation. Biblical history informs us that Ahab built a palace inlaid with ivory (III Kings (LXX) -1 Kings 22:39). Of course, all kings had nice places to live, but this was Ahab's 2nd palace. He had one palace in Jezreel but also this one in Samaria. Archaeologists have excavated the likely ruins of Ahab's palace in Samaria and have recovered over 200 ivory figures, plaques and panels in just one storeroom. How much more ivory was looted over the years we don't know, but Ahab certainly had a taste for imported ivory. By the way, it is not unusual for any one of us to have something that we like or we want very much. The problem with Ahab was that he wanted everything in excess. He was loaded with greed. He was overwhelmed with owning (many and varied) possessions which became his drug addiction.

In III Kings (LXX) - 1 Kings 20:43 we find Ahab angry. Instead of destroying the Aramean king Ben-Hadad, one of Israel's enemies, Ahab had made a treaty with him and let him go free. Then when God's prophet rebuked him, Ahab was sullen and angry (20:35-43). He lost face. He evidently felt disrespected as a man and as a king.

So, Ahab was brooding in his Samaria palace when he saw Naboth tending a beautiful vineyard. Maybe Naboth was whistling to himself, and Ahab wanted to be happy too. When we see someone with something we don't have and they seem happy, we often assume that what they have is the reason for their joy.

And since Ahab didn't resolve his emotional state by repentance, he went shopping (III Kings 20 (LXX) - 1 Kings 21:1-4)! Ahab decided to give himself an emotional boost by trying to buy Naboth's vineyard. No doubt it had worked before. Because Ahab was rich, he could generally buy what he wanted and that made him feel good for a while. But Naboth wouldn't sell him his vineyard, So, Ahab was even more depressed! So, in his frustration over not being able to buy something he wanted, Ahab made a really mature decision. He said, I won't eat (21:4).

It is almost funny, but we have to come to grips with the emotional aspect of our discontentment, envy and greed. It is all the same thing really. We over-shop, overspend, over-save, over-eat, obsess or hoard possessions very often because of unresolved emotional and spiritual issues.

Emotions fuel our greed. We have to admit our attachment to and our quest for material things quickly becomes an emotional dependency. Possessions can distract or appease us. We unwittingly feel that purchasing (buying stuff) is something we can control because there are other things we can't. [Here, it is worth reading the story of the Rich Fool in Luke 12:13-21].

Emotional issues are totally unresolved for Ahab. The only thing that could make it worse would be a wife like Jezebel. Ahab had married an equally dysfunctional and even more evil wife – Jezebel. She was not from Israel, but was rather a Sidonian Baal-worshiper. She certainly didn't embrace or even understand the contentment and trust that the true God of Israel could provide. III Kings 20 (LXX) - 1 Kings 21 records the horrific story of Jezebel taking situations into her own hands and executing Naboth based on bribed false testimony, so that Ahab could have the vineyard. She killed an innocent, godly Israelite who wanted to honor God's law by keeping his family inheritance (Leviticus 25:23).

What may be surprising to us about God's judgment is that although it was Jezebel's plot and murder, Ahab was held responsible by God for her actions! The prophet Elijah told Ahab, "This is what the LORD says: Have you not murdered a man and seized his property? This is what the LORD says: In the place where dogs licked up Naboth's blood, dogs will lick up your blood - yes, yours!" (III Kings 20: 17-19 (LXX) - 1 Kings 21:17-19)!

Being the leader of the family means that husbands are held responsible for their own financial mistakes as well as their wife's! The principle is found in the New Testament as well in the qualifications of deacons: "A deacon must be the husband of but one wife and must manage his children and his household well" (1 Timothy 3:12). Household leadership in this cultural context was not just about parenting; it was about managing the money.

God holds husbands responsible for the financial stewardship of their homes. Husbands are accountable to God for the family checkbook, savings and investments. Being the head of the home does not mean that husbands can buy the new shotgun, but their wife better not buy shoes! Leadership in a marriage means that husbands lead the team to best manage the money God allots them. As team leader husbands must respect that God will speak to both man and wife, but as leaders, husbands must take final responsibility for the financial stewardship of the home. So, how we deal with money in our household tells much about the marriage. Here we are definitely not speaking about dominance. Rather we strongly suggest that stewardship means that both spouses must give in to God about financial stewardship.

Ahab and Jezebel seemed to have had the wealth and the power to sustain their greed. But then God stepped in. Yes, Ahab got his vegetable garden – for a little while. And Jezebel got her way – for a little while. But what we gain by greed never brings lasting happiness. And in fact, it leads to death. Ahab soon met his end – being shot by an arrow in battle even though he traveled in disguise (III Kings (LXX) -1 Kings 22:35). And Jezebel was eventually thrown down to her death from a window by her servants and the dogs ate her (IV Kings (LXX) -2 Kings 9:33-36).

Greed has terrible endings. The story of Ahab and Jezebel is a terrible warning to us about the end of greed and discontent. Greed and discontent lead to destructive chaos in our emotions, in our marriage and of course in our finances. Discontent even leads to spiritual error and death. The example of Ahab must be in the mind of the writer when he wrote: "But each one is tempted when, by his own evil desire, he is dragged away and enticed. Then, after desire has conceived, it gives birth to sin; and sin, when it is full-grown, gives birth to death." (James 1:14-15). [We see a similar end with the Rich Fool. Just when he was content with his expansion of the barns, the angel of death came and took him We read in the story of Luke 12:20-21: "But God said to him, 'You fool! This very night your life will be demanded from you. Then who will get what you have prepared for yourself?' This is how it will be with whoever stores up things for themselves but is not rich toward God (NIV) - εἶπε δὲ αὐτῷ ὁ Θεός· ἄφρον, ταύτῃ τῇ νυκτὶ τὴν ψυχήν σου ἀπαιτοῦσιν ἀπὸ σοῦ· ἃ δὲ ἡτοίμασας τίνι ἔσται; οὕτως ὁ θησαυρίζων ἑαυτῷ, καὶ μὴ εἰς Θεὸν πλουτῶν"].

Paul also gives us a strong warning by saying: "People who want to get rich fall into temptation and a trap and into many foolish and harmful desires that plunge men into ruin and destruction. For the love of money is a root of all kinds of evil. Some people, eager for money, have wandered from the faith and pierced themselves with many griefs" (1 Timothy 6:9-10). [*Strong caution*: Paul and many Fathers of the Church warned us not to confuse wealth with problems. What they tell us and emphasize in many ways is that greed can fall onto the rich as well as to the poor. The problem is wanting wealth. Greed is not about the amount. It is the *wanting desire* to be rich. Why is this wrong? Because if that want becomes desire then we violate the stewardship principle of contentment. The result of this failure is a continual falling to other temptations].

Therefore, we need to address our greed at its core, which is the issue of desire. Our desires are the problem. It's our desire for nicer… bigger… and so on. To support this notion, it is worth listening to the words of 1 Timothy 6:9 which might simply take the form of suffering the slow thirst of finding life empty. We can discover after a couple decades of climbing the ladder of financial success that it's against the wrong building. You see, all of us look and fight for the money that we do not have and as such we fail to recognize that our ambition in this world is fundamentally the love of money, status, prestige and the power of what money brings us. We are completely off course – the ladder is indeed on the wrong building. We have and continue to have failed to recognize the real issue is spiritual, not circumstantial. So, unless we admit that our sinful nature is the reason for our greed, we will fail.

Furthermore, by studying the words of James (4:1-4 NIV) we receive a serious analysis of the issue of greed, thusly: "What causes fights and quarrels among you? Don't they come from your desires that battle within you? You desire but do not have, so you kill. You covet but you cannot get what you want, so you quarrel and fight. You do not have because you do not ask God. When you ask, you do not receive, because you ask with wrong motives, that you may spend what you get on your pleasures. You adulterous people, don't you know that friendship with the world means enmity against God? Therefore, anyone who chooses to be a friend of the world becomes an enemy of God."

So, in the final analysis we all must ask: Do we want contentment? Do we want to be released from the pressure to upgrade our life? The word of God suggests several concrete changes in mindset we must make once we've admitted that it really is a sin problem. The mindset change must take into consideration the following:

1. *Contentment means lowering our expectations*: Paul exhorts us to lower our expectations to the essentials in (1 Timothy 6:8). But if we have food and clothing, we will be content with that. Paul wasn't talking about gourmet food and designer clothing; he meant that we have to lower our expectations to appreciate that God has given us – His stewards – the essentials.

   This passage is actually just one of three times this particular Greek word for "ἀρκεσθησόμεθα – content" is used in the New Testament about finances. It simply means "we will be satisfied - enough." God's stewards agree with God that the essentials are enough. It is possible to be content with only food! Maybe God will even allow us a time in our life when we just have the essentials of food and clothing.

2. *Contentment means not assuming that the answer is more income*: John the Baptist once addressed the issue of discontent when he was questioned by some soldiers about what repentance would mean for them in (Luke 3:14) "Then some soldiers asked him, "And what should we do?" He replied, "Don't extort money and don't accuse people falsely - be content with your pay."

   Contentment with our pay is not the "world's" way. We have come to believe that abundance and getting ahead in life financially is our birthright – and our employer is generally the culprit in our way! All of us have felt or are feeling financial pressures. And when our needs seem larger than our income, we assume the answer is more money.

   Do you suppose that any of the Roman soldiers talking to John the Baptist had financial concerns? Of course, they did. Rome was not concerned with making sure its soldiers were well-paid. In the culture, the Roman government probably expected soldiers to use their position and weapons to extort money – as commonly as waitresses are expected to receive tips – regardless of the service they provide. According to John's words here, evidently one-way extortion was carried out was by threatening to accuse wealthy citizens of some crime against Rome – unless they paid up.

John said, Stop extorting money. Now they were supposed to make it on pay alone. God's word is telling us to be content with our pay, our income. More money is not the answer. That's a hard one to swallow.

Thinking about others who have more simply makes us more miserable. Envy, greed and discontent never brought anyone happiness. On the other hand, contentment does.

3. *Contentment means expecting peace from our relationship with God, not from money*: "Keep your lives free from the love of money and be content with what you have, because God has said, "Never will I leave you; never will I forsake you" (Hebrews 13:5).

Contentment can bring joy no matter how much we have, because contentment is based on our relationship with God! If our wages don't seem sufficient for our needs, we really can fall back on God who promised that He wouldn't leave us.

The real issue is not whether our money is enough, but whether God's promises are enough for us. Did we ever realize that our financial needs and desires are really meant to drive us to God? Let's not waste the opportunity.

Ahab and Jezebel let greed rule and ruin their lives because they were actually running from God! What if Ahab had confessed and dealt with his greed when He saw Naboth's vineyard? What a different story it would have been!

What if we would confess our discontentment as it occurred? What if we would begin to thank God instead – not just for our belongings (stuff), but for His presence? He is right there with us. He has promised to never forsake us. What if we began to realize that those feelings of discontent are actually invitations by God to find our satisfaction in Him? Those urges we have to upgrade are normal, but what if we learned to turn them over to Christ?

There's an old story of a humble Christian who sat down at a meal of only bread and water and prayed in gratitude, All this and Jesus too.

We will never be content until we are content with Christ. We will never be content unless we value our relationship with Christ more than possessing anything else, we naturally desire. This is the only answer to greed and discontent – contentment with Christ. Maslow's (1943) need theory explains some of this lack of contentment in his pyramid of needs – see note 1.

Is that possible? It is, but it means letting God pry our determined fingers off of whatever it is we want to keep or to attain.

4. *Contentment means finding satisfaction through Christ's strength whether we have too little or more than enough*: Paul described the experience of having Christ's strength even when he was hungry – lacking even the essentials (Philippians 4:12b, 13) "I have learned the secret of being content in any and every situation, whether well fed or hungry, whether living in plenty or in want. I can do everything through Him who gives me strength." This means that in reality, we can't be content in our own strength! We need Christ's strength – miraculously!

Paul uses a different Greek term for content here than he used in 1 Timothy 6:8. This term is similar, but it's a "food" word - χορτάζεσθαι. It means "satisfied" – as in having a full feeling after Thanksgiving Dinner. You literally are full and you do not want to even think of food. We are not hungry anymore. We are satisfied.

This is the term Paul used to say that he was "full" even when he was hungry – because Christ gave him the strength to be "full" even when his pockets and stomach were empty. That's miraculous contentment!

Contentment is first of all a test of our stewardship because it reveals if we consider ourselves owners or managers. But contentment is even more. Our financial needs and even our temptations to greed are actually a perfect God-ordained opportunity to develop spiritual intimacy with Him. Financial contentment really is not about the money; it's about the eternal possibility of drawing close to the God who promised to give us what we need and to trust Him with what we think we lack.

A new wide-screen TV can't bring you peace. A new Escalade or a Tesla will not make you happy – if it does, it will be temporary. But learning to live without either of them might just be the key to enjoying the riches of true contentment in our relationship with God.

People ruin their lives over financial rights, inheritance squabbles, and suing people they think cheated them. But God is calling us to think different – to be stewards – to just faithfully manage what God gives us.

Note 1: Maslow's hierarchy of needs is a motivational theory in psychology comprising a five-tier model of human needs, often depicted as hierarchical levels within a pyramid. From the bottom of the hierarchy upwards, the needs are: physiological, safety, love and belonging, esteem, and self-actualization. These needs are generally depicted as a pyramid in the following form – Figure 1.1.

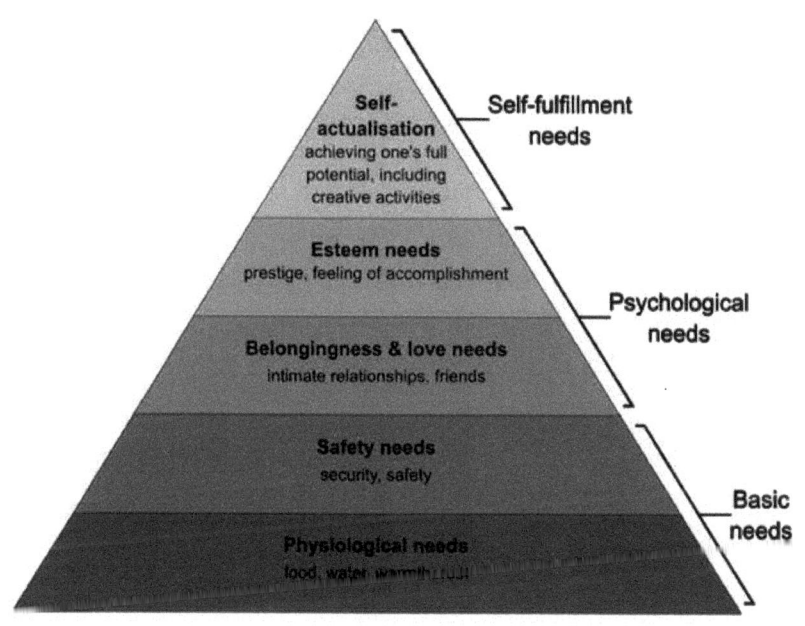

Figure 1.1. The Maslow's pyramid of needs

Chapter 2
Connecting to God through Giving

There is no other area of spiritual growth where we make the assumption that believers will grow without reminder and exhortation. I have come to realize that we are not mature disciples if we have not embraced the reality that materially we are stewards instead of owners. I have come to realize that as Orthodox Christians we are in need of fundamental teaching in faith and behavior including practices that support our growth in spirituality and connectivity with our God. One of the most underrepresentation in our day is the lack of understanding *stewardship*.

Our clergy have communicated somehow that "stewardship" messages are primarily about fund-raising (quite often with bingo games, festivals, raffle tickets and so on), and even then, the emphasis is on being "generous" without specificity. It seems that the Orthodox Church considers "stewardship" as an old-fashioned practice and modern-day taboo. Of course, as we already have pointed out in the introduction and chapter 1, that is not the truth. Stewardship is not fund-raising; it is basic discipleship. But in a similar sense, each believer must come to understand that giving is not just about "doing their duty." Giving is actually a deeply personal indicator of our spiritual maturity as well as our love for God. If we understand Jesus' words that our "treasure" is an indication of our "heart," how can the Church and the clergy avoid teaching on the important issue of giving? Yet, they do.

Giving is a spiritual issue and in fact, a relational issue with God. In order to truly yield to God's ownership of our possessions, we must evaluate carefully what may be the most telling evidence of our stewardship – the part we give. Just as we decide on what we spend on an appliance or how much we will put in a savings or retirement account; we must also decide how much money we will give. Even to give nothing is a decision. Stewards are accountable in each decision to please the owner.

Many see the responsibility of giving as a burden. How sad that is in light of Paul's reminder that God loves a cheerful giver. Giving is actually a relational decision. In the process of making giving decisions we really establish our agreement with God about stewardship. As we continually decide to give, we constantly affirm how much we value our relationship to God as His children. And as God's stewards, giving decisions are simply a matter of thinking through how He wants us to allocate His money.

An amazing benefit of giving as stewards is that it releases us from the real burden of our own financial needs. As we learn to trust God through giving, we can live confidently on what is left because we know that God is taking care of that. *Giving is a freeing experience as it connects us more closely to God relationally.* The ultimate outcome is that those who give as stewards experience a sense of intimacy with God that all followers of Christ long for. *Giving becomes worship.* Giving becomes a way of saying *thanks to God for His grace and promised provision.* Giving becomes a deep part of our *personal connection to God.* Some examples from the scriptures prove these points

1. *The Widow of Zarephath – 860 B.C. (III Kings (LXX) -1 Kings 17:7-14):* This passage tells us the story of God providing for a widow in a small-town northwest of Galilee along the Mediterranean Coast. After a 3 ½ year drought, God sent Elijah to this widow living in financial fears. There had been a terrible ominous fear growing in her heart for several years. There was no rain in the land. She could not grow anything. There was no welfare – especially in pagan Sidon. This wasn't Israel where people at least knew they were supposed to care for the widow and the poor. As far as she knew, the starvation process would begin after this meal. There was nothing to eat anywhere.

   And then the prophet Elijah showed up. First, he wanted a drink. His brook had dried up and he was thirsty. She must have had some source of water, so in spite of her own desperate plight, she does the proper oriental thing and aided the traveler. But his next request stopped her in her tracks. Bring me bread, he asked.

   I have no bread. I'm about to die with my son, and you want me to bring you bread. But Elijah does not back down on his request. He sets in place a test of this woman's heart. He says, don't be afraid. Go make bread like you said, but make mine first (III

Kings (LXX) -1 Kings 17:13). To be sure, by our modern standards, Elijah's request sounds very selfish indeed. However, Elijah represents the God of Israel. And the God of Israel and heaven and earth is sovereign – and He has to be obeyed. So, God's representative, Elijah promises her a miracle – but she has to make his cake of bread first.

Now the woman has a decision to make – just as all of us. Do I divide my very last meal? This means that I and my son will not even have the hunger pains subside today – in the scant hope that something might be found tomorrow. It means the hunger starts today, not tomorrow.

Shall I do it, she had to wonder – just like all of us. This is a man of God, representing the living and true God. He has promised to provide miraculously for me. But do I really believe it? Do I believe it enough to give this man bread that leaves me hungry today? These questions are always present for everyone who is about to decide about giving. In any case, she decides to trust God, but perhaps not without a large degree of doubt. Maybe she even had a "What do I have to lose?" attitude. So, she made the bread – dividing the little she had and giving to Elijah first.

How does it work out for this widow? III Kings (LXX) - 1 Kings 17:15-16 tells, us, "She went away and did as Elijah had told her. So, there was food every day for Elijah and for the woman and her family. For the jar of flour was not used up and the jug of oil did not run dry, in keeping with the word of the LORD spoken by Elijah."

God did the miracle! The widow was perplexed. She could not believe what happened. But it did. The story does not tell us *how* or *when* it exactly happened, but we know that it did happen and the replenishment lasted until the famine was over with.

The widow's experience makes all of us ponder the notion of God and His power. Can you imagine the joy that the widow found her the moment that the flour and oil were replenished? I suspect that her life after this experience was never the same. Why? Because the God whom she only knew at a distance was now her Divine Provider. He cared personally for her.

So, now the question is: Does God still do that? And the answer is a categorical and emphatic, YES. That is the way God is. He cares about us personally and reaches out to us relationally when we are devoted to Him. "For the eyes of the Lord move to and fro throughout the earth that He may strongly support those whose heart is completely His" (2 Chronicles 16:9). It should be no surprise to anyone that God uses the area of financial giving to test our heart and then to draw us close as we trust and obey Him. The example of the widow is astonishing. However, we can make some observations that might fit our situation in today's world:
    a. She was a believer in the true God.
    b. She had serious financial needs herself.
    c. She was asked to give away a big part of the little she had.
    d. She heard God's promise to provide for her if she gave.
    e. She believed God's promise and first gave obediently to God.
    f. God showed His care by providing for her needs miraculously!

2. *The Widow and Jesus At the Temple – 30 A.D.*: Jesus and His disciples were at the temple in Jerusalem sitting where people put in offerings for the temple treasury. It was Passover time and the town was extra full. At feast times like this, people who came to the temple would often give extra gifts. *This was not the tithe. It was not obligation. These extra gifts were special gifts that were supposed to be given as personal worship.* It is important to note here, that worship is not proven by a gift or anything external. Worship is what goes on in the heart. And that is what we learn by the Bible's account of what took place next. The Orthodox Church represents this event with the following (icon 2.1) shown here.

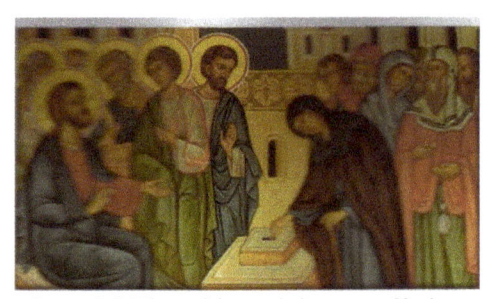

Icon 2.1 The widow giving an offering

The text in Mark tells us the story: "Jesus sat down opposite the place where the offerings were put and watched the crowd putting their money into the temple treasury. Many rich people threw in large amounts. But a poor widow came and put in two very small copper coins, worth only a fraction of a penny. Calling his disciples to him, Jesus said, "I tell you the truth, this poor widow has put more into the treasury than all the others. They all gave out of their wealth; but she, out of her poverty, put in everything - all she had to live on" (Mark 12:41-44 NIV).

Jesus doesn't say anything against the wealthy people who gave at the temple this day. He doesn't say that the wealthy were wrongly motivated. But Jesus noticed a particular widow whose heart was *genuinely committed* to giving as worship. And Jesus makes the divine observation that this woman gave MORE than the wealthy!

She gave the smallest of all imaginable gifts. It was two tiny coins. These coins – *lepta* – were little bronze pieces weighing less than a gram each. (A penny weighs about 3 grams.) Together these two coins equaled $1/16^{th}$ of a denarius. We know that a laborer could earn a denarius per day (Mathew 20:9-10), so for comparison, the amount she gave was about what a laborer today would earn in a half hour (a half hour of minimum wage).

So, on one hand what made her gift remarkable was how small it was. But ironically, what made her gift remarkable to Jesus was how large it was! What make this gift so large was that it was *all the money she had.*

The story does not tell us the particular finances of the woman, but what we know is enough to marvel at her decision to give *all she had*. Mind you, she did not have to give. In fact, she had every reason NOT to give. The incredible part of the story however, is the *willingness to worship*. That is what caught Jesus' eye and that is why He made the comment, she gave more than those who gave large amounts out of their wealth. The gifts given by others were expendable income. It didn't affect them really in any way. Her gift was essential income. Here it is interesting to notice that Jesus did not make any promises to her. In fact, we do not even know if He spoke to her. We do strongly suspect however, that the woman would be taken care of by the providence of God in her future needs. Why do we suspect this? Because God always sees the *sacrifice of giving.* That's where the worship of giving really happens. It costs. King David once said, I will not sacrifice a burnt offering that costs me nothing (1 Chronicles 21:24). By contrast, in our modern world, we honor the large amount of giving (of whatever utility) rather than the intent of the giver and individual sacrifice. See note 1 for three examples.

Jesus pointed her out because He recognized the sincerity of her heart. This woman has stood through the ages as a model for giving, not simply because her giving ratio exceeded the gifts of others, but because the sacrifice indicated her deep love for God. *Love for God is the goal*. Sacrificial giving is a means of establishing and expressing that closeness with Him. However, the story allows us to make the following observations that might fit our situation in today's world:
    a. We are never too poor to give.
    b. Giving generously means trusting God for the future. That is what faith is!
    c. God is honored by our degree of sacrifice, not the amount.
    d. Giving is worship that expresses our relationship to God.

Here is one more true story of a widow who gave.

3. *The Widow and God's Business*: A remarkable story for anyone who doubts the power of giving. The story begins with a couple having a business about to lose it when all of a sudden, the wife "Ruby" suggested that they should give $1,000 to their local church even though they had no money. They were about to go bankrupt. By the time the check cleared the bank not only there was enough money to pay the check but there was enough money to pay all the outstanding bills which were overdue by 36 months.

   Ruby's husband died within two weeks of this event but Ruby continued to write a check of $1,000/month for a year. The business improved and the giving as of the time of Ron Blue's book she was contributing $20,000/month to the church. For the entire story see Blue (1997). Obviously, this is one story. However, the giving principle is abundantly clear throughout the Bible as well as anectodical stories from many of us.

These three stories are not just about God's reward for giving. They pull back the curtain on God's desire to connect relationally with us. The widow who fed Elijah believed God's promise and got to know and enjoy God because she trusted Him. The widow at the temple already was a worshipper. She didn't come to the temple that day the way we often come to church – *asking, what will I get out of it*? She came to give as worship. And Ruby in those months of grieving while learning to manage a business certainly drew closer to God as the One who would now provide for her as she trusted Him through giving.

Giving was the crucial element that connected each of them to God as they stretched out to Him in personal trust. Giving connects us relationally with God. Giving is not about us; *giving is about our relationship to God*. Giving connects us to God relationally in several significant ways.

4. *Giving establishes our humility before God*: What does the IRS call the money that we can deduct from our income because we gave it away? It is called "charitable giving." How is charitable giving defined by our world? It's giving some of what we have to help out people who are needy or suffering. That is a good thing to be sure, but in the world's way of thinking, we are benefactors

if we give. Those to whom we give are recipients. There is a certain superiority in that concept. Benefactors are put on pedestal because they gave something away. They are called *philanthropists* – friends of humanity. Recipients feel small because they are in need of someone else's generosity.

If that is what giving is to us, it is not biblical giving. Giving does not make one superior at all. God of course is not in need of my gift. Giving is about me expressing to God that He is my superior. Giving is about me putting myself into a rightful humble relationship with God because He is the Owner and I am the steward. I am simply giving something to Him to express that I understand His ownership.

Deuteronomy (26:8-10 LXX) describes how giving expresses humble dependence: "And the Lord brought us out of Egypt himself with his great strength, and his mighty hand, and his high arm, and with great visions, and with signs, and with wonders. And He brought us into this place, and gave us this land, a land flowing with milk and honey. And now, behold, I have brought the first of the fruits of the land, which thou gavest me, O Lord, a land flowing with milk and honey: and thou shalt leave it before the Lord thy God, and thou shalt worship before the Lord thy God;"

The steward who gives to God is not superior at all. He is to bow before God the recipient! *Giving here is how Israel expressed its humble gratitude to God for what He let them enjoy.* You gave it to me, Lord. You are really the owner, the benefactor. Biblical givers are not superior because they are stewards. Obviously, owners are superior to stewards.

On a human level, giving doesn't elevate us over others either. In fact, giving is not a people thing at all; it's always a "God and me" thing. That's where the world's view and the biblical view of giving are going in totally different directions. When we give, we are recognizing our relationship to God as a manager of his money. It places us in our proper position under God.

If we give financially to other people with a smug attitude of superiority and condescension, we have tipped our hand that we are not really a steward of God at all. Or *if we give to have our name in print or placed on a bronze plaque, we better enjoy it, because that's all that we will ever get.* Jesus said of people like that, they have their reward in full (Matthew 6:2). [Strong warning here: As Orthodox we seem to take pride when we give. We want everyone to know it. It is not unusual to find churches with parishioner's names on individual bricks and or branches of trees or plaques announcing what they have given and how much. In the case of the brick the more you give the closer the brick is placed to the sanctuary (Ναο); in the case of the branch, the more money you give your name is engraved in bronze/copper plaques on the higher branches; in the case of the plaques, in a typical church you find them everywhere: In many icons, analogia (icon or book stands), pews, etc. If you give at least $100,000 the Church hierarchs nominate you and accept you as a member of the "Leadership Team and or Archons," and the list goes on – for examples of these issues see note 1. These are quite different than the *Tamata* (see note 2) which hang on the bottom of a particular saints. These are specific promises of a believer that petitions a particular saint or the Theotoko to help in a specific situation – usually a health condition. (In the Orthodox Church there are certain saints who are known to be famous for particular healings of a specific disease or ailment. For example. St. Paraskeve, is the saint for eyes or eye ailments; St. Nectarios for cancer and so on). So, a *tama* is a votive offering or promise made of a rectangular piece of metal with miniature body parts].

What Moses was saying in Deuteronomy 26:8-10 is that God gave them their land and God gave them their blessings. His point is that our gifts are really just recognition of who God is. By giving, the Israelites were saying back to God, You have placed Me in charge temporarily of this little bit of real estate. I am

bringing my gift to you not because I'm big or wonderful, but because You are. That is the attitude God is seeking in us.
5. *Giving is worship:* The computer program, *Google Earth*, allows all of us to zoom down from a picture of the globe to the level of our house – via satellite photo. When I zoom down to a picture of our church property, I can see my car parked out front on the day the satellite took the picture. When I zoomed down to my house – in Greece - I could even see my grill on the patio. But what strikes me as the computer is zooming down is how very, very, very tiny my place is – in the perspective of the earth. Even if I owned an entire city of land and houses, I would still own very little.

But God owns the earth (Ps. 23(24):1)! So, what posture should a person have as they bring their gift? Bow down. Bow down! God is great. The Israelite had in his hand a tiny portion of a single crop, but it served to acknowledge the greatness of the God who made all the crops throughout the world in all ages. Our gift might be big to us because it's a sacrifice, but to God it is big only because it acknowledges His infinite ownership. This little bit I call "giving" is actually just my way of saying, You own it all.

The tiny cake of bread for Elijah, two lepta for the temple, a measly 1,000 dollars from Ruby, or our check to support the church is big in God's grand scheme only if the gift acknowledges and worships the real giver, the real Owner. Giving is literally worship. Proverbs (3:9 LXX) says, "Honor the Lord with thy just labors, and give him the first of thy fruits of righteousness." The Hebrew word "honor" means to "glorify" or to acknowledge the importance of something. Its root meaning is that something is heavy or weighty and thus significant or important. When applied to God, honoring Him means that we ascribe to Him the significance that He deserves as God. When we bring our "first fruits" we express how important God is. In the final analysis, when we give to express our worship and honor, there will arise within us an expectation and confidence that God is so powerful and faithful that He will not only use our gifts for His larger eternal purposes, but also that God will meet our needs as well.

6. *Giving expresses our trust in God*: Do we trust what God is doing in our human relationships, our careers, and our health? Do we really trust God? How do we develop trust in God? Financial giving is actually one of God's key training grounds to produce a trust connection between us and Him. Giving is a test. So in Malachi (3:10 LXX) we read: "And ye have brought all the produce into the storehouses; but there shall be the plunder thereof in its house: return now on this behalf, saith the Lord Almighty, [see] if I will not open to you the torrents of heaven, and pour out my blessing upon you, until ye are satisfied. The NIV translation reads: "Bring the whole tithe into the storehouse, that there may be food in my house. Test me in this," says the LORD Almighty, "and see if I will not throw open the floodgates of heaven and pour out so much blessing that you will not have room enough for it."

    Giving really is about trusting God. Because, like the examples earlier, we saw that giving means that we have less. It's simple math. 100-1=99. I have less if I tithe. However, we still do it because of trust. There is nothing more relational than *trust*. Even in our daily life, *trust* is always based on a relationship. Once we have gotten to know someone's character, we can predict much of what they will do. But even in the times when we don't know for sure what they will do, we don't worry about it, because we know their character well enough to trust them to do what is in our best interest.

    So, it boils down to: Do we know and trust God? Do we know His character? God wants us to know and trust Him so that even when we can't see for sure what He is doing, we don't doubt Him. Financial concerns seem to be an area that tests the trust of all people no matter what economic level they are. God wants to use this constant tangible area of life to draw us closer to Him. As *we give back to God in sacrificial worship, we are telling God that we really do trust Him*. As a result, He is honored and we are more likely to find the peace of trusting God with our financial situation.
7. *Giving develops a giving heart*: So far, we have strongly suggested that stewardship is an issue of trust. However, it is also

a matter of the heart and it must be developed early on in our life or be an illumination of conversion to Christ later in our life. [Remember my father's violin story, in the introduction?] In either case it is a *work in progress*. An old story may make my message more understandable.

Long ago, a father gave his son two dimes as he was going to Church on Sunday morning. He told His son, that one dime was for the offering tray at the church – his personal offering – and the other to buy some candies after church. As the boy walked down the muddy road – it had rained all night long – he tripped and one of his dimes fell out of his hand. He stopped and he looked in the mud to find it but to no avail. The dime disappeared. The boy after some time searching for his money, stopped for a moment looked one more time with no results and then slowly but steadily looked toward the sky and said. Well God, there goes my offering for you today.

You see, even this simple story tells us that even a child generates war (an uncomfortable feeling) inside him when it comes to give what is his. Of course, for a child it is difficult to comprehend the principle of stewardship, but it is imperative that we teach that all belongs to the Almighty God, we are just managers of what he has bestowed us. To be sure, not to criticize the child in the story but all of us - adults – believe that just because something we call *ours* or it has *our name on it*, is really ours. If for any reason someone else wants to take it away, that creates discomfort, tension and even a physical fight.

So, who really determines where our money goes? Will I really use my financial and material things exactly how God wants me to? How would I know how to proceed? The answers are dependent on whether or not we all understand the *concept of stewardship* for God's richness. The driving force for such an understanding is our *heart*.

The usage of the word *heart*, in Scripture and in the language of the Fathers, is often a metaphor of our *will*. It's where we make up our mind if we will do what God wants. We can only understand what God says about financial giving if we *align our heart with his*. Two examples may solidify and contrast my argument. The first one is from a wealthy man in Jerusalem with a selfish heart in 1,000 B.C. and some believers with a willing heart in 100 A.D. in the northern part of Greece – known as Macedonia.

We want to contrast today a wealthy man in Jerusalem with a selfish heart in 1000 B.C. and some believers with a willing heart in 100 A.D. who lived in Macedonia (modern Greece). The first story comes to us from reading the text in (III Kings (LXX) -1 Kings 10:14-11:13)." And the weight of gold that came to Solomon in one year was six hundred and sixty-six talents of gold. Besides the tributes of them that were subjects, both merchants and all the kings of the [country] beyond [the river], and of the princes of the land. And Solomon made three hundred spears of beaten gold: three hundred shekels of gold were upon one spear." Obviously, Solomon was very rich. [Just in case you are curious, 666 talents of gold = about 800,000 ounces. At today's price of about \$2,000/oz, that's $\$1.6 \times 10^9$ (1,600,000,000, billion). That was just yearly revenue in gold, not counting taxes and tariffs from all kinds of people and governments.

Solomon also had a nice place to sit. (III Kings (LXX) - 1 Kings 10:18-20) "And the king made a great ivory throne, and gilded it with pure gold. The throne [had] six steps, and calves in bold relief to the throne behind it, and side-pieces on either hand of the place of the seat, and two lions standing by the side-pieces, and twelve lions standing there on the six steps on either side: it was not so done in any [other] kingdom.

God had blessed Solomon due to his priorities and godly prayer request in the early days of his kingdom *asking for wisdom instead of riches*. So, God promised him, "And I have given thee what thou hast not asked, wealth and glory, so that there has not been any one like thee among kings" (III Kings (LXX) -1 Kings

10:23). Solomon's riches clearly came from God. Solomon wasn't an owner either. He was a steward like you and me.

Never enough

But there was something about material possessions that were never enough for Solomon. (III Kings (LXX) – I Kings 10:22-27) "For Solomon had a ship of Tharsis in the sea with the ships of Chiram: one ship came to the king every three years out of Tharsis, [laden with] gold and silver, and wrought stones, and hewn stones. This was the arrangement of the provision which king Solomon fetched to build the house of the Lord, and the house of the king, and the wall of Jerusalem, and the citadel; to fortify the city of David, and Assur, and Magdal, and Gazer, and Baethoron the upper, and Jethermath, and all the cities of the chariots, and all the cities of the horsemen, and the fortification of Solomon which he purposed to build in Jerusalem and in all the land, so that none of the people should rule over him. All the people that was left of the Chettite and the Amorite, and the Pherezite, and the Chananite, and the Evite, and the Jebusite, and the Gergesite, who were not of the children of Israel, their descendants who had been left with him in the land, whom the children of Israel could not utterly destroy; and Solomon made them tributaries until this day. But of the children of Israel Solomon made nothing; for they were the warriors, and his servants and rulers, and captains of the third order, and the captains of his chariots, and his horsemen. And Solomon increased beyond all the kings of the earth in wealth and wisdom. And all the kings of the earth sought the presence of Solomon, to hear his wisdom which the Lord [had] put into his heart. And they brought everyone their gifts, vessels of gold, and raiment, and stacte, and spices, and horses, and mules, a rate year by year. And Solomon had four thousand mares for his chariots, and twelve thousand horsemen: and he put them in the cities of his chariots, and with the king in Jerusalem: and he ruled over all the kings from the river to the land of the Philistines, and to the borders of Egypt. And the king made gold and silver in Jerusalem as stones, and he made cedars as the sycamores in the plain for multitude."

If you notice the translation of the NIV is different. Here it is: "The king had a fleet of trading ships at sea along with the ships of Hiram. Once every three years it returned, carrying gold, silver and ivory, and apes and baboons. King Solomon was greater in riches and wisdom than all the other kings of the earth. The whole world sought audience with Solomon to hear the wisdom God had put in his heart. Year after year, everyone who came brought a gift--articles of silver and gold, robes, weapons and spices, and horses and mules. Solomon accumulated chariots and horses; he had fourteen hundred chariots and twelve thousand horses, which he kept in the chariot cities and also with him in Jerusalem. The king made silver as common in Jerusalem as stones, and cedar as plentiful as sycamore-fig trees in the foothills" NIV.

What could Solomon have been thinking when he sent his ships to Egypt for more horses? Yes, I know I have 10,000 horses and 1,000 chariots. That was my old goal. Go get another 2,000 horses and 200 chariots. That's my new goal. Yes, get more gold, more apes and baboons. Build more cages. I love my zoo. Yes, Yes, Yes.

It's like Solomon had little buttons inside his heart. One was labeled "Enough." The other was called, "More." Solomon seems to have set a golden brick on the "More" button and just let it run.

But money and horses are not all Solomon was accumulating during what seemed to be his "glory days." He also accumulated 700 wives and 300 concubines (III Kings (LXX)- 1 Kings 11:1-4). We can't even try to understand the idea of 1,000 women in his life. He married for many political and personal selfish reasons, but the result was that in his effort to please many of them, he built them places of pagan worship and they indeed turned his heart away from the Lord.

It was exactly what God had warned about in the law, a copy of which must have lain somewhere in the great temple Solomon had built earlier in his reign. "The king, moreover, must not acquire great numbers of horses for himself or make the people return to Egypt to get more of them, for the LORD has told you, "You are not to go back that way again." He must not take many wives, or his heart will be led astray. He must not accumulate large amounts of silver and gold. (Deuteronomy 17:16-19)

Solomon blew it on each detail of God's warning. And thus he "followed after other gods." It was an awful downward spiral. Why? His heart was turned. His heart not fully devoted to God. Now God had promised early on to bless Solomon with wealth, so it wasn't necessarily wrong that Solomon was wealthy, but somewhere he crossed the line that God warned about here of "accumulating" large amounts of it. That was a heart issue!

But Solomon simply did what most people and many Christians would do if we had the capability. Solomon just bought everything his heart desired that he could afford. It's just that he could just afford more than we can. But the warning is that what we can afford can actually turn our hearts astray from being devoted to the Lord.

The second story is of a giving heart found in the gospel of Matthew. In contrast to Solomon, Jesus told us to store up treasures in heaven as an expression of a devoted heart. "Do not store up for yourselves treasures on earth, where moth and rust destroy, and where thieves break in and steal. But store up for yourselves treasures in heaven, where moth and rust do not destroy, and where thieves do not break in and steal. For where your treasure is, there your heart will be also" (Matthew 6:19-21).

Jesus was greatly concerned about our heart. Our heart will naturally attach to physical things that moths destroy – speaking of valued cloth and clothes – or things that rust destroys or corrodes or anything valuable that thieves take.

As if to prove Jesus' point about the temporary nature of material things, we can think back to realize that most of Solomon's vast treasury of wealth disappeared just 5 years after his son Rehoboam ascended his throne (III Kings (LXX) - 1 Kings 14:25). The king of Egypt attacked Jerusalem and carried off the treasures of the temple and the palace. Rehoboam had to replace those gold shields with bronze shields. And what treasure remained was stolen over the coming generations by more invaders or used as tribute to buy off attacking kingdoms.

Money sure gets away easily, doesn't it? (Proverbs 23:5 LXX) "If thou shouldest fix thine eye upon him, he will disappear; for wings like an eagle's are prepared for him, and he returns to the house of his master." In contrast, Jesus urges us to store up treasures in heaven. Jesus is calling us to think differently about treasure. Attach your heart to things that last forever, Jesus says.

We've all heard the expressions, *you can't take it with you*, or, *you don't see a hearse pulling a U-Haul.* But Jesus is saying something different in Matthew 6:20. He is saying that you can't take treasures with you, but you can, however, send treasures on ahead! If we invest our lives in things that are eternal instead of material and financial, then treasures will be waiting for us in some sense when we get to heaven.

Treasure in heaven is permanent and yet it is personal! Jesus said to lay up treasures for yourselves. There is some kind of real and personal way in which our investment in eternal things is really "ours!" They will have our name on them somehow. There is some kind of eternal reward or enjoyment by which, when we get to heaven, we will arrive and receive our treasure! We can keep it eternally!

The real issue is that where our treasure is, our heart is. Period. This passage is not specifically talking about giving money to God or ministry, but it is teaching us something crucial about a decision we must make prior to any giving. Where is our heart? Which do we value – financial or eternal treasure? Public recognition or anonymity?

Giving or tithing is going to be meaningless at best if we think like some who teach that giving is a way to have financial success, or a way to impress God, or impress people, or a way to feel good about ourselves. Then our goal – our heart – is still focused on ourselves and not on eternity.

Jesus' main point was to ask us which we want. Which one do we value – earth's treasure or heaven's? We might pretend that we want a diversified portfolio – earthly and heavenly treasure. I want it all, we might say. But we can't. Jesus makes sure we understand that.

In the next two verses (Matthew 6:22-23) Jesus tells a little parable about how our eyes are either blind or seeing on this subject. Some people are blind to heavenly treasure. How great is that darkness, Jesus says.

Many people in all religions and non-religious communities do not understand it either willingly or unwillingly. They will never switch from material goals to eternal goals. And Jesus makes it clear we must choose. "No one can serve two masters. Either he will hate the one and love the other, or he will be devoted to the one and despise the other. You cannot serve both God and money" (Matthew 6:24).

We can serve God or money, but not both! We can only have one heart, one devotion. Some areas of life must be single-minded. So, no matter what we have or how much we have, we must act as a good steward. Period! God wants our whole life, not just our money, but God uses our money – particularly our giving – as a key indicator and even a method by which to transform our heart.

A generous heart can develop in us if we are close to God's grace. In fact, generosity develops in us as we align our hearts with God's and imitate His grace. 2 Corinthians 8 tells us about a remarkable group of believers – in fact whole churches in the first century – who got it. The light turned on and they had eternal treasure on their minds. Their generous new way of thinking was so amazing that Paul called it God's gift (grace) to them.

"And now, brothers, we want you to know about the grace that God has given the Macedonian churches. Out of the most severe trial, their overflowing joy and their extreme poverty welled up in rich generosity. For I testify that they gave as much as they were able, and even beyond their ability. Entirely on their own, they urgently pleaded with us for the privilege of sharing in this service to the saints" (2 Corinthians 8:1-4).

These people are not normal, are they – pleading with Paul for the privilege of giving even though they were poor? This is not the typical Christian way and certainly it is not the Orthodox way of today's world.

You see, Paul was raising funds to send from the new churches planted all around the Roman Empire to take back to the founding Jerusalem church. A famine there, as well as spiritual persecution, had left families jobless with empty flour bins and hungry stomachs.

But things evidently weren't much better up in Macedonia the church Paul describes ≈500 miles (1,621 km) NW of Jerusalem – which included the churches at Philippi and Thessalonica. These Christians were undergoing severe trial. We don't know all they went through, but the Greek term Paul uses (severe trial - ἐν πολλῇ δοκιμῇ θλίψεως) suggests that it lasted a long time.

Macedonian believers had overflowing joy in their giving during that time of trial! "Overflowing joy" in financial trials is not possible unless we have adopted an "eternal treasure" mindset that God uses trials to produce something more valuable to us eternally.

Paul uses two pairs of words in verse two that are essentially an oxymoron. "Their extreme poverty welled up in rich generosity - βάθος πτωχεία αὐτῶν ἐπερίσσευσεν εἰς τὸν πλοῦτον τῆς ἁπλότητος αὐτῶν." It's like Paul is saying that you really can squeeze blood out of turnips. They gave in spite of their poverty. This is much like the widow we studied previously who gave her two tiny copper coins – all she had. But it wasn't an emotional televangelist who manipulated these impoverished believers into giving; it was the Holy Spirit working within them.

Notice the phrases used to describe the work of God in their hearts about giving. They gave "even beyond their ability… entirely on their own… urgently pleaded…pleaded with us for the privilege." How do you give more than you are able? How do we wrap our minds around that?

Something had happened in their hearts. And whatever it was, that's what God wants to happen in us. How do we get this deep-down desire to give? Is it just a spiritual gift that they uniquely possessed? No. We see in verse 5 that they first gave themselves to God – and then to a financial need in Jerusalem. (καὶ οὐ καθὼς ἠλπίσαμεν, ἀλλ᾽ ἑαυτοὺς ἔδωκαν πρῶτον τῷ Κυρίῳ καὶ ἡμῖν διὰ θελήματος Θεοῦ v. 5)

The order is significant. Giving is just a meaningless duty or a guilt trip until we first give ourselves to God. When we give ourselves to God, it means that we begin to care about the same things God cares about. To give ourselves to God means to begin thinking like God. And that's how we get a heart much like God's.

How do we know if we have that? How do we know if we care about what God cares about? How do we know if we are generous like God is?

Giving money is just one of the results. The Macedonian churches first giving themselves to God is very important to notice. Then generosity follows and must be a complete lifestyle and a ministry attitude, not a financial principle to benefit ourselves. A good inventory of what it takes to know if our heart is in the right place is:

- Do we offer to help our spouse, or try to stay busy so we don't need to?

- Do we gladly let someone else in the family use the bath /shower /sink first when we both wanted it at the same time?
- Do we willingly give up the last piece of the dessert?
- Do we give up watching our show for someone else to watch what they want? Do we try to get the best seat in the room to watch TV?
- Will we skip a lunch break to help a co-worker finish a project?
- Do we clean up after others in the breakroom at work, offer to do dishes at home, or help clean up or put away chairs after a church potluck?
- Do we seek out younger women or men in the church to mentor or encourage?
- Do we try to say yes if we are needed in the nursery, to help someone move, do a car repair or give someone a ride to the doctor?
- Do we look for opportunities to have people over for a meal?
- Do we willingly loan our vehicles or other valuable things to others?
- Do we take interest in children?
- Do we offer help to someone older or disabled – when no one sees.
- Do we ask questions and listen attentively in conversation, or do we impatiently wish they'd quit talking so we could make our comment or tell our story?

I hope you noticed that none of the questions deal with money. You see, stewardship of money comes from that same heart that is a steward of time and ability and plain old kindness – putting others first.

If we sense true guilt about some of these questions, then we have to start at the bottom and first recommit to giving ourselves daily to the Lord. And then God will teach us generosity on the heart level. Now how does God do that? Admonition, exhortation and encouraging us to try harder, right? Guilt always does the trick, right! Wrong. We will "become poor" for the benefit of others only if we are motivated by the grace of Jesus Christ who "became poor for us so that we might be rich [spiritually]" (2 Corinthians 8:9-19).

Of course, all that "material" sounds good but how do we accomplish it? Well, in Scriptural giving, that is accomplished through ONE WAY and that is through GRACE and never by guilt. A giving heart only starts as we contemplate and comprehend how Jesus could trade heaven and its glorious perfection for this earth and a human existence and the pain of a crucifixion. Only as I appreciate God's grace to me, will my heart be changed into a giving heart. Grace motivates giving that pleases God. God is honored by giving when we are imitating Him – the One who gave his only Son to die for us.

We have all heard pleas for money that were based on guilt. What kind of Christian are you if you don't give to this need? We may have heard exhortations to give trying to motivate us based on our own greed. God will make you wealthy if you give. We may have been urged personally by someone to give until we felt awkwardly obligated. Please give to this desperate need. Or we may have been motivated to give by being told we will be on the "gold list" of donors.

2 Corinthians 9:7 talks about compulsory motivations like this. *Giving under compulsion is not a biblical motive. Neither is pride.* Jesus spoke in Matthew 6:1-4 about hypocrites who gave to be seen and praised by men. *Jesus said we should give privately.*

In contrast to all those motives, biblical giving is grace-motivated giving. The Macedonians Christians fall in that category. When they heard about a need, their thinking was so saturated by the thought of Christ becoming poor for them that the idea of becoming a little bit poorer by a financial gift was not a foreign idea at all. They wanted to give! In fact, they desperately pleaded for the privilege "μετὰ πολλῆς παρακλήσεως δεόμενοι ἡμῶν τὴν χάριν καὶ τὴν κοινωνίαν τῆς διακονίας τῆς εἰς τοὺς ἁγίους" (2 Corin. 8:4). That's the difference grace makes. Yes, they were abnormal compared to their society, but they were not abnormal compared to Christ. It just seemed normal to give because they had a heart like Christ, transformed by Christ.

But Paul is not writing this to the churches of Macedonia, like Philippi and Macedonia; he was writing to Corinth. They were maybe more like many of us. They needed to rethink the whole issue of giving – as part of the Christian walk. Paul recognized that even the Corinthians wanted to give ("your eager willingness to do it - καθάπερ ἡ προθυμία τοῦ θέλειν" – 2 Corinthians 8:11). Yes, it was a stretch for them at this point in their spiritual maturity, but he urges them to respond to the desire that God already implanted in them.

God has implanted in every believer a desire to give. Some respond and some don't. We may be afraid to – afraid we won't have enough; afraid we'll have to give up something we enjoy. But God did implant that desire. If we are true believers of Jesus Christ, we are already spiritually equipped to give the way God wants. We know what to do. It's just a matter of responding and carrying through with what God is doing in our life. "For you know the grace of our Lord Jesus Christ, that though he was rich, yet for your sakes he became poor, so that you through his poverty might become rich" (2 Corinthians 8:9).

Note 1: *Giving under compulsion and or pressure is not a biblical motive. Neither is pride*. Jesus spoke in Matthew 6:1-4 about hypocrites who gave to be seen and praised by men. *Jesus said we should give privately*. The following three pictures identify the vainglory of giving publicly. It contradicts Proverbs 27:2 and Matthew 6:4 which emphasize secrecy for the glory of God and not one's glory. The pictures are blurred ON PURPOSE so that the individual names are not recognizable. Also, ON Purpose I have not identified the location of the Churches.

Bricks with names	**Tree leaves with names**
St. George Greek Orthodox Church: Bricks engraved with parishioner's names. The greater the giving, the closer to the physical church the brick with the donor's name is placed. A reminiscent of the Middle Ages *indulgences*.	St. Nickolas Greek Orthodox Church: The leaves of the tree have been engraved with the names of the parishioner's names. The leaves at the bottom indicate a low amount of giving where the leaves at the top indicate a high amount of giving.

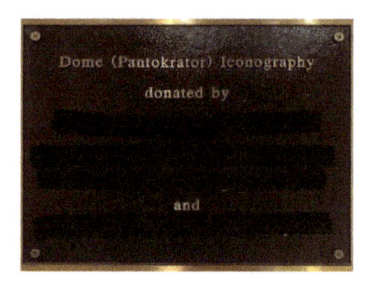

Annunciation Cathedral. The most often display of giving of an icon, or liturgical item. It is always engraved with the donor's name.

P.2.1 Three different examples of public recognition for giving: a) name on bricks; b) names on tree branches and c) name on a plaque (the most common)

Note 2: *Tama* (votive), is a votive deposit or ex-voto used in the Eastern Orthodox Churches. It is a confirmation of a promise to honor a saint or the Theotokos for a specific need that a believer may have. It is asking for a mediation; influence of the person given the Tama to intercede with Christ for a favor decision on behalf of the giver. It is always a personal activity and it usually is hung in the icon of the saint or Theotoko without a name. The Tama is usually silver, tin or aluminum hardly ever gold and it depicts the particular item of concern. Examples may be: eye, leg, hand and so on.

Icon 2.2. St. Nectarios Church. Greek Orthodox church. The *tamata* are shown at the feet of the saint.

In this case they are depicting the entire human body. Remember that St. Nectarios is the Patron Saint for the whole body's sickness *i.e.* cancer and other series illnesses It is very important to notice that there are no names associated with the Tama, since this is personal request and promise.

Chapter 3
Tithing in a historical context

What comes to our mind when one hears the word, tithe? Most often, people think of tithing in terms of obligations, rules, and demands. The message of tithing seems to be something like TITHE or PERISH! We confuse tithing with giving and stewardship as a Way of Life. *Tithing* is a compulsory giving. A tithe is 10% of your income given specifically to your local church. *Giving* is to grant; to allow; to permit. In Malachi 3:10-12, giving is the one thing God tells us to test Him in. ... It sets a model that generosity in God's people should be sacrificial. Stewardship on the other hand, can be consciously defined as: utilizing and managing all resources God provides for the glory of God and the betterment of His creation. The central essence of biblical world view stewardship is managing everything God brings into the believer's life in a manner that honors God. This is very important because most of us forget that one hundred percent of what we have comes from God. In the Divine Liturgy we are all called to "commend ourselves, one another, and our whole life to Christ our God," not merely five, ten, fifteen, or even fifty percent.

A small example will demonstrate the concept of giving and generosity. A rich man testified that God had blessed him with wealth. He said, "I am rich because when I was a young man with only a dollar in my pocket, I heard a homily on sacrificial giving and the Spirit inspired me to put everything I had in the plate. So, I put the dollar in the offering plate." "I dare you to do that again," said his priest. That's the spirit of Christian stewardship - to dedicate all that we have and are to the Lord. But stewardship is wise management (see the story on Acts 4:32-37 which emphasizes total giving for the benefit of the Church).

Within this way of life, good stewards must make decisions and choices concerning our offerings for the support and advancement of the Church and sharing with the poor. And that's where tithing comes in (and not before). A man asked Saint Basil whether God willed that some be healthy, rich, and admired. Basil answered, "Some men are given these [health and riches] for stewardship's sake." He went on to say that the good man treats whatever God gives him as loans for his *administration* (Basil, 1994 pp 178-79).

So then, the matter of tithing is a matter of practical administration of what is already dedicated to God. Such *administration* (that is, management) requires some computations. But according to what calculus? If we treat tithing according to the old calculus self-interest, then we would count how much we can keep instead of considering how much we can give. We might as well be instituting another form of dues, howbeit on a sliding scale. I'm here to say that there is another way to look at "tithing." Tithing has a place in practice of Christian stewardship as a way of life. But to appreciate that place, we need a fresh understanding of it that doesn't get caught up in the old calculus of legalism.

How do we arrive at the meaning of a concept like stewardship? According to the philosopher Wittgenstein (1958), meaning not only depends on what is said but the context in which it is said. As he put it, "For a large class of cases…the meaning of a word is its use in the language." It is just as we are taught in school. When we come across a new word in a story, we look for clues to its meaning in the context of the story. Meaning varies with context as we see in the very Greek word *oikonomos* which is variously translated as "dispensation, management, arrangement, administration, order, plan, training," or, if you will, "stewardship." With that in mind, it is helpful to go back to the way tithing is used in the historical contexts of the Old Testament. We know that tithing is prescribed in the Law of Moses. For example, in the book of Leviticus we read: "Now all the tithe of the land, whether seed of the land or fruit of the tree is the Lord's: it is holy to the Lord…" (Leviticus 37:34).

There is no doubt that this sounds like a legal rule. In fact, the books of Leviticus, Numbers, and Deuteronomy set out three categories of tithes for the Chosen People (Israelites) to obey). [1st Tithe (to Levites): Numbers 18:20-24 (no time indicated); Leviticus 18:30. Tithe of a tithe: (Levites to priests) Numbers 18:25-32 (no time indicated); Deuteronomy 2nd Tithe (at Temple) Deuteronomy 12:11; Deuteronomy 14:22-26; 3rd Tithe (for poor) Deuteronomy 14:28 (every third year)]. These were laws given in the desert, looking forward to the return and occupation of the Promised Land. But let's not go too fast. Let's ask some questions. What was the use of these laws? To whom did they apply? How were they practiced?
https://www.acrod.org/assets/files/PDFS/Stewardship/Resource%202/Tithing%20PPT%20SCRIPT.pdf

When we study the historical books of the Old Testament, we find that the reference to tithing is set within the cycle of apostasy and repentance. The neglect of tithing for the support of the priests/ministers of worship is a sign of the unfaithfulness of the Chosen People. Conversely, the restoration of tithing is a part of comprehensive programs of cleansing of idolatry and restoration of true worship. It appears in a repeated pattern of renewal of the reforms of Hezekiah, Josiah, Nehemiah, and the Maccabees (701 B.C.: Hezekiah's Reform: Southern Kingdom (before the Babylonian Captivity facing the threat of Assyria); 444 B.C.: Covenant Renewal under Ezra the priest and Nehemiah the Governor (after the Babylonian Exile); 164 B.C.: Cleaning of the Temple and Restoration of Sacrifices by the Maccabees). For example, if we look at the example of the King Hezekiah around 700 B.C. The book of 2 Chronicles records that the righteous Hezekiah a) instituted a reform (2 Chronicles 30) b) then he announced a gathering of all the people in festival, the Passover (2 Chronicles. 29:3 ff) c) the festival was so successful that it was extended for another week d) the king installed and organized the minister of worship in the temple (the whole assembly rejoiced along with the priests and Levites… "So, there was great joy in Jerusalem for since the time of Solomon…there had been no feasts like this in Jerusalem" (2 Chronicles 30:26) and e) for their support, he reinstated the system of tithing (2 Chr. 31:4-11).

Now we find that the response of the people was overwhelming. The offerings were so great that they piled up on the ground in heaps. Storehouses had to be built in the temple and the Levites charged with overseeing them. In summary, for Hezekiah (as for the other temple reforms) (Minor reforms (no mention of tithing): Minor: Asa (1 Kings 15:11-15); Jehoshaphat (1 Kings 22:43-46); Azariah (2 Kings 15:3-4); Jotham (2 Kings 15:34-35; 2 Chr. 27:2) tithing was part of a comprehensive program of renewal of the worship of the One True God (1. Purging of idols and idol worship 2. Centralization of the cult in Jerusalem and destruction of sacred shrines elsewhere 3. Cleansing and refurbishing of the Temple in Jerusalem 4. Re-establishment of the orders of priests and Levites for service in the Temple 5. Provision for the support of priests and Levites as well as the poor by the system of tithes) and in every case, the response of the people was enthusiastic and the collection of tithes resulted in overwhelming abundance. How different is this report of the exuberance of tithing from our usual picture of tithing in our churches?

So, there is no question then, that tithing was active in the *OT* times. However, it was active just as much in the *NT* as we see the Apostle Paul warning us about those profiting from Christ's message (2 Cor. 2:17). By the middle to the end of the 1st century, tithing was creating a tension point in the church. Even during the years of 33-105 A.D. where the Apostles were with us, there was a constant discussion about the issue as we read in Acts (4:32-35): So, we *"Now the full number of those who believed were of one heart and soul, and no one said that any of the things that belonged to him was his own, but they had everything in common. And with great power the apostles were giving their testimony to the resurrection of the Lord Jesus, and great grace was upon them all. There was not a needy person among them, for as many as were owners of lands or houses sold them and brought the proceeds of what was sold and laid it at the apostles' feet, and it was distributed to each as any had need."*

So, we see that whether out of necessity or conviction, the first-century church viewed their possessions and giving differently, quite differently. As the church grew, the discussion of tithes and offerings became a big issue again. Were these new Christians obligated to give ten percent like their Israelite forebearers? Were they expected to have all things in common like the early church? How exactly should church leaders communicate the responsibility of Christ followers to be generous and giving? I have gathered some quotes from the early centuries of the church's existence and on generosity. So, in the 2nd century we have:

- **IRENAEUS** (C. 130-202 A.D.): (*Against Heresies*, Book IV, Chapters 8 and 17). *"The Jews were constrained to a regular payment of tithes; Christians who have liberty assign all their possessions to the Lord bestowing freely not the lesser portions of their property since they have the hope of greater things."* In Irenaeus' economy, the tithe was actually a constraint or a lid placed on the giving of the Israelites. In the Christian economy, we're free to give above and beyond the tithe because all that we have is the Lord's. *"And for this reason did the Lord, instead of that [commandment], `You shall not commit adultery,' forbid even concupiscence; and instead of that which runs thus, `You shall not kill,' He prohibited anger; and instead of the law enjoining the giving of tithes, to share all our possessions with the poor; and not to love our neighbors only, but even our enemies; and not merely to* *be liberal givers and bestowers, but even that we should present a gratuitous gift to those who take away our goods."* In keeping with the previous quote, Irenaeus provides examples of Christ's law superseding Moses by cutting directly to our heart's motives. Instead of a law that simply dictates a percentage of our possessions, we willingly and liberally share our belongings with those in need—and with our enemies. In other words, Irenaeus argues that freedom in Christ does not exempt us from our obligation to bring tithes and offerings to the church. What has changed is that now we don't give as a mere legal obligation but instead do it joyfully and freely.

- **The Shephard of Hermas:** (Lightfoot and Harmer, 1992. p 377). "Work at that which is good, and out of your labor, which God gives you, give generously to all who are in need, not debating to whom you will and to whom you will not. Give to all, for God wishes that from His own gifts, gifts should be given to all."

- **Justin Martyr** (C. 100-165 A.D., ANF. VOL. 1. CH. 14. P 167): *"We who valued above all things the acquisition of wealth and possessions now bring what we have into a common stock and share with everyone in need."* In this one sentence, Justin gives us a picture of that very thing. Where people once valued the hoarding of money and things, their new Christ-centered posture makes them see their possessions differently.

- **Tertullian** (C. 155-240 A.D.): ANF: Apology, XXXIX, pp. 46-47: *"We would ask God for material goods if we considered them to be of use; without a doubt, He to whom the whole belongs would be able to concede us a portion. But we prefer to hold possessions in contempt than to hoard them: it is rather innocence that is our aspiration, it is rather patience that is our entreaty; our preference is goodness, not extravagance."* [To paraphrase Tertullian, I offer my interpretation: Our leaders are elders of proved worth, men who have attained this honor not for a price, but by character. **Every man brings some modest coin once a month or whenever he wishes, and only if he is willing and able; it is a freewill offering.** You might call them the trust-funds of piety; they are spent . . . on the support and burial of the poor]. You see, for Tertullian, possessions are infinitely precious for building up of the kingdom, but can worm their way into our hearts and defraud us of our innocence. From Tertullian's perspective, giving was more than duty, it was an act of preservation.

- **Clement of Alexandria** (C. 150–215 A.D.): *"The tithes of the fruits and of the flocks taught both piety towards the Deity and not to* *covetously grasp everything. Instead, one should share gifts of kindness with one's neighbors. For it was from these, I reckon, and from the first fruits that the priests were maintained."* What's interesting here is how Clement addresses the tithe as an Old Testament principle being taught in retrospect, and not as an ongoing practice he's advocating. Ultimately, the tithe was a tool to instruct the Israelites in kindness and altruism—traits that Clement believes Christians should exemplify.

In the 3rd century we have a situation of an outbreak of financial misappropriation in the church. Running the church like administrators of secular businesses, ministers were using the gospel for private gain. Cyprian's frustration included the horrible example it gave to those who were looking for leadership. So, tithing came back in the discussion with Cyprian as the major proponent:

- **Cyprian** (C. 210–258 A.D.): *"Each one was intent on adding to his inheritance. Forgetting what the faithful used to do under the Apostles and what they should always be doing, each one with insatiable greed was absorbed in adding to his wealth. Gone was the devotion of bishops to the service of God, gone was the clergy's faithful integrity, gone the generous compassion for the needy, gone all discipline in our behavior.*

  "Too many bishops, instead of giving encouragement and example to others, made no account of the ministration which God had entrusted to them, and took up the administration of secular business: they left their sees, abandoned their people, and toured the markets in other territories on the look-out for profitable deals."

- **Didascalia Apostolorum.** (3rd Century- 230 A.D.): Latin for *The Teaching of the Apostles*, Chapter IX, ii, 35. mentions the word "tithe" fourteen times. The ninth chapter instructs laypeople on how they should conduct themselves. It says: "Present to the bishop your tithes and offerings that you may be blessed." See http://www.earlychristianwritings.com/text/didascalia.htm

In the 4th century we have:
- **St. John Cassian** (A.D. 360 – c. 435). *The Conferences,* Chapter XXIX: "He who retains his goods of this world, or, bound by the rules of the old law, distributes the tithe of his produce, and his first fruits, or a portion of his income, although he may to a considerable degree quench the fire of his sins by this dew of almsgiving, yet,

however generously he gives away his wealth, it is impossible for him altogether to rid himself of the dominion of sin, unless perhaps by the grace of the Savior, together with his substance he gets rid of all love of possessing."
- **Jerome** (385 A.D.) saw the clergy as being in the line of tribe of Levi and the Jewish priesthood and therefore **due tithes**. In comments made on Malachi 3, Jerome said that Jesus commanded Christians to sell everything and give the proceeds to the poor. Since Christians are unwilling to do that, at least they should "imitate the rudimentary teaching of the Jews" in giving tithes for the poor and the clergy. Otherwise, Christians are "defrauding and cheating God."
- **Ambrose** (374 A.D.), the Bishop of Milan, was unequivocal that Christians **are required to tithe**. If Christians neglected to give God his tenth, then God will take what they have. He clearly supported the concept of tithing.
- **Augustine** (400 A.D.), Bishop of Hippo, is one the most often cited church fathers by all Christians. He said that while the paying of tithes occurred before him, presently Christians were not adequately paying their tithes. Augustine believed that Jesus' command to sell one's possessions and give the proceeds to the poor was binding upon Christians. He lived this out in his own life. However, since Christians were unwilling to give all, they should at least imitate the Jews and give a tenth. Therefore, Augustine supported tithing through concession.
- **The Constitutions of the Holy Apostles** (375-380 A.D.) 2.4.25 (*ANF* 7:408); 7.29 (*ANF* 7:471). See also statements at 2.4.27; 2.4.34; 8.30–31 and *ANF* 7:388). In the fourth century, the *Apostolic Constitutions* gave separate instructions for bishops regarding two issues: (1) tenths and first fruits; and (2) free will offerings. This document also states that tithes were "the command of God." Furthermore, the Constitutions likened bishops with priests and Levites, and the tabernacle with the Holy Catholic Church. It exhorted all Christians to give their first fruits and tithes. While the Constitutions contains the strongest statement about tithing in the Ante-Nicene period, this passage may be of a much later date than the rest of the document.
- **Nikitas Stithatos** (1995 p. 163) the tithe that we offer to God is in the true sense the soul's Passover – its passing beyond, that is to say, every passion-embroiled state and all mindless sense-perception.

- **John Chrysostom** (C. 349–407 A.D.): *"Woe to him, it is said, who doeth not alms; and if this was the case under the Old Covenant, much more is it under the New. If, where the getting of wealth was allowed and the enjoyment of it, and the care of it, there was such provision made for the succoring of the poor, how much more in that Dispensation, where we are commanded to surrender all we have? For what did not they of old do? "They* [old covenant believers] *gave tithes, and tithes again upon tithes for orphans, widows, and strangers, whereas someone was saying to me in astonishment at another, 'Why, such an one givest tithes.' What a load of disgrace does this expression imply, since what was not a matter of wonder with the Jews has come to be so in the case of the Christians? If there was danger then in omitting tithes, think how great it must be now"* (4th *Homily on Ephesians*, v. 2:10. P 69).

In addition, Chrysostom said that the Christians of his day should return to tithing or face dangerous consequences. He understood the Old Testament to be inculcating multiple tithes, not one ("tithes again upon tithes"). Commenting on Matthew 5:20, Chrysostom calculates that the Jews gave about half of their income. He concluded that if when giving half "achieves no great thing, he who doth not bestow as much as the tenth, of what shall he be worthy." While Chrysostom thought that Christians fulfilled the Old Testament law by tithing, he also believed Christians should not need law.

So, if the Jews had to tithe to take care of the poor, Chrysostom argues, how much more are Christians expected to give? The fact that Christians would marvel the tithe of the Israelites was a sign to the archbishop that Christ's followers didn't fully grasp how their faith should inform their views about possessions.

It is interesting to note that Constantine the Great, even though he officially embraced Christianity, there is no record of him accepting or recognizing or practicing tithing. On the other hand, Basil of Caesarea (370 A.D.) **exhorted Christians to pay tithes** and Gregory of Nazianzus (c.a. 365) mentions first fruits, but no reference to tithes has been found in the writings of Gregory of Nyssa (c.a. 365). Hilary of Poitiers (366 A.D.), when commenting on Matthew 23:23, concluded that while Christians should place a greater emphasis upon justice and mercy, tithing **was still required**.

Most Orthodox churches (today) object to tithing because they claim that it belongs to the Old Covenant and is no longer applicable to the New. However, we forget or ignore that the early Church practiced tithing as we read the writings of the first century, such as the *Didache* (13:8) recommends tithing for the support of the ministers of the Church. Furthermore, *The Apostolic Constitutions* also echoes the same practice for the support of the bishop, priests, and deacons (*Apostolic Constitutions* 375-380 A.D.) and so many other sources, including Church Fathers as Basil the Great, John Chrysostom, and John Cassian, among many others, who advise tithing. [These individuals deserve a similar study of how the concept was used and practiced in their contexts].

St. Irenaeus (2nd Century) as we read earlier claims that tithing did not apply to the early Church. He stated that the Jews had their tithes but Christians in liberty "set aside all their possessions for the Lord's purposes…" "since they have the hope of better things hereafter." However, in full context he wrote: "Concerning sacrifices and oblations and those who truly offer them. And for this reason they (the Jews) had indeed the tithes of their goods consecrated to Him, but those who have received liberty set aside all their possessions for the Lord's purposes, bestowing joyfully and freely not the less valuable portions of their property, since they have the hope of better things [hereafter]; as that poor widow acted who cast all her living into the treasury of God" (Irenaeus *Against Heresies* 4:18:1). This is an incredible and powerful statement that suggests that the giving MUST be higher than the 10% of the Jews. He based this notion on Acts 4:32-37.

But let's not take this quotation out of context, as many do. St. Irenaeus. begins the thought with the observation that "first fruits" and sacrifices (*oblations*) have not been set aside in the Church. The difference is not in the offerings but in the "character" of the action. The motivation and spirit are different. Those under the New Covenant now give "not out of compulsion, for God loves a cheerful giver" just as St. Paul said (1 Cor. 9:7). In the same vein, Irenaeus says that liberty is the key to Christian giving.

Tithing, therefore, must never be demanded but that does not mean it cannot be recommended. The continuing pattern of the Old Testament historical books is that of the cycle of an apostasy and covenant renewal. When one reads the church fathers in context, we find another pattern, at least in the fourth century. Saint John Chrysostom (375 A.D.) says that

Christians living in the New Covenant are called to **surrender** all they have to Christ. The Jews gave "tithes upon tithes" yet now Christians are amazed if someone tithes. So, if the Jews were warned against neglecting tithes, how much more are Christians in danger. (See the full text above).

Ambrose (374 A.D.) echoed the same thought. Moreover, Jerome (385 A.D.) said that Christians are commanded to give all they have to the poor, but if they are unwilling, at least they should follow the *rudimentary practices* of the Jews.

Augustine (400 A.D.) shared the same idea. Study will discover that throughout these changing contexts, the uses of the tithe remained constant though they took different forms. There were three types of tithes in the Old Testament:

1. Tithes to provide supplies for the feasts of worship
2. Tithes to support the Levites (and priests) as ministers of the House of God
3. Tithes for the relief of the poor

These carried out the functions of:

1. Worship and thanksgiving
2. Support of ministry
3. Relief of the poor

We can find these in different contexts: Old Testament, Deutero-Canonical, and the Church Fathers (Ante-Nicaea). Today, tithes can still be a helpful guideline for our decisions about the support of these same basic things. The subject of tithing is a mirror in which we see our own attitudes toward financial stewardship whether they be based on self-interest, legalism, or faithfulness. To use the categories of Saint Paul, it comes down to whether we choose "to sow sparingly" or "to sow bountifully" (that is, generously - (2 Corin. 9:6)) and urge others to do the same in our parishes. No one who is a generous and cheerful giver should feel threatened by the suggested promotion of the tithe as a fitting standard for Christian giving. Rather, think of tithing in historical context as more than an arbitrary rule and as a general guide to giving. Using tithing can enhance your personal renewal of faithfulness and it can be a starting point to understand the responsibility of stewardship.

Again, let us not forget the words from scriptures: "Where your treasure is there will your heart be also" (Matthew 6:21). All that we have is on loan from God. It is all a gift. However, because of its significance, the Scriptures have no less than 2,350 verses having to do with money and money management. Both the OT and the NT discuss the issue. Jesus speaks about money and money management more than any other topic including heaven, hell, salvation etc. Therefore, the topic is very important for the Christian life.

In the book of Genesis, the mysterious paradigmatic priest of priests Melchizedek appears to perform one task alone: to collect the tithe from Abraham and to thus confer a blessing upon him on behalf of the Lord (Genesis 14:18-20 – see Appendix A). This clearly shows that Abraham in his righteousness before God gave of his first fruits (his best fruits) unto the Lord and in turn was blessed. This is precisely what God is calling us to do. We as believers are each called upon to give sacrificially of our best resources first and God will take care of the rest as He did with Father Abraham.

As individuals, when we become burdened with a mindset of materialism (*i.e.* non-stewardship focused giving) we become slaves to our wealth instead of our wealth becoming our servants for the promotion of God's Kingdom. This clearly is not the way that God intended it to be. Inevitably, we squander the gifts of our resources. Then a multitude of other problems emerge namely the bondage of debt. For truly, as the Preacher teaches in Ecclesiastes and Proverbs, "the borrower is a slave to the lender" (Proverbs 22:7).

If you want to know the spiritual state and strength of a church, just look at its stewardship report. Invariably, it tells it all because what people do with their money speaks volumes. We make disciples by giving people Jesus through preaching, teaching, the sacramental life, the liturgical life and outreach ministries. It is to this end that our giving should be focused. If the *ecclesia* will do its job, Jesus has promised to be faithful and do His. **Sacrificial giving for the Christian is not an option, but a joyful obligation.** St. John Chrysostom in the 4th century speaks of this joyful obligation in his book *On Wealth and Poverty* when he writes that the Christian owns nothing because God owns everything (Chrysostom, 1984 – see especially the III Homily). [Some portions here, have been adopted from J. Panagiotou article as it appears in http://orthochristian.com/78020.html. Retrieved on August 16, 2020].

With these things in mind, proper Christian stewardship for individuals and congregations should include the following four principles: 1) the glorification of God should be the focus; 2) giving should be sacrificial; 3) giving should be of the best of the first fruits of one's resources; and 4) debt has no place in this paradigm.

Where do we stand?

It is somewhat encouraging to see that the early church had many of the same issues regarding materialism and offerings that we do. It's also challenging to see how seriously they took it. Maybe it's time we all prayerfully reconsidered our relationship to our possessions ("the" *stuff).*

The tithing conversation in church can get uncomfortable very quickly, even when the sermon incorporates the truths about how difficult it was for Old Testament figures. Talking about tithing is always going to be awkward, but necessary.

Orthodox Christian Stewardship

"Where your treasure is there will your heart be also" (Matthew 6:21). These words of Jesus have resonated within the hearts of people for over two thousand years. What was Jesus talking about? What do Jesus, the Bible, and the Church Fathers have to say about tithing and giving to God?

The Scriptures have no less than 2,350 verses having to do with money and money management. Jesus speaks about money and money management more than any other topic including heaven, hell, salvation *etc*. The topic is very important for the Christian life. In an often-misquoted verse, St. Paul the Apostle writes, "the love of money is the root of all evil" (1st Timothy 6:10). St. Paul teaches that our Lord realizes that we have needs to meet in order to live and to carry out His work.

God is, however, a jealous God and demands our full commitment with nothing else taking precedence over His Lordship in our lives. That is why the Apostle Paul warns his first century Greek congregation that ***the love of money is evil***. All that we have is on loan from God. It is all a gift.

What we do with our time, talent, and treasures will have to be given account of on the last day. This was the great sin of disobedience by Adam in the Garden of Eden. He abused his gift of stewardship. King Solomon who was the richest and wisest man of all time, expressed his feeling of the emptiness of materialism apart from God when he said, "vanity of vanities, it is all a bubble that bursts" (Eccles. 1:2).

All of these principles not only apply to the individual Christian, but to the life of a congregation as well. Jesus is clear in the New Testament when He says that He would build and grow the Church and that the task at hand *for believers is to make disciples who are followers of Jesus amongst the nations. That is what the core culture of a parish and diocese should be all about.* That is what the ultimate focus of any and all monetary collections should be about. As the late great Russian theologian Florovsky (1948) would write on the matter: "The primary task of the historical Church is the proclamation of another world "to come." The Church bears witness to the New Life, disclosed and revealed in Christ Jesus, the Lord and Savior. This it does both by word and deed. The true proclamation of the Gospel would be precisely the practice of this New Life: to *show faith by deeds* (cf. Matt. 5:16). The Church is more than a company of priests, or a teaching society, or a missionary board. It has not only to invite people, but also to introduce them into this New Life, to which it bears witness.

It is a missionary body indeed, and its mission field is the whole world. But the aim of its missionary activity is not merely to convey to people certain convictions or ideas, not even to impose on then a definite discipline or a rule of life, but first of all to *introduce them into the New Reality, to convert them, to bring them through their faith and repentance to Christ Himself, that they should be born anew in Him and into Him by water and the Spirit.* Thus, the ministry of the Word is completed in the ministry of the Sacraments (Florovsky, 1948).

The *ecclesial ministry in its essence is not about buildings, budgets, and bodies. The model that we ought to follow is that the Church should be viewed first and foremost as the family of God, not just as another corporation or business.* When that happens, the Bible tells us that inevitably God's presence and blessing can be seen manifest in the local eucharistic community because its focus is on Jesus - the Author of our salvation. It is then when we see the fullness of the Faith express itself, not only in the transformation of the elements into the Body and Blood of Christ, but when the celebrant and those worshipers present are transfigured into the Body of Christ as well. (Some of this text has been adopted from *www.aoiusa.org.* October 21, 2016).

If we would incorporate these four principles of economics into our lives and the life of our congregation, the Lord has promised to do mighty, mighty works in our life and in the lives of all around us. A proper understanding of stewardship is not a luxury in our private life as a Christian and in our collective life as the *Ecclesia*. For us to be truly "called out from the world – see John 15:19 - as the word *ecclesia* connotes, is to take up the mantle and responsibility of stewardship and all that it entails.

Chapter 4
How Giving Makes You Joyful

Money is mentioned in the Scriptures over 800 times. On the other hand, issues concerning finance and possessions are dealt in over 2350 verses (Baumer and Cortines (2016). That is more verses – more material – than all 13 letters in the New Testament that Paul wrote! This means that finances for all of us are quite important. However, the finances have two components. The first is to generate money, possessions and wealth in general. The second is spending. So, now the question is how do we spend this wealth that we accumulate. Obviously, there are many ways. However, one of the key spending activities is giving liberally and with joy to others and God. So, God obviously cares about our view of possessions to instruct us that much about it.

At this point, one may ask why should "I" give what "I" have worked for to someone else and God. The simplest answer is that: in reality none of us own anything. Everything we have belongs to God. We are just "stewards" of His wealth. As such, we must learn to share with others, the Church and certainly God. But sharing is not enough. It must be shared with JOY. But how can giving make one happy and joyful? A good example of this, is the letter to the Philippians by the Ap. Paul (4:10-20).

1. *Giving revives our concern* (v. 10). The word rejoiced ('Εχάρην) in verse 10 pictures something that was dead and now is coming to life (ἀνεθάλετε). The word sometimes is translated as revived. It reminds us of a tree or plant that is barren in the winter, but when spring comes, the tree or plant blossoms with new shoots and flowers. The Philippian Christians had been barren in expressing their concern for Paul [because of lack of opportunity - ἠκαιρεῖσθε δέ] but now, with the gift of money they sent him, they were blossoming anew with concern for Paul's welfare. Paul reminds us that giving takes the focus off ourselves and puts it onto someone or something else. Giving becomes a tangible way we can express concern and love to other people. But more importantly giving glorifies God for His benevolence.
2. *Giving teaches us contentment* (v. 11). Paul did not want this church to think that his joy rested on whether he had money. Paul had schooled himself to be satisfied with whatever he had (αὐτάρκης). He had joy in his life, not because his purse was full,

but because he had learned contentment. The Greek stoics used the word content to describe self-sufficiency. Paul believed his sufficiency was in Christ (Read Hebrews 13:5- emphasis is on ἀρκούμενοι τοῖς παροῦσιν). Paul believed that whether you were naked or clothed, hungry or filled, rich or poor, if you had the Lord in your life, you had everything you needed. So, how does one define contentment? Contentment is not trimming down your desires. Contentment means living with a sense of God's adequacy, a conviction that God is adequate for any need we face. Therefore, we can give joyfully, knowing God will supply our needs. This is supported by reading verse 13 - πάντα ἰσχύω ἐν τῷ ἐνδυναμοῦντί με Χριστῷ.
3. *Giving makes us partners in ministry* (v. 14). Paul said about this gift of money that it was good of them to send it. The word "share" is the same word often translated as "fellowship - συγκοινωνήσαντές." The word also denotes partnership. Each time we give to the Lord's work, we partner with other Christians to help advance the kingdom. That exciting thought puts joy in our hearts.
4. *Giving pays spiritual* dividends (vv. 17-18). Paul made clear he was not looking for monetary gifts for his own benefit - οὐχ ὅτι ἐπιζητῶ τὸ δόμα. Giving blesses the one who gives more than the one who receives the gift. The phrase "credited to your account" (ἐπιζητῶ τὸν καρπὸν τὸν πλεονάζοντα εἰς λόγον ὑμῶν... ἀπέχω δὲ πάντα καὶ περισσεύω· πεπλήρωμαι δεξάμενος παρὰ Ἐπαφροδίτου τὰ παρ' ὑμῶν, ὀσμὴν εὐωδίας), implies that giving to the Lord is like investing in kingdom matters. Kingdom work pays spiritual dividends. Giving from the right motives and for the right reasons becomes a pleasing gesture to God (θυσίαν δεκτήν, εὐάρεστον τῷ Θεῷ). This language from the Old Testament shows that our giving becomes an act of worship and devotion to God. Sacrifices to God fill our hearts with great joy (see Ps. 4:4-7).
5. *Giving grows our faith in God* (v. 19). Perhaps some of the members of the church at Philippi had given to Paul's ministry but were worried they might not have enough money left to meet their own needs. Paul gave them a great promise to stand upon. Today's Christians have many items on the plates. The expenses are indeed overwhelming. However, verse 19 encourages us to take the step of faith and to give, trusting God to meet our needs

(ὁ δὲ Θεός μου πληρώσει πᾶσαν χρείαν ὑμῶν κατὰ τὸν πλοῦτον αὐτοῦ ἐν δόξῃ ἐν Χριστῷ Ἰησοῦ). In the final analysis of verse 19, we are assured that a) God meets our needs personally ("my God") b) He meets our needs liberally ("all our needs") and c) He meets our needs gloriously ("according to his glorious riches in Christ Jesus"). Why are these things important? Because through our giving the Church spreads the message of salvation through Christ; the church can help people in need; the church can help current followers of Christ develop their spirituality; the church can pay the bills of everyday operations and above all it helps the Church shine as a lighthouse to the world.

Now that we have an idea of what giving can do for the *giver*, let us examine the definition of the biblical steward, and the relationship as well as the responsibilities of the administrative efforts of the keepers of the money – the *Steward (οικονομος)*.

1. *Financial Stewardship*: It's all God's money. Many Christians would nod their head in agreement with that statement, but when it's time to open the wallet, it is as if we have completely forgotten. Suddenly it is our money and we try desperately to get or keep as much as possible.

   My reason for writing this book is to transform the way Orthodox Christians think about money and giving. We need to think about money the way God thinks about money. An adjusted view of money and material possessions is part of the renewing of the mind that God intends for us, as we grow spiritually (Romans 12:2). Financial decisions can actually be one of the most effective means of drawing close to God and glorifying Him, by trusting our future, our wants, our hopes and expectations in Him.

   Jesus' model prayer (Matthew 6:9-13) seems to include all of the core elements of our relationship to our heavenly Father. His prayer did not only consist of lofty issues like worship, a coming kingdom and God's will. Jesus urged us to relate to our heavenly Father by becoming reliant on Him for *daily bread*. Just as earthly children naturally stay close to their parents because they need

food, we can also draw close to God as our Father by acknowledging that we are financially dependent on Him.
2. *Stewards, Not Owners: Facing how we think about money*: Financial advice comes from everywhere: From friends, family members, culture, advertisements, financial planners, personal advisors, book-helps and of course the Church leaders with the unending refrain – BE GENEROUS. However, the most persuasive financial advice we receive, is from the voice in our own head. Somewhere in the process of life we develop our own private financial philosophy and values. Of course, we make mistakes, but then again that is our human characteristic. Part of the problem is that we face financial decisions based on the Axiom: "**W**hat **I**s **I**n **I**t **F**or **M**e (WIIFM)," which indicates selfishness and or ignorance. Selfishness because we want to be "part of a group and it makes us feel good" and ignorance because no one has taught us about the benefits of giving.

Jesus said, "Where your treasure is, there will your heart be also" (Matthew 6:21). He is saying that what we do with our money and our possessions reveals our real priorities. It is that simple. In no uncertain terms God is talking to us about a spiritual thermometer – a way to measure what is really going on in our heart with Him. This notion is identified with God's words in I Kings (LXX) or 1 Samuel 16:7: "But the Lord said to Samuel, look not on his appearance, nor on his stature, for I have rejected him; for God sees not as man looks; for man looks at the outward appearance, but God looks at the heart."
3. *Material things in the beginning*: A good place to begin a study of the subject of money and material things is Genesis 1:1. "In the beginning God created the heavens and the earth." We learn here as the Bible opens that God owns everything because He created everything.

David wrote, (Psalms 23(24):1-2 LXX) "The earth is the Lord's and the fullness thereof; the world, and all that dwell in it. He has founded it upon the seas, and prepared it upon the rivers." Therefore, God made the whole earth so it is all his and if God made it, He owns it. He then put man in it and gave Adam the first job – to rule over the animals and to tend the garden. As their salary Adam and Eve could eat of anything in the garden – except one tree of course.

Like Adam and Eve, we were also created by God. We have been given food by God. We have been given a place to live by God. We belong to God along with everything we think is ours. It is all God's!

It was a great garden residence that God gave Adam and Eve. The garden even had gold and other valuables (Genesis 2:10-12). But anything they "had" really must not have been theirs. We know that because when they sinned, they were driven from the garden and didn't take anything with them (Genesis 3:24).

They lived in God's garden and enjoyed God's food gifts and everything else, but it was all God's. Because of sin, they lost access to it all. This is very important for all of us to remember: Everything – NO EXEPTIONS – we have, God gave it to us and as a consequence He can also take it away.

4. *You can't take it with you*: If we don't learn it by life experiences, there is something we should learn from every funeral. We don't "own" anything because we don't take it with us. Solomon, the wisest man ever, said, "As he came forth naked from his mother's womb, he shall return back as he came, and he shall receive nothing for his labor, that it should go [with him] in his hand" (Ecclesiastes 5:14 LXX). The apostle Paul concurred, "For we brought nothing into the world, and we can take nothing out of it" (1 Timothy 6:7). Job, at his lowest point worshipfully agreed, saying, "I myself came forth naked from my mother's womb, and naked shall I return thither; the Lord gave, the Lord has taken away: as it seemed good to the Lord, so has it come to pass; blessed be the name of the Lord" (Job 1:21 LXX).

In the Orthodox funeral service, we are reminded of this temporary world with the following words in some of the hymns: "Where is the pleasure in life which is unmixed with sorrow. Where is the glory which on earth has stood firm and unchanged? All things are weaker than shadow, all more elusive than dreams…" Another hymn reminds us: "like a blossom that wastes away, and like a dream that passes and is gone, so every mortal into dust resolved…" Yet another one reminds us: "vanity are all the works and quests of man and they have no being after death has come; our wealth is with us no longer…"; Where is now our affection for earthly things? … where is now our gold, and our silver? … All is dust, all is ashes, all is shadow" (Vaporis, 1997, pp 106-108)

God didn't stutter about how temporary material things are. We only have them for a little while. Therefore, the message is loud and clear: *Stewardship* is the most basic of all biblical concepts about material things. So, what is a steward? Very simply, stewards manage the property of others. An excellent example is found in Genesis by reading and meditating the story of Joseph the Steward.

The story is quite explicit: "And Joseph found grace in the presence of his lord, and was well-pleasing to him; and he set him over his house, and all that he had he gave into the hand of Joseph. And it came to pass after that he was set over his house, and over all that he had, that the Lord blessed the house of the Egyptian for Joseph's sake; and the blessing of the Lord was on all his possessions in the house, and in his field. And he committed all that he had into the hands of Joseph; and he knew not of anything that belonged to him, save the bread which he himself ate" (Genesis 39:4-6a LXX). Joseph didn't own anything in Egypt at this point. He was a slave of Potiphar. But that didn't keep Potiphar from *entrusting to him all that he owned.* He seemingly even did the books, because a few verses later (Genesis 39:9) it is clear that he was in charge of everything except Potiphar's wife.

Here it is very critical to recognize that often *stewards* can enjoy the things they manage. It's a perk and it is biblical! "Thou shalt not muzzle the ox that treads out the corn" (Deut. 25:4 LXX). The idea here of not muzzling an ox while it is working to produce grain is that the ox deserves to partake in some of his own labor and so the command is to not to muzzle the ox. This means they allow him to eat from part of his labor while he treads out the grain. It seems cruel to make an animal work for man to produce food while depriving it of the same thing.

Paul repeats this in "You shall not muzzle an ox when it treads out the grain. Is it for oxen that God is concerned" (1st Cor 9:9)? When anyone in the New Testament says "It is written" or "You have heard it said of old" so Paul was using the example of Deuteronomy 25:4. The context of 1st Corinthians 9 is that Paul has the right or those who preach the gospel have the right to be supported in their ministry. It is the same principle of showing mercy to the servant of God for his or her labor and being merciful to the servant of man (the ox) for their labor and that neither should be muzzled and not be able to partake in the fruits of that labor. Paul writes, "If others share this rightful claim on you, do not we even more" (1st Cor 9:12) and to make sure everyone knows exactly what he is writing about, he continues by writing, "Do you not know that those who are employed in the temple service get their food from the temple, and those who serve at the altar share in the sacrificial offerings?

In the same way, the Lord commanded that those who proclaim the gospel should get their living by the gospel" (1st Cor 9:13-14). That could not be any clearer to the reader. You don't need to be a theologian or Bible scholar to understand that "those who proclaim the gospel should get their living by the gospel" (1st Cor 9:14). You cannot reach any other possible conclusion with these verses than to not muzzle the ox and not support those who are laboring in the fields of the world.

5. *The Steward's real job is Faithfulness*: God has clear instructions for stewards. "Now it is required that those who have been given a trust (literally, stewards - οἰκονόμους μυστηρίων Θεοῦ), they must prove faithful - ἵνα πιστός τις εὑρεθῇ" (1 Corinthians 4:1-2). The Greek term "steward" here includes a form of the word, house. It describes a household manager in the ancient Greek world who handled the finances for the owner. Managers are accountable to owners for how they use their finances or material possessions. So, owners *DO* hold managers accountable! And God (as owner) will hold us (being the stewards) accountable for anything He has entrusted to us.

Now back to Joseph. We know that Joseph was falsely accused and was thrown into jail. That doesn't sound fair for someone who was a faithful steward, does it? However, at the end of the story, where is Joseph? He is a steward again – in a big way! Joseph became the prime minister of Egypt, in charge of the palace, in charge of everything and everyone except Pharaoh himself. And Joseph evidently could even use Pharaoh's signet ring any way he chose (Genesis 41:40-42)!

Why did this happen? God made it happen because Joseph was a faithful steward. So, we learn two principles from Joseph about the way God views stewardship. 1) Stewards manage the property of others. 2) Stewards who are faithful receive greater privileges.

6. *How God rewards our good stewardship*: Managing a little, leads to managing a lot. This is also biblical. Jesus said it in Luke 16:10) with these words: "Whoever can be trusted with very little can also be trusted with much, and whoever is dishonest with very little will also be dishonest with much." What is Jesus talking about? Was He promising to make us richer financially if we are faithful stewards of our money, as some in the prosperity movement teach? No, He isn't. Although I imagine that the apostle Paul was faithful with any money he handled, he certainly wasn't wealthy. In fact, he was often in complete poverty – and content with that (Philippians 4:10-11).

So, if the promise of financial wealth is not what Jesus is teaching, what is He teaching? He is teaching the surprising truth that God uses our stewardship financially to determine how much He can trust us with spiritually. Jesus explains it. "So, if we have not been trustworthy in handling worldly wealth [money, material things], whom will we trust with true riches [spiritual things]? And if we have not been trustworthy with someone else's property [money], who will give us property of our own?" (Luke 16:11-12).

What did Jesus mean by "property of our own?" It is eternal things! Jesus is saying that God is testing our financial stewardship to determine who He can trust among us with spiritual and ministry privileges that last forever. Our management of money affects the eternal impact that we will have. That is the "property" we can keep. It is eternal!

Jesus never promised us worldly wealth here on earth, but He does say that the way we manage whatever amount of money or worldly possessions we have is really a spiritual test. And God is grading that test. *How much we have is not an indication of our spirituality; how we manage what we have is an indication of our spirituality.*

Stewardship testing starts early and lasts throughout life. Grade school children are tested when they get an allowance. High school students with a part-time job are being tested. Our management of money continues through our working life and retirement. God is looking for people he can trust with real eternal things – and He uses our management of entrusted money and possessions in that evaluation. So, every financial decision is a spiritual decision. *Stewardship means a whole different way of thinking.*

7. *Stewards think differently than owners:* What does God want me to do with this paycheck? That's the real question, because it is really God's paycheck. Our budget is His budget. How does God want me to allocate what He has given me? How does God wants me to use this house? It is His house. How should I use extra money? How much should I save, invest, spend or give away? It is all His. How should I use it? Should I buy this car, this piece of furniture or even this book or candy bar? The size of the purchase isn't the issue. What matters is that it's all God's money and I must decide how He wants me to use it.

10 Essential Truths about Christian Giving

Very often, people ask or wonder "what are the basic biblical principles for Christian giving?" As we seek God's answer to that question and as we contemplate our own giving to the Lord's church in response to the clear teaching of His Word, perhaps it would be wise and helpful to review some of those principles here.

First, let us go to the Word of God itself, without comment:

- **Matthew 6:1-4:** Beware of practicing your righteousness before men to be noticed by them; otherwise you have no reward with

your Father who is in heaven. So, when you give to the poor, do not sound a trumpet before you, as the hypocrites do in the synagogues and in the streets, so that, they may be honored by men. Truly I say to you, they have their reward in full. But when you give to the poor, do not let your left hand know what your right hand is doing, so that your giving will be in secret; and your Father who sees *what is done* in secret will reward you.
- **1 Corinthians 16:1-2:** Now concerning the collection for the saints, as I directed the churches of Galatia, so do you also. On the first day of every week each one of you is to put aside and save, as he may prosper, so that no collections be made when I come.
- **2 Corinthians 8:9-15:** For you know the grace of our Lord Jesus Christ, that though He was rich, yet for your sake He became poor, so that you through His poverty might become rich. I give my opinion in this matter, for this is to your advantage, who were the first to begin a year ago not only to do this, but also to desire to do it. But now finish doing it also, so that, just as there was the readiness to desire it, so there may be also the completion of it by your ability. For if the readiness is present, it is acceptable according to what a person has, not according to what he does not have. For this is not for the ease of others and for your affliction, but by way of equality - at this present time your abundance being a supply for their need, so that their abundance also may become a supply for your need, that there may be equality; as it is written, "HE WHO *gathered* MUCH DID NOT HAVE TOO MUCH, AND HE WHO *gathered* LITTLE HAD NO LACK."
- **2 Corinthians 9:6-7:** Now this I say, he who sows sparingly will also reap sparingly, and he who sows bountifully will also reap bountifully. Each one must do just as he has purposed in his heart, not grudgingly or under compulsion, for God loves a cheerful giver.

In these four passages we find at least ten (10) principles for Christian giving. They are:

1. **The Lord Jesus expects and requires us to give.** Jesus said to His disciples, "when you give" not "If you give" (Matthew 6.2)! Hence, Christian giving is not optional, but rather essential. We often hear folks say: "in the Old Testament they had to give, but not in the New - now we only give if we want to." This is clearly

not Jesus' teaching. He expected all His followers to be givers. Christians will give. *Are you giving?*

2. **The Lord Jesus wants us to give for the right reasons.** Jesus warned His disciples not to give for the sake of being admired by men. "Beware of practicing your righteousness before men to be noticed by them," He said (Matthew 6:1). When we give, we must be careful to examine our motives. We ought to give for the glory of God and the good of His people. We must desire His approval of our giving, rather than the praise and admiration of people. *Are you giving for God's praise or man's?*

3. **The Lord Jesus wants us to practice benevolent or charitable giving.** Jesus said "When you give to the poor . . .." (Matthew 6:2-3). Jesus is specifically teaching about "alms" in this passage: aid, charity, or benevolent offerings for the needy. *Do you give amply enough to the Church that she can be generous in benevolent giving?*

4. **The Lord Jesus reminds us that our giving is ultimately to the all-seeing heavenly Father.** Jesus said "When you give . . .; your Father who sees *what is done* in secret will reward you" (Matthew 6:3-4). When we give, we are not simply adding to the Church budget, we are giving up a thank offering to the Father Himself. Thus, we must all give "as unto the Lord." Our ultimate goal in giving is to please Him. *Are you conscious of the fact that your giving is to the Lord and seen by the Lord?*

5. **The Bible teaches that Christian giving is an act of worship.** In connection with the previous point, we see this truth stressed in another way in Paul's word's "On the first day of every week each one of you is to put aside and save" (1 Corinthians 16:2). Paul here teaches the Corinthians that their taking up of *the collection is an act of worship* which *is to be a part of their regular Lord's Day worship*. When we put our money in the plate, we are worshiping Almighty God in accordance with His Word. Note well, Paul is speaking here of a "collection for the saints" - this is giving by the Church to the Church for the Church. *Did you realize that giving is a part of worship? Is your worship in this area abundant or inhibited? Is giving to the Church a priority with you?*

6. **The Bible teaches that Christian giving should be done in light of the incarnation.** Many Christians argue about whether the tithe (10% of our income) is still the standard for our giving to the

Church (disputants usually want to show that less than 10% is fine). Paul scuttles the whole debate in one verse. He says: "***For you know the grace of our Lord Jesus Christ, that though He was rich, yet for your sake He became poor, so that you through His poverty might become rich***" (2 Corinthians 8:9). *Christ's self-giving is now the standard for our giving!* We *begin from the base of the tithe and aim for emulation of His self-sacrifice.* Our giving is to be inspired and instructed by Christ's inexpressible gift. In light of such a challenge, who could possibly satisfy himself with asking "how little a percentage is acceptable for me to give?" *Do you try to get by with giving as little as possible to the Lord, or do you give in view of the Lord's costly sacrifice?*

7. **The Bible teaches that Christian giving should be done in accordance with our means.** Paul is quite clear on this: "For if the readiness is present, it is acceptable according to what a person has, not according to what he does not have" (2 Corinthians 8:12). Put another way Paul is saying that you should give in proportion to what God has given you. He said it this way in 1 Corinthians 16:2, "each one of you is to put aside and save, as he may prosper." This means at least two things: (1) since we are all supposed to give proportionately, those who have more money are expected to give more [we who are particularly blessed materially must remember this], and (2) the Lord never asks us to give what we do not have, or contribute beyond our means. *Are you really giving in proportion to the material blessings that the Lord has given you?*

8. **The Bible teaches that the liberality of God's blessings to us is connected to the liberality of our Christian giving.** Though it may seem strange, both Jesus and Paul emphasize that there is a relation between our giving to the Lord and the Lord's giving to us. As Paul says in 2 Corinthians 9:6 "Now this I say, he who sows sparingly will also reap sparingly, and he who sows bountifully will also reap bountifully." Jesus reminds us of this in Matthew 6:4, where He teaches that our reward in giving comes from our heavenly Father. As someone once said: "The desire to be generous and the means to be generous both come from God." *Do you realize that the Lord has given you much, so that you can give much?*

9. **The Bible teaches that Christian giving must be willing giving, free giving.** We learn this in 2 Corinthians 9:7 "Each one must do

just as he has purposed in his heart, not grudgingly or under compulsion." But doesn't this contradict what we learned under the first principle, that Christian giving is not optional? The answer is, of course, no. True Christian giving is both mandatory and voluntary. It is required by God, but always willingly given by the believer. *Is your giving to the Church something you do wholeheartedly, or indifferently, or grudgingly?*

10. **The Bible teaches that Christian giving ought to be cheerful giving.** As Paul says "God loves a cheerful giver." This is a truly amazing assertion. Paul assures us here that the Lord takes a special delight in those who are joyful, energetic, merry givers. *Is there joy in your heart as you give? Can you truly be characterized as a **cheerful giver**?*

In any discussion of giving eventually the discussion gravitates into the" "first fruits" and "best fruits." We will address this important issue in chapter 8.

Chapter 5
God's Giving Promises

Everyone knows that rewards work for both humans and animals. In psychology we call it *positive reinforcement*. For example: If you are going to train a seal or a dolphin to do tricks, you better have some fish in your pocket. On the other hand, whether we talk about the airline industry or a credit card industry or any business entity, we are accustomed to receiving some kind of rewards in the form of coupons or money/points credit in our account.

We all are expecting (just like Pavlov's dog experiment) something in return if we make a purchase. It is our human nature to look for rewards or return. [*Pavlovian theory* is a learning procedure that involves pairing a stimulus with a conditioned response. In the famous experiments that Ivan Pavlov conducted with his dogs, Pavlov found that objects or events could trigger a conditioned response. ... As he gave food to the dogs, he rang the bell].

So it is, with giving to God. Many of us may wonder what would happen if we did begin to give what we think God wants us to give. Are we getting a reward? Would anything change for me? Would I be better off financially? Would I simply be better off spiritually? What would happen?

Hebrews 11:6 says that God "rewards those who earnestly seek him." God rewards. It is just the way God is. God is not in anyone's debt. The rewards however, are not considered a deal we can make with God. He is sovereign and we can't make Him do anything. Here we must always remember Paul's request to remove his "thorn," but God's response was, My grace is sufficient "And lest I should be exalted above measure by the abundance of the revelations, a thorn in the flesh was given to me, ... I pleaded with the Lord three times that it might depart from me. And He said to me, 'My grace is sufficient for you... for My strength is made perfect in weakness.' Therefore, most gladly I will rather boast in my infirmities, that the power of Christ may rest upon me, Therefore, I take pleasure in infirmities, in reproaches, in needs, in persecutions, in distresses, for Christ's sake. For when I am weak, then I am strong" (2 Corn. 12:7-10 NKJV). Therefore, our motive must remain rooted in simple thankfulness for His grace. But we can know that when the books of earth are closed someday in eternity, no one will ever say that they gave more to God than He gave to them.

There are many examples of generosity from God, but one that stands in my mind is the story of the generous woman found in IV Kings (LXX) - 2 Kings 4: 8-37; 8:1-6). The story is recorded as:

Around 850 B.C., a wealthy woman in Shunem, about 5 miles south of Nazareth, one day asked Elisha the traveling prophet to eat at her home (IV Kings (LXX) - 2 Kings 4:8-10). He did so and her house soon became a regular stop whenever Elisha came through the area.

Helping Elisha must have somehow been rewarding to the woman, because she began to think of ways that she might be able to bless him even more. She told her husband that she wanted to build a small addition onto the home to give Elisha his own furnished room when he came. Then he would be able to come and relax there. What a blessing! And that's exactly what they did.

Now this woman didn't do this to "get" anything. She didn't make a deal with God that if she built this room for Elisha, she expected certain things back from God. She seemingly just gave as God led her. But what happened? Elisha wondered aloud if there was a way that He could bless her and his servant Gehazi mentioned that she didn't have a son ((IV Kings (LXX) - 2 Kings 4: 11-13). Evidently it was a real desire of her heart that so far had not been fulfilled. So, Elisha the prophet promised her a son. And God came through as Elisha promised! This woman who had been childless had a bouncing baby boy! God is certainly a rewarder! The blessing of a child was a far greater blessing to her than she had even been to Elisha. Indeed, God came through with generosity.

But the story doesn't end here. This child grew and as a boy one day working with his dad in the fields, he suddenly died. Of course, the woman was heartbroken – and even angry at God and Elisha. She laid the body of her only son on Elisha's bed in his room and went to find Elisha. In her bitter grief she said, "Did I ask you for a son, my Lord?" she said. "Didn't I tell you, 'Don't raise my hopes" (IV Kings (LXX) - 2 Kings 4:28)?

So, Elisha went to her house, prayed and laid himself over the body of the boy and God gave her son life again. God gave her a son to begin with and then God raised him from the dead, giving him to her again.

God is a giver. But we learn that when we give to God, there is no guarantee that life will suddenly be wonderful and without pain. When we give, we will still be tested.

There was yet another time when this Shunamite woman was tested – this time financially (IV Kings (LXX) - 2 Kings 8:1-6). Elisha told this woman to leave the land of Israel because God had revealed to him that a seven-year famine was coming.

Evidently the Shunamite woman's husband who was older had died by then because now she was a widow. So, she left the country of Israel to avoid the famine. But what evidently happened in those days is that if you left the country for an extended time, your abandoned land would become either the property of the king or perhaps of a relative. But whoever had it, evidently it was no sure thing that you would get it back.

So, when the Shunamite woman came back to the land, she went before the king to beg to get her land back. This is where God's rewarding character is again obvious. When this woman comes to King Joram, Gehazi, Elisha's servant, just happened to be talking to the king. Imagine that! And the king just at that moment had asked Gehazi to tell him about his master Elisha's miracles.

In (IV Kings (LXX) - 2 Kings 8:5-6) we read the story: "Just as Gehazi was telling the king how Elisha had restored the dead to life, the woman whose son Elisha had brought back to life came to beg the king for her house and land. Gehazi said, "This is the woman, my lord the king, and this is her son whom Elisha restored to life." The king asked the woman about it, and she told him. Then he assigned an official to her case and said to him, "Give back everything that belonged to her, including all the income from her land from the day she left the country until now."

So how did this woman's generosity work out in the long run? Her gifts to God were initially just meals for Elijah and then she built and furnished a small room for him. God's gifts to her included the birth of a son, the resurrection of her son, advance warning of a 7-year famine and

105

then God made sure she received her land back – plus seven years income!

God is an incredible rewarder to those who give to Him out of a *grateful heart.* But along with the principle we find in the Old Testament scriptures the principle that those who refuse to give miss out on God's blessings.

In yet another scriptural story we read the events that took place as a result of robbing God of tithes under the Old Covenant. Here is the story as written in the book of the prophet Malachi.

In the time of Malachi, the prophet (about 400 B.C.), there were serious spiritual problems in Israel. The book of Malachi addresses several of them. The Israelites were bringing God sacrifices consisting of their maimed animals (1:7-8). The priests had stopped teaching the word of God accurately (2:1-9). Furthermore, the Israelites had married unbelievers (2:11-16) and were divorcing their wives (2:13-16). They were even saying that evil people were good (2:17). Included in God's rebuke through the prophet Malachi was proof that they had turned from God as shown by the fact that they *stopped giving their tithes* and *offerings* (Malachi 3:7-9).

At first, they denied that they had turned from God (Malachi 3:7). They seem to have protested that they had done nothing wrong, what do you mean, return to God? I'm doing fine with God. I don't need to change anything. And then interestingly Malachi uses as their failure to give financially as evidence of their spiritual state. He tells them, you've robbed God. Now they are really sputtering. How do we rob God?

(Malachi 3:8-9) "Will a man rob God? Yet you rob me. "But you ask, 'How do we rob you?' "*In tithes and offerings.* You are under a curse--the whole nation of you - because you are robbing me." The failure to bring their tithes and offerings is called robbing God.

Tithes are a largely misunderstood part of Bible teaching about giving. "Tithe" is a Bible term that means 1/10th. *Tithing was an obligation under the covenant of the Old Testament law*. The first 10% of their crops went to God. The following short outline shows the basic tithing requirements under the Law.

1. Regular Tithes = 10% of crops (income) given each year to the Lord (Leviticus 27:30) OBLIGATION
    a. Provided regular income for Levites and Priests serving at the temple in Jerusalem (Numbers 18:21-26)
    b. Provided means for having three special feasts in Jerusalem each year (or if they lived too far away, they could bring money – Deuteronomy 14:22-26)
2. 2nd Tithe every 3rd year = 3.33% OBLIGATION
    a. Used to support the local Levites and the needy (Deut. 14:27-29)
3. Personal Offerings – Any other gifts (IV Kings (LXX) - 2 Kings 12:4); Mark 12:41 – voluntary vows, gifts). VOLUNTARY

This list is not definitive, as even today scholars debate the details of the per centages. However, even though there may be a discrepancy of the actual numbers, what is known is that the tithing of an Israelite was more than 10%. For example, it is possible that the feasting tithe (1/a above) was actually a 2nd separate tithe and thus it would mean an additional 10% tithe was required. This would actually make the annual "tithe" a total of 23.3% of one's yearly income. But we'll assume for now that it was part of the 1st tithe. Even then, the basic Israelite farmer would be giving an average of 13.3% per year as an obligation. Then they could and should give offerings above the tithe as thanks or praise.

These additional personal offerings were personal worship decisions. An example of this would be the widow at temple who gave her two small copper coins while the wealthy threw in large amounts (Mark 12:41). These gifts were over and above tithing. When Josiah collected money to restore the temple, that was all above the tithes (IV Kings (LXX) - 2 Kings 12:4). And these financial offerings still did not account for many of the sin offerings and other offerings that involved animals or produce of the field.

So, under the giving system of the Law, an obedient Israelite would be giving 13% (or maybe 23%) that was their obligation, plus whatever God led them to give above that in personal offerings.

Malachi rebuked the Israelites of his day who for the most part, were not giving their tithes and offerings. He said that they had thus robbed God. As it turns out, they were actually robbing themselves of God's blessings.

Notice the promise of God to the Israelites if they were to repent of their failure to give.

The prophet does not finish here. He continues in Malachi 3:10-12 to say: "Bring the whole tithe into the storehouse, that there may be food in my house. Test me in this," says the LORD Almighty, "and see if I will not throw open the floodgates of heaven and pour out so much blessing that you will not have room enough for it. I will prevent pests from devouring your crops, and the vines in your fields will not cast their fruit," says the LORD Almighty. "Then all the nations will call you blessed, for yours will be a delightful land," says the LORD Almighty."

God is promising Israel financial success as a reward for tithing. Now before we start planning on building a new home and buying that yacht because we are going to give, we need to remember several things. 1) God's purpose in rewarding us is not so that we can become selfishly wealthy. 2) We do not have the promise about tithing repeated today in the New Testament. We live under the new covenant and we actually don't have a tithing law in the New Testament. No one can tell you that you must give 10% or 13% plus other voluntary offerings. That was the Old Covenant.

In fact, as Orthodox Christians we say that there is no tithing. However, there is giving! The amount depends on the individual, but if we go by what the New Testament writers and many Fathers of the Church have written about, *we give it all for the glory of God*. After all, it would seem very strange that we would make it our goal in this age of grace to do less than what was required under the law. In His teaching Jesus often challenged people to live by a higher standard now under grace than what Moses had required under the law (*e.g.* Matthew 5:27 - 28).

So, although the law of tithing and the financial promises of tithing are not in force today – at least in the Orthodox Church - we find from the words of Jesus, from the epistles of the New Testament, the Fathers of the Church, and the Holy Tradition, that the general principle of God's promises to givers are still true.

Jesus taught the basic principle that God rewards those who are generous not only financially, but *generous in spirit*. Listen to the words of Christ.

But love your enemies, do good to them, and lend to them without expecting to get anything back. Then your reward will be great, and you will be sons of the Most High, because he is kind to the ungrateful and wicked. What kind of reward? It doesn't say – perhaps here, perhaps heaven. Be merciful, just as your Father is merciful. "Do not judge, and you will not be judged. Do not condemn, and you will not be condemned. Forgive, and you will be forgiven" (Luke 6:35-37).

People who do good to others generally find themselves blessed with the same kind of graciousness with which they treat others. God makes sure that happens somehow. Jesus says next that God gives back even more than a generous merchant. The thunderous words are: "Give, and it will be given to you. A good measure, pressed down, shaken together and running over, will be poured into your lap. For with the measure you use, it will be measured to you" (Luke 6:38).

A "good measure" meant that when you bought grain in the market, the merchant didn't do to you what the cereal manufacturers (and others) do to us. When we open the cereal box, we find it half empty when we think it is going to be full. But a generous merchant would fill his measure to the brim and then press it down and shake it so it settles so he could get a little more in before giving it to you as the costumer. [Profit and greed are overpowering]. On the other hand, think of the cheerful baker. Generally, he is generous with his baker's dozen – an extra item of whatever the dozen purchase is.

Jesus says God is like that generous merchant – only more so! God will reward us in such abundance of blessings that they will be overflowing our basket and filling the robe in our lap. God is just that way! He will not be out-given. What kind of giving is Jesus talking about? He could mean money, but He could also be referring to anything of ours that we give away – time, concern for others, encouragement, money or other material things. And what kind of return or blessing is Jesus promising? God may give back to us in many ways. In His miraculous way He can choose to bless us financially through finding us good deals, preventing high expenses or by providing raises or more hours and overtime. But it could also be that God blesses our "giving" by rewarding us with unexpected time to relax even though we had given away time to serve others. It could be that God miraculously blesses our marriage, restores relationships or health or any number of good things.

Those who give time regularly to serving others in their church, family and community are not shortchanged in the long run. Providentially, God takes care of the time needs of those who gave time, the financial needs of those who give financially and the encouragement needs of those who give encouragement.

From what we've seen from the Shunammite woman and from the tithing promises of Malachi and Jesus' words to us here, we can be sure that God will reward our financial giving. We may not get wealthy, but no one will get to heaven and think, boy, I got the raw end of that giving.

In the New Testament, God's promises to givers include a great variety of both spiritual and financial blessings. In 2 Corinthians 8 and 9 Paul urges the church at Corinth to give to an offering he is collecting for famine relief for believers in Jerusalem. At the end of his exhortation he lists some of the blessings they will experience if they do.

If God is working in our heart to produce a new attitude of giving based on stewardship, contentment, trust and worship, then what God wants us to know very clearly from the following passages is that we will never regret it. The general principle is exactly what Jesus taught: God blesses givers; "Whoever sows generously will also reap generously" (2 Corinthians 9:6-14). Here are other blessings Paul describes that will come just from participating in this offering for needy believers in Jerusalem.

1. We will have enough to live on (8). "…having all that you need."
2. Our ministry will multiply (8,11). "You will abound in every good work… [God] will enlarge the harvest of your righteousness.
3. We will have enough to give more (10-11). "[God] will also supply and increase your store of seed … You will be made rich in every way so that you can be generous on every occasion"
4. People will thank you for supplying their needs (12) "… your generosity will result in thanksgiving to God … supplying the needs of God's people…"

5. People will praise God for your obedience to God and generosity (13) ... "Men will praise God for the obedience ... and for your generosity in sharing with them and with everyone else."
6. People will pray for you (14) "And in their prayers for you their hearts will go out to you, because of the surpassing grace God has given you."

If we are privileged to live the kind of life described above, our life will be richly blessed indeed! To appreciate God's rewards, we have to adjust our expectations. Those who teach that it is God's will that Christians should be wealthy appeal to the selfishness of our hearts. They suppose that "godliness is a means to financial gain" (1 Timothy 6:5). The problem with that thinking is first of all that God never promises that in the New Testament and secondly, that if we give in order to live selfishly, we forfeit the real rewards God promised here.

If we struggle with a constant desire to be better off financially, we must note in the passage above what Paul promised the Corinthians. The reason why God will bless them financially is not so that they can spend it on upgrading their lifestyle, but so that they could give more. "[God] will also supply and increase your store of seed ... You will be made rich in every way so that you can be generous on every occasion" (2 Corinthians 9:10-11). It is profoundly important to recognize that the principle is not that we should "Give to Get." This is only partially true and needs to be augmented with the full response saying: "Give to Get, so that, to Give more." God rewards that kind of an unselfish heart.

Paul's letter to the Philippians reveals his own financial struggle and how he learned to be content through Christ even when he was hungry (Philippians 4:11-13). But in this section Paul stresses that he really did appreciate the financial gift that the church in Philippi sent him. Paul had received a gift from them for his support, just as a church budget pays salaries for pastors and missionaries.

Philippi is one of those Macedonian churches who gave to the offering for Jerusalem out of their poverty (2 Corinthians 8:1-5). Since this letter to the Philippians was written about seven years later, we realize that they didn't quit giving with that single offering. Philippians 4:10-20 is really

Paul's thank you note for that gift. And in his note, Paul includes additional promises of rewards from God for giving.

Eternal Rewards are placed on our account (Philippians 4:17-19) "Not that I am looking for a gift, but I am looking for what may be credited to your account. Where are these rewards? These are rewards awaiting us in heaven!

1. We have the Privilege of Pleasing God (4:19) "I am amply supplied, now that I have received from Epaphroditus the gifts you sent. They are a fragrant offering, an acceptable sacrifice, pleasing to God."
2. All our needs including money will be supplied by God. And my God will meet all your needs according to his glorious riches in Christ Jesus."
3. All means all. God is promising not only material blessings. This is a much better promise than even the Old Testament promise of material blessings. *This is a promise of incredible blessing throughout our lives.*

Will life still be hard at time for givers? Yes. Will it actually be hard to give at times? Yes. Will there be doubts and fears about giving? Yes. But God will bless. We can just leave that part up to God. **Should we give to get? *No.*** We should give out of gratitude for what God did for us through Christ. But God wanted us to know that He will not ignore our gift or be out-given. *God rewards those who give.*

Now, if giving is new to us, or if God is working in our heart in some new way, we need to make some practical decisions about where to give and how much. The New Testament describes three crucial parts of a giving plan. They are: 1) Give proportionately (Mat. 23:23) 2) Give consistently according to a plan (1 Corin. 16:2) and 3) Give personally, willingly and cheerfully (2 Corin. 9:7) and 4) Privately (Mat. 6:3).

1. *Give proportionately*: Two key passages from Paul to the Corinthians make the point that God expects our giving to reflect our income in some proportionate sense. Our giving should be a reflection of the income God has given to us. Paul called it giving "according to your means" (2 Corinthians 8:11). Even clearer are his instructions when the offering for the Jerusalem church was first announced. (1 Corinthians 16:2) "On the

first day of every week, each one of you should set aside a sum of money in keeping with his income, saving it up, so that when I come no collections will have to be made."

A *George Barna* poll in 1999 revealed that, "Evangelicals are the most generous givers, but fewer than 10% of born-again Christians gave 10% or more to their church" (George Barna. News release by Barna Research Group, April 5, 2000.) Also, according to Barna, in 2000 14% of evangelicals said that they tithed. In 2001, 12% claimed to tithe. After 911, in 2002, the polls showed that it fell to 6%.

In 2018, another research group, *share faith,* reports that 28% of all tithers are debt free (https://www.sharefaith.com/blog/2015/12/facts-christians-tithing/. Retrieved on August 31, 2020

In 2020 the *Non-profit source* research organization reports the following. (All numbers are composite numbers and there are no specific denomination giving. (https://nonprofitssource.com/online-giving-statistics/church-giving/. Retrieved on August 31, 2020. Some key statistics are the following regarding giving to Churches:

- 49% of all church giving transactions are made with a card.
- 8/10 people who give to churches have zero credit debt.
- 60% are willing to give to their church digitally.
- Tithers make up only 10-25 percent of a normal congregation.
- Churches that accept tithing online increase overall donations by 32%.
- Only 5% tithe, and 80% of Americans only give 2% of their income.
- Christians are giving at 2.5% of income; during the Great Depression it was 3.3%.
- Only 3-5% of Americans who give to their local church do so through regular tithing.
- When surveyed, 17% of Americans state that they regularly tithe.
- For families making $75k+, 1% of them gave at least 10% in tithing.
- 3 out of 4 people who don't go to church make donations to nonprofit organizations.
- The average giving by adults who attend US Protestant churches is about $17 a week.

- 37% of regular church attendees and Evangelicals don't give money to church.
- 17% of American families have reduced the amount that they give to their local church.
- 7% of church goers have dropped regular giving by 20% or more.
- About 10 million tithers in the US donate $50 billion yearly to church & non-profits.
- 77% of those who tithe give 11%–20% or more of their income, far more than the baseline of 10%.
- 7 out of 10 tithers do so based on their gross and not their net income.
- The average number of updates that a successful campaign owner post is 4.
- Crowdfunding campaigns get 126% more donations when owners update supporters.
- Campaigns that are shared fewer than 2 times have a 97% chance of failure.
- Crowdfunding campaigns with personal videos raise 150% more than those that don't have videos.
- Over half of people who receive an email about a crowdfunding campaign made a donation

However as accurate as the statistics may be, it's nonetheless obvious that only a small number of those who claim to be believers and to acknowledge the Bible as God's word are giving even at the most minimal Old Testament standard. In fact, the *New York Times* has reported that there is a 50% decline in giving or tithing since 1990 (https://www.cdfcapital.org/tithing-generosity/. Retrieved on August 31, 2020. [As of this writing, there are no published giving or tithing data for the Orthodox Church].

To be sure, there is no specific contribution that has to be met in the Orthodox Church. Even Paul would not say that we must tithe, but tithing can serve us as a basic principle for proportionate giving. For some who are beginning, it might be a target to plan toward. For some it might just be a starting point. On the other hand, as believers today we must give with a full understanding of God's grace and of God's promises. So, while the tithe should not obligate us, it also should not limit us!

What Paul seems to say in 1 Corinthians 16:2 is that we should simply decide on a percentage of our income to give regularly. Then it is just a simple pre-spending decision that comes off the top of every paycheck or other source of income. In one sense it is as simple as taxes – just a lot more fun. Beyond what we decide to give proportionately, there may be many other occasions when God shows us a need to which He prompts us to give.

Giving in any form is a financial decision. Therefore, we can simply pray and decide what percent we should begin with or move toward. The need to give is part of the whole issue of living as stewards. Some of us might think that we can't afford to give up a certain percentage. It is possible for one to go through a hardship when we cannot afford our set tithe. However, if we begin our journey as stewards and worshippers, God begins to make it possible. That's where trust begins and God's promises kick in.

So, tithing is not a rule, but proportionate giving is God's plan. The second principle we find in Paul's instructions to the Corinthians is that proportionate giving needs to be regular.

2. *Give consistently according to a plan*: Paul taught the Corinthians to give regularly. (1 Corinthians 16:2) "On the first day of every week, each one of you should set aside a sum of money...." Paul was telling them to get ready for the offering by setting aside a regular amount each week when they came together to worship. This does not establish a rule that everyone must give every week, but it does establish the principle that regularity is key to proportionate giving. Just giving when we feel like it will probably lead to less and less commitment.

Obviously if you have a steady salary, say every week, then the proportion of giving is easy to figure. However, if your pay is erratic you can figure your annual income and divided by 52 and that becomes your base for your weekly contribution. What is important here is consistency. We have complete freedom in how much we give and how often, but as in all areas of life, we need a plan that has some regularity. Consistency holds us accountable and it also enables the Church and its programs to be able to count on the gifts they need. For this to happen, there must be transparency of the incoming funds and how they are spent. They should not be secret and controlled by the Bishop, priest or a few council members.

3. *Give personally, willingly and cheerfully*: As God moves in our hearts to be faithful givers as His stewards, probably the most important decision we make is about our attitude. Paul states it directly, "Each man should give what he has decided in his heart to give, not reluctantly or under compulsion, for God loves a cheerful giver" (2 Corinthians 9:7).

No other person can tell you how much exactly to give. But as we seek God in prayer, God will direct us. If giving is an issue between me and God, then it is also crucial that we give willingly and with a cheer.

Paul's word cheerful here is the Greek word - ἱλαρὸν γὰρ δότην ἀγαπᾷ ὁ Θεός) hilaros which is where we get our English word hilarious. The Greek term does not quite have the connotation of hilarity, but the general idea is that when we give in gratitude for God's grace to us, it should be a happy occasion.

So, we have seen that the Old Testament tithe went to support the worship and ministry of Israel at the temple. It was essentially the Old Testament equivalent of the local church. The local church would seem to be the biblical place to start giving proportionately. The epistles of the New Testament describe the need to support elders/priests who teach the word (1 Timothy 5:17-18; Galatians 6:6). The point was that when we receive our regular spiritual "food" and encouragement from those who teach and lead us in the local church, they should be supported financially.

Along with such teachers are the financial support needs of others who preach the gospel such as Paul – who was financially supported much like missionaries today (1 Corinthians 9:4-14). Most missionary support today goes through the local church as well – in the form of the *Philoptohos* (Friend of the poor). Finally, benevolence gifts are also frequently channeled through local churches as well - through the *Philoptohos*.

So, the local church would seem to be the primary place to give financially based on the worship precedent of the Old Testament as well as the support principles of the New Testament. However, giving is not restricted only for the church. We are free to help the poor, orphanages missionaries and other worthy activities that may be necessary to proclaim the Gospel directly and or indirectly.

Generally, for most people the giving is by the way of cash. However, other forms of giving are possible. Going back to Old Testament times, people gave material, valuables and other items needed to build, assemble and furnish the tabernacle (Exodus 35:22-29). Today a person might give items that they know a missionary or someone else needs. IRS laws in the US allow tax deductions for "gifts in kind" just as it does for direct cash gifts. Stocks, bonds and wills are another way of giving.

When the church started in Jerusalem people sold items of value and gave it to support people in the church (Acts 2:44-45). Acts 4 tells about people who sold some of their assets of land to make significant gifts to the new church at Jerusalem and gave it to the apostles to distribute to those in need (Acts 4:34-37).

Christians today can give creatively and substantially to the Church needs to which God directs them by selling items of value, donating stocks, or including a church or ministry in their estate plan.

God prompts and provides ways for us to give that are uniquely part of his plan and fit us perfectly. Then God rewards and blesses our giving in many ways.

Yes, indeed God rewards giving and builds His church through the faithful financial worship of His people. To begin teaching the biblical way of giving and tithing one may start a regular and systematic training based on 1 Corinthians 16 and 2 Corinthians 8 & 9.

Chapter 6
Stewardship of the Money We Don't Give

If you received a 10% on a paper you turned into your teacher as a student, you wouldn't feel really good about it obviously. You would have seriously failed the assignment to miss 90% of the material somehow. Yet it is possible to get that grade on God's financial stewardship test – even if we gave a tithe from every paycheck! How can that be? Well, that is how far off we can actually be from living as God's stewards if we think that we can do whatever we want with whatever is left after we give.

If God owns everything, then we declare our agreement with God that we are stewards by giving back to God a regular sacrificial percentage. But what about that part that is left? Isn't that God's as well? It really is, if we are stewards. We get to choose how to use it, but it still belongs to God.

God's word claims that He owns the cattle on a thousand hills (Psalm 49(50):10). Although human beings claim ownership of livestock, God is saying that He has a prior ownership claim. People simply manage God's cattle whether they acknowledge it or not.

We have only grasped stewardship if we realize that all our money must be under God's control. And that is actually the path to financial freedom. You see, if I consider all of my money to be under God's control, then I can seek and find God's help in every decision about material things. What a relief! God is not only the owner of my possessions; He's my advisor about how to manage it all!

This chapter addresses some other places our money goes – spending, saving, investing, debt repayment and so on. Obviously, not all the principles and ideas we discuss in this chapter are for everyone. You might not have any debt. Good for you. Likewise, we are not all supposed to spend the same or have identical financial priorities. For example, today I'll make some specific suggestions for living conservatively. God might be leading one person to buy generic and stop spending money on entertainment. The next person might follow God's will to buy name brands and get season tickets to the Detroit Tigers baseball team, *etc*.

We can't judge each other, but there are some principles about stewardship wisdom that we must apply and cannot ignore. Our challenge today is to put all our money on the table before God and seek His wisdom.

Perhaps a good beginning is to recognize a good steward within our family. The woman of the house – wife. It is biblical! This woman seemed to be a wise steward of her financial resources – all of them. She teaches us that stewardship is far more than giving money. Stewardship touches our work ethic and all the ways that we spend and invest. So, we read in (Proverbs 29: 30-31 LXX or 31:10-12 Masoretic): "Charms are false, and woman's beauty is vain: for it is a wise woman that is blessed, and let her praise the fear of the Lord. Give her of the fruit of her lips; and let her husband be praised in the gates." Even though the two verses are a bit different, they both say practically the same thing. The Masoretic text reads: "A wife of noble character who can find? She is worth far more than rubies. Her husband has full confidence in her and lacks nothing of value. She brings him good, not harm, all the days of her life."

By reading the text of the Proverbs we learn about the fundamental *"traits"* which are essential to every Christian who wants to be a good steward financially. The traits are: 1) She works hard and 2) she spends wisely. It is interesting to note that these two traits are expanded in a form of a list in Proverbs 29:10-21 LXX. The same list is found in the Masoretic text in (Proverbs 31:13-21). For our discussion here we use the Masoretic text for simplicity. "She selects wool and flax and works with eager hands. *She works hard. She is like the merchant ships*, bringing her food from afar. *She spends wisely. She gets up while it is still dark. She provides food* for her family and portions for her servant girls. *She works hard. She considers a field and buys it*; out of her earnings *she plants a vineyard. She spends wisely. She sets about her work vigorously*; her arms are strong for her tasks. *She works hard. She sees that her trading is profitable. She spends wisely*, and *her lamp does not go out at night. She works hard.* In her hand *she holds the distaff and grasps the spindle with her fingers. She works hard.*"

And as a result of her hard work and wise spending, she is truly a wise steward in two additional ways: In Proverbs (31:20) she opens her arms to the poor and extends her hands to the needy. *She gives freely.* When it snows, she has no fear for her household; for all of them are clothed in scarlet. *She plans ahead.*

A good cash flow depends on hard work first of all. We won't have any money or belongings or even food of which to be a steward unless we work hard. [St. Paul remind us in 2 Thes, 3:10 "If a man will not work, he shall not eat (NIV, MIT) - τοῦτο παρηγγέλλομεν ὑμῖν, ὅτι εἴ τις οὐ θέλει ἐργάζεσθαι, μηδὲ ἐσθιέτω"]. By working hard in fact, this woman minimized her expenses, making some things herself that she wouldn't have to buy in the market. She was also wise about spending and investing. This woman looked for ways to make her money grow.

Finally, we learn from her example that when you work hard and spend wisely and plan ahead there is money left to give generously. Quite frankly the reason why we often feel we can't give is because we have not been faithful stewards by working hard and spending wisely. So, if God is speaking to us in these days about financial stewardship, we will need to ask Him which of these areas to address.

The first step to becoming a wise steward of our spending is to set a lifestyle limit financially – **have a budget**.

The writer of Proverbs 30:8-9, Agur (an epithet of Solomon), declares, "Keep falsehood and lies far from me; give me neither poverty nor riches, but give me only my daily bread. Otherwise, I may have too much and disown you and say, 'Who is the LORD?' Or I may become poor and steal, and so dishonor the name of my God." Really, he was praying for the ideal financial condition. He prays that God would not give him too much or too little. Is this a prayer that God would answer? Agur asks just for "daily bread." Interestingly, this is exactly the financial prayer Jesus taught us, "Give us today our daily bread" (Matthew 6:11).

For us, even today, maybe we are praying or at least desiring the wrong things, as such maybe that is the reason that we are struggling with our finances. Agur, clearly is teaching that there is a "just right" place to be financially sound. If God owns everything and has determined how much we should have, then there really is a *sweet spot* for us financially. The world says that the *sweet spot* is always to have more. God's word says no.

We all seem to forget that God's will for how much money we should have is the amount we have right now. However, when we accept that, we have a significant challenge and that is: What does God want us to do with what we have? What lifestyle does God want us to live at spending-wise? Do we assume that if we can afford a certain lifestyle, then it's

God's will that we live at that level? Have we ever considered that God might want us to set a lifestyle limit below our income level?

The answer to these questions is very personal and critical. Never-the-less it requires much thought and a radical change in our behavior if we follow the biblical principles. There are at least three choices, no matter what income bracket one belongs to. They are"

1. *Living above our means*. This lifestyle will mean increasing debt and stress to be sure. This can be represented as: **expenses > income**.
2. *Living within our means*. This is what we all assume is the right way to live. It will result in a steady, balanced cash flow and will give a person freedom from the bondage of debt and significant financial worries. This can be represented as: **Expenses $\leq$ income.**
3. *Living below our means*. This is the lifestyle many Christians have never considered, but need to. It will also result in a steady, balanced cash flow and freedom, but it also accomplishes more. Living below our means really prepares us to experience some additional blessings. This can be represented as: **Expenses < income.**

The question now is: Why should we consider living below our means? First of all, it is the key to contentment – because we constantly realize there are things we choose not to buy. I learn daily what I can live without because I actually have the ability to buy more, but I don't.

Secondly, when we spend less than we earn, we are free to give more than we even planned. When I spend less than I have, I discover that God has allowed me more money which He wants me to manage. Then when opportunities arise, I am free to give as God leads me.

Thirdly, when I spend less than I earn, my stewardship has a good chance of outlasting my own life. For one thing, if I'm a parent, I can be an example to my children. Many young adults and families struggle financially in their early years because they are used to the lifestyle of their parents. But our adult children may or may not be able to live at the level we live. Maybe the larger problem often is that children follow the philosophy of their parents that they should spend all the money they get. But if we as parents consistently demonstrate contentment by limiting our lifestyle, that's the principle they can learn. And we are doing them and our grandchildren a huge favor.

The other way that our stewardship can outlast the years we have on earth is by leaving money to ministries. Indeed, leaving an inheritance to children is a good thing. In Proverbs 13:22 LXX we read: A good man shall inherit children's children; and the wealth of ungodly men is laid up for the just. Therefore, the lesson of controlling the finances is to control the string on the purse (πουγκί). A typical purse is shown here:

Figure 6.1: A typical purse

How to live below our means

So, what do we do when we want things we can't afford? When that want or desire comes, we assume that the solution is to either increase our income or to increase our debt. Right? If we want something we can't afford right now, we think about how we can get more money either from more income or more borrowing. But the Proverbs tell us two simple truths that can change our entire financial situation. I'm warning you; the Bible uses a strong term to describe us if we think this way. Ready? (Proverbs 17:16) "Of what use is money in the hand of a fool, since he has no desire to get wisdom?" In the LXX translation we read: "Why has the fool wealth? For a senseless man will not be able to purchase wisdom. He that exalts his own house seeks ruin and he that turns aside from instruction shall fall into mischief." If we only want money, not wisdom, God calls us fool.

So, more money is not the solution. The Proverbs further tell us that it's foolish to have what we can't afford (Proverbs 19:10) "It is not fitting for a fool to live in luxury…" In the LXX translation we read it as: Delight does not suit a fool…" So, we are not misunderstood here. We are not suggesting that there is something wrong with luxury as one defines it. Not at all. What we are talking about here is: It is not right to want or live in luxury however it is defined for you, if you cannot afford it.

Unfortunately, many think, that there is nothing they can change in their spending. They use the refrain: there is nothing more I can cut out. I just need more money. I have to go into further debt or get more income! I am afraid that is not the correct attitude and solution. There is plenty one can do. For example, some ideas to live within or below your means are:

1. Doing without
2. Accepting less convenience
3. Older technology and styles
4. Budgeting, and keeping it
5. Used instead of New
6. Waiting and shopping longer
7. Sales, coupons, rebates
8. Planning ahead
9. Keeping the old one – little longer
10. Buying quantity – take advantage of membership stores such as; BJ's, Casco, Sam's warehouses
11. Giving up things that are fun to do/have
12. Giving up what tastes best
13. Buying lesser/generic brands
14. Making instead of buying
15. Fixing instead of replacing
16. Renting instead of owning
17. Learn to live with less instead of more
18. Smaller instead of bigger
19. Combine trips
20. Less entertainment
21. Shorter showers, and other utilities
22. Value instead of vanity
23. Selling off what I don't need
24. Give to charity what you have not used for t lest six months (*e.g.* Purple heart, Salvation Army or any other charity group)
25. Don't use the credit card. If you have to use a credit card, do so very sparingly. Remember the interest alone on a typical credit card is anywhere from 19 to 30%, depending on your card carrier and your financial credit history.

Obviously not all items are for all. However, I am sure with the proper humility we can apply some of these ideas to control our appetite for "more," "luxury," and keeping pace with the neighbors. Frugality is the answer to spend less! Let us never forget that our God gives us all things richly (abundantly, Ephes. 3:20-21) TO ENJOY.

So, are we learning that it is God's will that we never spend more than we absolutely need? (1 Timothy 6:17). God delights in rewarding us with special blessings. Some might be gifts. Some we can indeed splurge on with freedom at times as God's blessings. But the tendency of our society is to consider splurges to be rights and soon splurging becomes our routine. And it's an enslaving lifestyle that we often cannot afford. We need to consider if a certain splurge really is God's blessing or not. Proverbs 10:22 tells us that, "The blessing of the LORD brings wealth, and he adds no trouble to it." If our so-called blessing is bringing us financial debt and family stress, it's probably not God's blessing at all.

It is of profound importance here to differentiate what our needs, our wants and our desires are. They are not the same. Need is essential in the present. A want is something "better" an upgrade from what we have – it is not essential. We can live without it! A desire is something we strongly wish for but we fundamentally know that we cannot afford it. Sometimes God leads and enables us to enjoy our wants and desires (see Figure 1.1). But often He doesn't. Instead he wants to teach us wisdom, contentment and frugality in some way to enable us to have the financial freedom of living below our means.

The discussion of needs, wants and desires leads us to the important stewardship issue of savings. Why? Because it is through savings that we can "really" expand our needs to "wants" and "desires." Biblically we have the admonition of Proverbs 6:6-8 that tells us that ants have enough sense just by instinct to work hard when the weather is good so that they have enough in the winter. And to close the thought Proverbs 21:5 tells us, "The plans of the diligent lead to profit as surely as haste leads to poverty." Therefore, the answer to our appetite of "more" is in savings and planning. If we miss these two, then no matter how much money we bring in we can still live in poverty if we spend it all and can't meet the bills. If we don't restrain our spending so we have enough money to do what we need to do, that's poverty. So, planning means some kind of budgeting or plan unless there is a shared and accepted standard of thrift in the family.

Here we may have a dilemma and that is: how can we plan and save if we are already living paycheck to paycheck. The answer may be found in Proverbs. Specifically, we are warned in Proverbs 21:20 thusly: "In the house of the wise are stores of choice food and oil, but a foolish man devours all he has." So, saving is part of living within or below our means. We simply can't use up all the money we have now if we are going to have it when we need it. Therefore, a saving plan- no matter how small - is an essential part of planning. A wise steward will seek to set aside some portion as savings in anticipation of those unexpected needs.

At this point of our discussion, we must emphasize that investing IS NOT ONLY for the rich. Everyone benefits. The farmer invests in seed so that he can have a larger amount of harvest; the businessman invests to receive a better return on his investment, individuals invest what they have for a new business and so on. A good example of this "investment concept" is found in Proverbs 31:16. Yet another benefit of investing is the opportunity a) of having a good retirement fund but also b) to leave an inheritance (Proverbs 13:22) "A good man leaves an inheritance for his children's children). [A word of caution is necessary here. To be sure savings and or investment must be in balance with always the wisdom of an excellent steward. However, one can overdo it and that leads to excessive selfishness and pride. The biblical example is from the rich man found in the story of Luke 12:16-21. The story tells us that he built bigger barns and said, There, I have plenty laid up for years. Eat, drink and be merry. But then the man died. Jesus said that his problem was that he was not rich toward God. His investing was all selfish and excluded God].

Understanding the biblical sense of saving and investing is fundamental to avoid debt. Unless we get rid of debt, we become slaves to the lender. It is important to understand that some debt is unavoidable. For example, most of us could not own a home without a mortgage, the same for a car if we do not take a loan. If we are a business, we may need a loan for expanding this business provided there is a low risk in the investment.

The real culprit of most debt problems is consumer debt – paying finance charges on credit cards or any loan that we really can't afford buying things that depreciate in value.

What does the Bible say about debt? It says that debt is slavery and obligation. In (Proverbs 22:7) we read: "The rich rule over the poor, and the borrower is servant to the lender." The term, servant is really, slave. Debt is bondage. The Bible doesn't say that it's always wrong to borrow; it just tells us that debt is bondage. How much bondage do we want – because debt is an obligation to repay? Debt is also a major cause of conflict. Jeremiah 15:10 complains, "Alas… I have neither lent nor borrowed, yet everyone curses me." This makes the interesting observation that 2500 years ago debt was already causing conflict.

If we are sensing God working in our lives about stewardship, what do we do about our debt problems? There is hope, but it starts NOW, with spiritual decisions to realign our finances with God's principles. It starts NOW, with making significant changes in our mindset and financial management. It starts NOW with deciding to put God in the driver's seat where He has belonged all the time.

The NOW principle, reminds me of an old saying that I have heard since my childhood: no matter how far down the wrong road you've gone, turn back, NOW. Therefore, applying this principle of the *now* we can overcome debt problems by stopping borrowing more, and starting to live on less and beginning to pay back what we owe. In the final analysis, getting rid of debt and becoming a good steward is up to the individual.

So, is the money we give more holy than the money we spend or save? If our "tithe" could talk to the rest of our money could it claim to be "holier than thou?" Actually, No, not at all. If indeed God owns all that we have, then the way that we spend, save and invest is just as much a spiritual matter as any money we give to the Lord. If He is Lord of all, then we must be stewards of all the money or other possessions God entrusts to us.

Chapter 7
Learning and Teaching Stewardship

Learning is the way by which we become efficient in something. It is a process and sometimes it takes a long time. However, during this process we make mistakes and hopefully we learn from them. In everyday language we call this "learning experience" and it becomes a path for our future improvement.

When we deal with financial decisions, we realize – after the fact – that we have made a bad mistake(s) - sometimes. We become aware of our mistake(s) – even though we do not share it (them) with anyone else. We recall them because we know the actual consequences we experienced from those decisions.

Quite frequently when we make a decision, we challenge our own decision with *cognitive dissidence.* That is: we ourselves asking (sometimes challenge) ourselves if we did the right decision. So, the real concern is whether or not we are using "our" money as it belongs to God. In other words: Are we being good managers (stewards) of His money in hard as well as good times?

As we have said several times, true stewardship is a radically different way of thinking, because it challenges our *status quo* of giving, especially in hard times. To circumvent this difficulty, one must have trust in God and have faith in the stewardship principles that He has bestowed on us.

The stewardship principle in hard times is demonstrated in the story of a woman in 850 B.C. in IV Kings - 2 Kings 4. She was a godly woman married to one of the prophets led by Elisha. It is even possible - based on the term that is used to describe her husband *sons of the prophets* - that he wasn't yet a full-fledged prophet, just a man studying and preparing to be one.

The story tells us that a tragedy strikes this family. The husband dies leaving a wife and two sons. To compound this woman's grief, they are also in debt to a certain man. How the family got into debt we don't know. But now there was no one to support this family and Jewish law allowed the creditor to enslave the children of those who owed them money. And that is exactly what their creditor intended to do. He was about to take this woman's two young sons and use them as servants and or slaves as payment for the money they could not repay. So, what did the woman do? In desperation, she cried out to Elisha. The story is recounted in IV Kings - 2 Kings 4:1-4, thusly: "The wife of a man from the company of the prophets cried out to Elisha, "Your servant my husband is dead, and you know that he revered the LORD. But now his creditor is coming to take my two boys as his slaves." Elisha replied to her, "How can I help you? Tell me, what do you have in your house?" "Your servant has nothing there at all," she said, "except a little oil." Elisha said, "Go around and ask all your neighbors for empty jars. Don't ask for just a few. Then go inside and shut the door behind you and your sons. Pour oil into all the jars, and as each is filled, put it to one side."

There is a basic violation of a law of physics in Elisha's instructions, it seems. She has a "little oil," in a flask maybe. And Elisha asks her to use it to fill as many whole jars as she is able to borrow from her neighbors. And the obvious question is, what will be the source of this oil? Where is the hose supplying the oil, Elisha?

Obviously, God had many options to provide the oil or something else of value to the woman However, God chooses to use the little oil this woman had and require her to invest time, effort and most importantly, her faith. God wanted to use what she already had. God generally uses us in His process of meeting our needs. God does more than just supply; God is always teaching us and helping us grow. To be sure it is a miracle what happened but it also shows us that God will supply us our needs and wants and desires when we work and provide our time to fulfill our requests. It is also very interesting to note that God make the woman use what she had and to follow his strict requisition. She had to go borrow vessels.

What do you say to people when you trust God in a profound way? It can sound arrogant to claim that you expect God to supply miraculously, but indeed she did expect God to supply, because she obediently gathered the jars. Having gathered all the jars, the moment of truth and trust had come. The room was shut for privacy as Elisha had instructed. This was God's personal miracle. Now it is just her and her sons. Did she explain to her sons how God would supply? Did she express her faith to them? This moment of faith would mark their lives. Our children are watching our faith when it comes to money. We are always teaching.

The story continuous in IV Kings - 2 Kings 4:5-7 thus "She left him and afterward shut the door behind her and her sons. They brought the jars to her and she kept pouring. When all the jars were full, she said to her son, "Bring me another one." But he replied, "There is not a jar left." Then the oil stopped flowing. She went and told the man of God, and he said, "Go, sell the oil and pay your debts. You and your sons can live on what is left."

Again, she acted on her faith in a seemingly ridiculous situation. She held a small table top flask containing only a little oil. But she was poured that little oil into a larger empty jar. It made no sense. But as she poured, God did a miracle! She kept pouring and the oil kept coming. God kept the divine spigot open as long as there were vessels to fill. Only then it stopped. She had been in debt. Now she was in the oil business! She paid her debts, plus she had enough oil to evidently sell and live on comfortably for the rest of her life.

Indeed, an incredible story of having faith, of trusting in God, and being a good steward. Furthermore we – just like the woman – learn that our God is trustworthy, even in the hardest of our predicaments. Yes, without the smallest doubt and unquestionably, God is in the miracle-working business when we trust and obey His words. God *always* shows His faithfulness continually to those who trust Him. Period!

This widow found that God was faithful and supplied their needs. But the events of the story generate several very important questions. The questions now become: What if we are responsible for the mess we're in? What if we have violated the stewardship principles we have studied, borrowed to the hilt, lived too high, didn't plan, or didn't work hard enough? What if there is nagging guilt in addition to the financial mess were in? Does God care about us then? Does God help us then?

Surprisingly the Holy Scriptures give us various examples of self-inflicted financial problems – several of them just in Proverbs 6. Maybe we will see ourselves in some of these situations.

1. *Unwisely formed partnerships* (Proverbs 6:1-3) "My son, if you have put up security for your neighbor, if you have struck hands in pledge for another, if you have been trapped by what you said, ensnared by the words of your mouth, then do this, my son, to free yourself, since you have fallen into your neighbor's hands: Go and humble yourself; press your plea with your neighbor!"

    The issue of surety was basically that a person had co-signed an unwise, high-interest loan. He just became a partner to a losing

proposition. It was a mistake. The writer of the Proverbs, Solomon, warns us: Get out of it, if at all possible.
2. *Lack of planning* (Proverbs 6:6-8) "Go to the ant, you sluggard; consider its ways and be wise! It has no commander, no overseer or ruler, yet it stores its provisions in summer and gathers its food at harvest."

Ants are smart enough by instinct to know winter is coming and they put grain aside. And the simple reality is that many of our financial problems come from just not looking ahead. We may have signed on some dotted line to buy something. We talked ourselves into it without really doing the math.
3. *Laziness (Proverbs* 6:10-11) "A little sleep, a little slumber, a little folding of the hands to rest - and poverty will come on you like a bandit and scarcity like an armed man."

Employers are often frustrated when an employee gets paid on Friday and then he does not show up for work on the weekend and Monday, because they celebrated on the weekend without concern for work. Of course, there is another issue here: Some people do not want to work at all. They would rather depend on government help and or begging on some busy street corner. On the other hand, we do recognize that some people are legitimately not working but there are those who out of pure laziness refuse to work or are not working hard enough to keep up with their own expenses.
4. *Dishonesty/Theft* (Proverbs 6:30-31) "Men do not despise a thief if he steals to satisfy his hunger when he is starving. Yet if he is caught, he must pay sevenfold, though it costs him all the wealth of his house." [A classic story was written by Victor Hugo in his *Les Misérables* novel in 1862. Hugo portrays the protagonist's - Jean Valjean - long struggle of 19 years to lead a normal life after serving a prison sentence for stealing bread to feed his sister's children during a time of economic depression and various attempts to escape from prison. Javert – the antagonist in the story - is defined by his legalist tendencies and lack of empathy for criminals of all forms. He is the epitome of legalistic mind and behavior. In the story, he becomes obsessed with the pursuit and punishment of the protagonist Jean Valjean after his violation of parole. In the

process of pursuing Jean, he lost the ability to differentiate between law and love. Javert sees Valjean only as the convict he once was, rather than the benefactor of humanity he has become. This dichotomy, over time, caused profound confusion - by the realization that the law is not infallible, that he himself is not irreproachable, and that there exists a superior force (identified by Hugo with God) to what he has known - lunges him into such a despair that he commits suicide].

If we are dishonest, we will probably get caught and have to pay the consequences. Unfortunately, family members also pay the price of dishonesty through the shame and even incarceration of someone who is caught in financial deceit.

5. *Presumption* (James 4:13-14) "Now listen, you who say, "Today or tomorrow we will go to this or that city, spend a year there, carry on business and make money." Why? You do not even know what will happen tomorrow. What is your life? You are a mist that appears for a little while and then vanishes."

Many business ventures fail because of presumption. We didn't have a sound business plan or the capital to risk. Some job searches fail because we presumptuously expect too high of a salary, too little work or a job that is beyond our capability. Most presumption can be avoided just by getting good counsel and recognizing the reality of the current events in one's situation. But a presumptuous person doesn't seek or listen to advice.

6. *Greed* (1 Timothy 6:9-10) "People who want to get rich fall into temptation and a trap and into many foolish and harmful desires that plunge men into ruin and destruction. For the love of money is a root of all kinds of evil. Some people, eager for money, have wandered from the faith and pierced themselves with many griefs."

Money of course is not the problem, nor does it cause problems by itself. The problem is wanting to get rich and loving money - Greed. It is often hard to even diagnose ourselves on this issue. The love of money is an internal condition that is not revealed by the size of a bank account or by what kind of car someone drives. A wealthy Christian who understands and lives by stewardship principles is not doomed to "ruin and destruction." And a

Christian living on minimum wage can actually be the one who loves money in this verse. Loving money is a heart condition that is found in all economic levels. And that greedy desire leads to risky investments, debt problems, personal conflict, excessive hours causing family strife, gambling, crime and almost always a spiritual decline for believers – wandering from the faith.

So, we may recognize ourselves in the list above. We may have made some of these mistakes, but the real question is whether it's possible to recover. How do we become a steward when we haven't been one? How do we crawl out of the hole of the financial trouble we created?

Believe it or not, there is good news available that we can overcome financial issues. However, there may be consequences that have to be addressed. A great advice of how to become a good steward is found in James 1:5. It addresses the first step to overcoming our financial mistakes. Then it follows with identifying the importance of wisdom in our decisions (James 1:2-4). Specifically, his words are:

Pray for wisdom to learn from the financial trial we created: Here is what James 1:5 tells us. "If any of you lacks wisdom [about coping with trials – James 1:2-4], he should ask God, who gives [wisdom] generously to all without finding fault, and it will be given to him." In simpler terms, James tells us to pray for wisdom to recover from and learn from trials. In context of James 1:1-4 is the many kinds of trials we face. Financial trials are obviously included. These trials are meant to mature us. How will that happen? James 1:5 gives the answer: If we pray for wisdom to learn from trials – even those we bring on ourselves – God is so gracious that He will help us attain the wisdom we seek.

God gives wisdom "without finding fault/reproach." God doesn't just give wisdom to people who did everything right! When we pray humbly for wisdom God gives it without accusing us. He of course knows already what we did. And when we acknowledge our mistakes as well, He is eager to help. We must realize that God wants to help us even if we got ourselves into the mess!

Yes, God is gracious and forgiving. However, we also must do something to deserve His consideration. The following steps are only an example.

1. *Be content* (1 Timothy 6:8): Just before Paul warned those who want to get rich (1 Timothy 6:9-10), he told Timothy the antidote for the problem of loving money. It is contentment. "For we

brought nothing into the world, and we can take nothing out of it. But if we have food and clothing, we will be *content* with that" (1 Timothy 6:7-8). Obviously, this kind of thinking is a revolutionary one for most of us. In fact, perhaps that is the reason why most people do not follow the principle of good stewardship. To follow Paul's admonition to Timothy we need to refocus from self to God's perspective. In simple terms that means without a blink of an eye we must forego the love of money and replace it with the love of God. Pride and greed have no place in stewardship.
2. *Pursue God instead of money*: "But you, man of God, flee from all this, [the love of money – v. 10] and *pursue righteousness, godliness, faith, love*…" (1 Timothy 6:11). Like a person coming off of an addiction, there has to be a plan to replace the substance or activity to which they are addicted. When money and possessions have gripped our lives, we need to replace that with a new focus on God and godliness. God must be our new desire. Becoming a steward of money is actually part of establishing an authentic relationship with God!
3. *Accept God's discipline*: "**God disciplines** us for our good, that we may share in his holiness…. it produces a harvest of righteousness and peace for those who have been trained by it" (Hebrews 12:10-11). We might wish that by confessing our financial mistakes we have taken care of the problems we have created, but life rarely works like that. There will be consequences. We must accept the pain of the discipline. It won't go away in a day or a year even. But we know that God disciplines us for our good.
4. *Listen to counsel*: A final crucial part of that process of overcoming poor stewardship is the step of listening to and heeding advice. "The way of a fool seems right to him, but a wise man *listens* to advice" (Proverbs 12:15).

A fool always blames other people or bad circumstances, but never looks in the mirror. The most serious financial problem we can have is to insist that we are doing the right thing. The most important financial step you will ever take may be to listen to advice. A wise person asks another wise person to be his or her mirror by giving advice.

There is hope, regardless of whether your financial hardship is because of circumstances beyond your control or the result of financial mistakes. And the amazing thing is that if we begin to submit to God's ownership as a steward, our hard times could be the greatest blessing we ever experience.

When we think of hard times for ourselves and or our country, I cannot help but think Tom Brokaw's expression "The Greatest Generation." For those of you who do not know T. Brokaw: he was a TV news anchor at NBC and in 1998 penned the book by the title *The Greatest Generation*.

His reference was to the generation that fought WWII on the battlefield abroad and on the home front. His contention is that those **hard times** made those individuals and America great. Not coincidently, that is the same generation which went through the *Great Depression* as teenagers and young adults. *The Great Depression of course was a financial crisis*. It was brought on partly by bad decisions and increasing debt across the nation, but was also exacerbated by the natural disaster of the *Dust Bowl*. [The Dust Bowl was the name given to the drought-stricken Southern Plains region of the United States, which suffered severe dust storms during a dry period in the 1930s. As high winds and choking dust swept the region from Texas to Nebraska, people and livestock were killed and crops failed across the entire region].

When the stock market collapsed in 1929, some people committed suicide – revealing how tied to money people can be. Life savings were lost as over 9,000 banks failed during the 1930's. Unemployment skyrocketed. The Dust Bowl hit in 1933 and farmers lost farms and people went hungry. But the many that persevered became Tom Brokaw's "greatest generation."

To be sure, at that time there was poverty and a serious financial crisis for many. However, they learned to get by and do without. They learned financial wisdom through hardship. And they created the prosperity that we may well squander because we perhaps have inherited their wealth without acquiring their wisdom.

As Christians though, we must not despair or lose hope or even worse, feel guilty. Rather we must have hope for the best. We all must learn from God's word and from the financial struggles that we experience. We must recognize and accept that God uses financial hard times for our good. They are indeed the proverbial *blessing in disguise*. Our challenge is to accept and take advantage of those financial struggles in some of the ways that God intended. Some biblical examples are:

1. *Need teaches us to appreciate God's presence and promises* (Hebrews 13:4; Philippians 4:11-13): St. Paul writing to the Hebrews exhorts us to be content because God has said, "I will never leave you or forsake you." Paul was actually content without food because He was strengthened by Christ (Philippians 4:13)! Can you imagine being content when you are hungry for a prolonged period? When we have real financial needs, dependence on Christ becomes a reality that only an impossible situation can create.
2. *God is praised when he provides our needs* (2 Corinthians 9:12-13 *"men will praise God...for your generosity"*): When the impoverished believers in Jerusalem received the offering of gifts that Paul had collected from other churches, they praised God. It became an occasion to worship that would not have happened without such a trial.

   On a personal note, even though I can share many instances where God has intervened in our lives, I will share with you the most unusual and perhaps most needed at the time. God has provided for Carla and me in an unexpected and powerful way when we had some financial need that our paycheck could not provide. Out of nowhere, we received a phone call from a friend and he voluntarily gave us a car – a Pinto. It was old but it was running. The driver door was not working – I had to keep it closed with a steel wire. It was very cramped for my family of six, but we managed for about a year. We did have a hard time but we never lost faith. We recovered and thankfully we bounced back in a normal life. Both my wife and I thanked and do thank God for his generosity. It is awesome to think that God with so many responsibilities, saw our financial need, heard our prayers for help and supplied something specific for us. The personal nature of this particular event overwhelmed us. Who are we to receive such personalized attention from the eternal God? We are nobodies. Never-the-less, it is reason to worship and glorify Him.
3. *Need teaches us the humility of accepting help from others* (Philippians 4:14-16 *"you sent me aid again and again when I was in need"*): What is harder than forced humility? It is a lot easier on our ego to give than to receive. In fact, much "charitable

giving" really is motivated by pride and the recognition that comes with it. (See chapter 2, Note 1). Receiving can be the much greater challenge to our character.

Paul knew the feeling of being a "receiver" that many poor as well as many in ministry who depend on the gifts of others experience. There is something about receiving that goes against our ego. But those times can be greatly used by God to actually confirm in our hearts that we are dependent on God. When we are forced to receive, we realize that we are not as capable or shrewd financially as we would like to think we are.

4. *Need helps us understand the struggle of others* (2 Corinthians 1:3-4 - *"who comforts us… so we can comfort"*): Going through financial hard times and seeing God work to correct and teach us is worth sharing with others who are going through similar struggles. Let's not waste the hard things or the good things God has done for us financially. Let our good experience of stewardship become a significant message to others.
5. *Need teaches us how to correct mistakes* (Hebrews 12:5 – *"it produces a harvest of righteousness"*). Very simply, we can learn from our mistakes. We should not be the same after God takes us through the process of making and correcting financial mistakes. If we think more like stewards managing God's money, we have also grown spiritually.
6. *Need gives us opportunity to teach our children about stewardship and God's financial provision* (IV Kings LXX- 2 Kings 4:1-7). Maybe the biggest blessing that parents can gain from financial struggle and learning stewardship will be seen in their children. We are responsible to teach financial stewardship to the next generation. And the best way to teach something is to have had firsthand experience. In Proverbs 22:6 we read, "Train a child in the way he should go, and when he is old, he will not turn from it." Certainly, that applies to teaching our children about money.

Money is not neutral in the battle for our kid's hearts. Materialism – wanting more of anything – is one of the most deceptive tools of Satan. Even if we can keep our kids off drugs and keep them pure morally, we could still lose them to the god of this world financially.

How can we pursue a better family financial legacy? We may not be mega-wealthy, but we are surrounded by prosperity. One of the reasons it's really hard to teach stewardship to kids is because so many people around us may at least seem to be able to afford most of their wants and desires. Added to that dynamic is the fact that many of us as parents who grew up without certain material things would like our kids to have them.

Money is a key tool for teaching children to know God and trust God personally. On one hand we should welcome any financial hardships, because they can easily be an asset in teaching stewardship. However, we need to first of all teach and model contentment, hard work, integrity (Proverbs 1:1-9). Proverbs 1, begins by urging us to teach wisdom and discipline, knowledge and discretion – to the young! Solomon repeatedly addresses his "son." The many financial principles found in Proverbs are really the teachings of a parent to a child.

We as parents are also the key models of trusting God and giving generously (IV Kings LXX - 2 Kings 4:1-36). Both of the widows that we addressed earlier in 2 Kings 4 had children. Two sons helped gather the vessels for oil and saw their mother trust God to supply. They saw the miracle. It was their personal miracle because they would not be sold as slaves. Our children have the opportunity to experience the blessings of God's provision when we give generously and trust God.

On a personal level, I was present in a miraculous event in my village in 1958 when the villagers (of Thisvi – Thivon) were praying fervently for rain. It was a drought and all the wheat, barley and other vegetables were withering. After praying for a week in the Church, the villagers decided to go out in the middle of the valley on a very hot and sunny day in early May. Not a cloud in the sky. Yet, many villagers brought rain coats and umbrellas so they could be prepared for the rain. They trusted God and believed in him, that He would send rain. Half way through the supplications of the celebrated Litany, all of a sudden, the heaven opened and rain came down abundantly. It rained, for two days. The crops ware saved and everyone praised and glorified God for His generosity.

However, the most memorable event of the moment was not the rain. For me, the faith, conviction and the trust in God that my mother and the other villagers had that rain was coming still makes me stand in wonder. Specifically, when I challenged her about the rain, telling her that the sky is clear and there are no clouds anywhere, she responded to me with a smile saying: "God will make the heaven open and rain will come." It did! I was there and I do remember the event.

But regardless of our level of prosperity, perhaps the most universal task is to teach our children stewardship by requiring financial discipline of each child. It's part of the discipline that God expects every parent to teach (Hebrews 12:9).

So, our first foundational task in teaching stewardship to our children is to teach work and the financial responsibility of money and possessions. There are some practical ways that we do that.

1. *Assign chores and insist on them – out of obedience.* Obedience enforces the simple value of work. Everyone in a family has to help because we all take the responsibility God gave us to meet our own needs and that of others. Doing chores is a financial principle. To not have chores teaches entitlement without responsibility.
2. *Make sure they do an assigned job well and completely.* It's not obedience if it's not done well or if it is half done. And it is bad stewardship because you have wasted someone else's time if they have to check up on you or finish what you started.
3. *Make sure they take care of toys and other property.* One of the most disturbing violations of stewardship is when young children are allowed to bang on toys or bang on other things with their toys. If they are harming something, they are wasting something that costs money. That's not stewardship. But even if they are not harming something, they are treating something with contempt that has value. That's not stewardship either.
4. *Don't give "allowances:"* This might be controversial, but it seems biblically that possessions are either needs, or gifts or else they must be earned. If children need something, we provide it as parents – like God does. If there are special things, we want them to have, they are gifts – like God gives us gifts. Otherwise, if there is something, they need that they can earn, we should let them earn it – in some age appropriate way. Even then we need to give guidance about what they can buy.

    It seems that the traditional "allowance" is teaching the exact opposite of stewardship. We are essentially saying, here's some money for you to go blow on whatever you want. What is that teaching? It is teaching that money is mine and that it exists to create pleasure for me. And how do children get over that idea when they are teens and young adults? Stewardship starts young.

I am not suggesting that we cannot "treat" our kids? To the contrary. I am all for it. Absolutely. God gives us special gifts at times to enjoy as well. But if we want to model what God does, He doesn't toss out money to waste; He asks us to be stewards. So, to imitate God, it would seem we should 1) Supply what they need. 2) Give them gifts at times to show our love. 3) Require them to work and earn other things. God does all those things, and we are attempting to prepare our children to function as mature stewards in God's world.

5. *Require them to get a job when they are old enough.* Getting a job requires a young person to begin budgeting both their money and their time. Although we need to make sure they don't work too many hours that it jeopardizes school work or church, a job will require a young person to use time more wisely. It also gives them an opportunity to learn about work in another setting – where we can still help guide them because they live at home. Let us not forget that the *hard knocks* experience of the workplace can reinforce in a young person the principles that we may have struggled to communicate at home.
6. *Make them pay or help pay for some needs (clothes, college etc.)*: The key seems to be that we should let our children learn the same things about money that we do as adults by paying for some of their actual needs. Money is not just for enjoying. And the more we spend unwisely, the less we have to pay for more important necessities.
7. *Don't rescue adult children*: This isn't an absolute. There may be times when it's appropriate to give a substantial gift to help out an adult child. But then it's a gift. The problem comes when an unhealthy dependence develops so that parents trap adult children in perpetual childhood always expecting mom and dad to bail them out. Too many parents subconsciously bail out their adult

children financially in an attempt to control or manipulate them. Hopefully we'll leave that for the movies and soap operas.

8. *Require simple budgets and stewardship – give, save and spend*: As I was growing up my mother gave me three piggy banks and she wrote on each piggy bank: Give; Save and Spend. She made it a point to remind me every day that those three piggy banks were hungry and it was my job to feed them. I remember that there was no strict definition of "how much" should go to giving, saving, or spending. However, it was a requirement that if I did have any money, I had to spread it between the three piggy banks. At the age of 12 my mother taught me about giving to church, saving for the future and spending on things that I "wanted." All of a sudden, I realized that splitting the money was much more difficult and demanded some thought and rationale. By the way, my income was generated from doing small jobs at the "general store" of the village – sweeping, straightening out shelves and delivering small orders to the elderly. My working hours were Monday, Wednesday and Friday after School. My income for the week was 10 drachmas - about fifty cents.

Here we cannot overlook that along with teaching our children, we also must model our behavior as parents. We should show and tell our children how we *give, save and spend* as much as possible. We must talk with our children about money, otherwise they will be ignorant of their responsibilities as they grow older.

A final thought on the subject. It is imperative that we start teaching our children about stewardship and responsibility. They have to learn the principles of giving, so that, they can educate future generations.

Chapter 8
First Fruits

It is important to understand that First Fruits is a biblical principle that is practiced and emphasized throughout the Bible. It begins in the stories of the Bible with faithful believers like Abel (in Genesis 4) and Moses (in Exodus 23) and continues into the New Testament through the Apostle Paul's writings.

It was Moses who said, "As you harvest your crops, bring the very best of the first harvest to the house of the Lord your God" (Exodus 23:19). King Solomon wrote about it too: "Honor the Lord with your wealth, with the first fruits of all your crops; then your barns will be filled to overflowing, and your vats will brim over with new wine" (Proverbs 3:9-10).

When we give the first and best of our fruit to God that is the fundamental principle of First Fruits. 'Fruit' in our modern-day context means: income, wealth and finance. So, at the start of each year, families and individuals bring a special financial offering that goes way beyond our normal tithing or offerings. We follow in the footsteps of great biblical leaders by coming to God and giving the first of our wealth and the best of it to God. Ecclesiastically, the new year begins on September 1. In the Orthodox calendar we call this the *indiction period* (αρχη της Ινδικτου – αρχη του Εκκλησιαστικού έτους). The indiction was first used to date documents unrelated to tax collection in the mid-fourth century. By the late fourth century it was being used to date documents throughout the Mediterranean. In the Byzantine (Eastern Roman) Empire outside of Egypt, the first day of its year was September 23, the birthday of Augustus. During the last half of the fifth century, probably 462 A.D., this shifted to September 1, where it remained throughout the rest of the Byzantine Empire and continues until today. In 537 A.D., Justinian decreed that all dates must include the indiction via *Novella 47*, which eventually caused the Byzantine year to begin on September 1.

Even today, the Church celebrates that date with a liturgy and thanksgiving prayers. It is also customary for the believers to bring a sample of their first fruits of the harvest. In some orthodox jurisdictions and parishes, the first fruits are brought to the Church for blessing on August 6 – the Transfiguration holiday; and in some on September 14 –

the Holiday of the Cross. Specifically, in the United States, even though the service may be held, there are hardly any first fruits presented. Generally, the fruits are monetary in nature and maybe a short service of the five loaves.

The idea of giving the first fruits (the harvest of the year) is based on the notion that we give to God in obedience and affection, He gives back to us. Let's read what King Solomon said again, "Honor the Lord with thy just labors, and give him the first of thy fruits of righteousness: that thy storehouses may be completely filled with corn, and that thy presses may burst forth with wine" (Proverbs 3:9-10 LXX). God fills our lives to overflowing! As a result, God moves in powerful and miraculous ways in situations that only He could resolve. We hear of breakthrough's in health and finance, relationships and families, careers and mental health. Literally when people put their faith in God, God reveals His faithfulness to His people.

So, the question is asked: Why do we bring our first fruits into the church? There are at least two reasons:

1. **God asks us to:** "As you harvest your crops, bring the *very best of the first harvest* to the house of the Lord your God" (Exodus 23:19). The house of the Lord is the Church; that's us! It is also a wonderful thing to think that the church we are building together is what God calls 'His House.' What an honor and what a privilege, to be able to support His house!
2. **You're investing back into your home; your spiritual family:** Why wouldn't we give extravagantly to our people and our vision. We are after all investing in our children and young people, in our men and our women, the broken who walk through our doors and the desperate who are touched by our community engagement, and all the generations and nationalities that call our church their home.

   The church is the vehicle by which the world is transformed and this includes the neighborhoods where we live and the people we work alongside. Our giving goes back into the community we belong to.

   Who spreads the love of God around the Church? (do we do this? Or are we interested in buildings and salaries?) We do, the church. Who blesses the poor and helps the broken find healing? We do. Who shapes the next generation in the ways of Christ? We do! Why wouldn't we bring the first and best of our fruit into His house?

Now that we have a good idea as to what the First fruits are all about, there is still a lingering question as to what it really means to us today. So, let us look at that question:

1. *We are making a statement for the year*: First Fruits is not a New Year's resolution; ***it is a declaration***. It is when we speak life over our future and our situation. We say the time to come, "God will win and so will I. I am planting my roots in God's soil and He is my provider."
2. *We prophecy to the future*: Watch out, Worry, and step aside, selfishness, forget about it, Fear, you no longer have a part in God's destiny for me. This year I put my faith in the God who sets me free. It is my time and it is my turn. These are powerful statements we make over our lives at the start of the year! In 2021 we are empowering the church to count the stars, to believe for the innumerable abundance of God's plan for your life and to be obedient to Him as you walk.
3. *We are starting as we mean to go on*: We begin the year in faith. We don't place our trust in anything because God is infallible and unconditional. We set out our stall and we position ourselves under God's banner of protection and love. We trust Him. We believe in His promises. He provides for our needs, for He is aware of ALL and He sees ALL. At least to me, (hope for you too). It makes sense to place our faith in His eternal grace rather than our own selves. Giving at the start of the year, places our faith in the right place and positioning ourselves under the abundance of our Heavenly Father.

   Jesus tells us: "Seek the Kingdom of God above all else, and live righteously, and he will give you everything you need" (Matthew 6:33). The problem is that if we do not plant, we cannot set up for a coming harvest. That is why we start with the first fruits to be ready for the harvest later. King Solomon tells us, when we give our First Fruits, our 'barns will be filled to overflowing' and our 'vats will brim over with new wine' (Proverbs 3:10). Imagine a harvest being more than your current containers can handle.

So, let's not make this about money either. Let's see God for who He is: The Lord of everything! Therefore, as givers, we are setting up a harvest of God's grace in any area of life. This might mean the restoration of our mental health or physical health, this might be a relational issue or struggles with others, or it could have to do with our work or neighborhood. A very good example of planting and expecting a bountiful harvest is the farmer. What farmer plants a seed not expecting a return? So goes the seed, so goes the harvest. We can expect the return according to the sacrifice. We give convinced of God's faithfulness and generosity because we know He is a good Father and He loves to give to His children (that's you and me by the way).

This point usually gets misunderstand as a "get rich quick" scheme. This is not the theology of the Orthodox Church. We do not promote the "prosperity Gospel" (that is a Protestant theology and practice) but we do promote the prosperity of the Gospel. Our motive for giving is not to receive but we give because we want to prosper the Gospel (the good news of Jesus Christ) in our lives as well as the town we seek to transform (this is our intention, our purpose. However, are we really doing this?) We give our first and best to God our of obedience and faith, that is our starting place, knowing that God will both increase our harvest and protect it too because that is His character. Let us not forget the words of Apostle Paul who tells the Hebrews "It is impossible to please God without faith. Anyone who wants to come to him must believe that God exists and that he rewards those who sincerely seek him" (Hebrews 11:6).

I am absolutely positive that most people want to give. However, the same people have a dilemma about what is the right amount to give. As we hinted all along, generosity is grounded on good stewardship and managing our money well. So, what and how do we give a First fruits offering that is both wise and extravagant? Here are some principles for making the most of your giving:

1. **Pray**: "If you need wisdom, ask our generous God, and he will give it to you. He will not rebuke you for asking" (James 1:5). God knows you and He knows your financial situation. Go to Him daily and ask Him: "God, help me out. I want to give generously. Show me what my 'first and best' is." One of two things will happen. He'll either bring a figure to forefront of your mind to give or He'll help you to

decide upon a figure. Our heart is to *give the first and best* to Him who has given us everything. Give what you believe to be generous and, of course, 'the best' to God.
2. **Plan**: Did you know that the gift for our First Fruits may be extended? In other words, it may be paid in payments – through pledging. In this way, people have an opportunity to maximize their gift by drawing down from a various account or spreading it over a few paydays. In any case, it gives us time to make a plan. It's whatever works best for you. St. Paul again comes to our rescue for encouragement with the words: "I pray that God, the source of hope, will fill you completely with joy and peace because you trust in him. Then you will overflow with confident hope through the power of the Holy Spirit" (Romans 15:13).
3. **Places**: Think creatively of about the places your income streams can flow from. Many of us don't just have one bank account and some of us have a number of other areas we can tap into. The beauty of pledging is that it helps in purposing various sources of wealth. It helps tremendously in budgeting. If we think creatively there may be different sources where we can retrieve funds. Why not think through where these lineup for you and be audacious in your offering?

Remember, that First Fruits is about attitude not just amounts. Some have much and some have little but whatever our financial status, all of us can give to the same measure of faith. We can all throw ourselves into obedience to God and believe in the outrageous wonders from Him. If you have little you can still believe much. And if you have much, you have a responsibility to show the ways in faith. So, give with as much faith as you can muster in relation to your circumstance! If you have surplus, believe big and give big. If you have little, believe big and give big! It's simple. This principle is the basis for the Orthodox Church not to have a definite amount of tithing. We must give ALL that we can. However, there is nothing wrong with keeping the tithe.

What is important in this discussion is to always remember: A farmer who plants only a few seeds will get a small crop - if any. But the one who plants generously will get a generous crop. Therefore, we all individually must decide in our hearts how much to give. And don't give reluctantly or in response to pressure. 'For God loves a person who gives cheerfully. And God will generously provide all you need. Then you will always have everything you need and plenty left over to share with others" (2 Corinthians 9:6-8).

A Short Guide to Understand First Fruits Offerings

Much has been written about understanding the *First Fruits Offering* by many authors. However, in this section of the book we will address the topic based on Wisnewski's (August 20, 2020) work, with his permission.

There are plenty of terms and phrases in the Bible one frequently hears in church but may not understand. One such term is the *first fruits* in the Bible. First fruits may be mentioned when priests talk about giving or generosity. But what exactly does it mean? Why is it good for the average church-goer to know?

So, what is first fruits in the Bible? *"When you come into the land which I give you and reap its harvest, then you shall bring a sheaf of the first fruits of your harvest to the priest"* (Leviticus 23:10). The concept of first fruits is rooted in biblical times when people lived in an agrarian society. Harvest time was significant because that was when the hard work the farmers had poured into their crops all year began to pay off. They were literally reaping what they sowed.

God called his people to bring the first yield—the first fruits—from their harvest to him as an offering. *This was to demonstrate the Israelites' obedience and reverence for God.* It also showed that they trusted God to provide enough crops to feed their family. Back then, there were plenty of rules associated with making first fruit sacrifices. They had to be brought to the temple priests. No other crops could be harvested until after the first fruits were presented. It was a complex process.

The Hebrew word for first fruit is *bikkurim* - literally translated to "promise to come." The Israelites saw these first fruits as an investment into their future. God told them that if they brought their first fruits to him, he would bless all that came afterward.

Obviously, we no longer live in an agrarian-based society. Most people reading this are probably not farmers. You likely don't worry about harvest time or giving away the first yield of your crops. But the idea of first fruits is still relevant - it just takes on a new meaning for us.

That transformation for the modern world is to present the first fruits however we accumulate wealth. That is harvest, from fields; return on investments from any financial transaction and so on. We surmise this thought from: *"Honor the Lord with your wealth, with the first fruits of all your crops"* (Proverbs 3:9). We see the term first fruits initially mentioned in the book of Exodus when Moses is leading God's people out of captivity in Egypt. God instructed the Israelites to give up the first of their crops so that they could understand the value of God's blessings. Through the first five books of the Bible, Moses brings up the idea, a total of thirteen times. That's because it was an essential concept for his people to understand. First fruits are mentioned throughout the Old Testament (OT), and it's even referenced in the New Testament (NT) books. [Do not confuse the giving sacrifice of Abel and Cain with that of the first fruits. They are different!]

In the New Testament, the term "first fruits" takes on a symbolic meaning. In 1 Corinthians 15:20, Paul mentions Christ as the "first fruits of those who have fallen asleep." Jesus was God's first fruits—his one and only son, and the best that humanity had to offer. God gave Jesus, who was raised from the dead, up for us, in the same way that we sacrifice the best we have for him. What started as a specific instruction for bringing crops to the temple priest was expanded on later in Scripture. It no longer refers to literal fruit—first fruits mean any income, wealth, or blessings that a Christian has received over the course of the year.

Furthermore, do not confuse the first fruits with tithing. They are different. *"The first of all first fruits of every kind and every contribution of every kind, from all your contributions, shall be for the priests: you shall also give to the priest the first of your dough to cause a blessing to rest on your house"* (Ezekiel 44:30). To give a *tithe* means that you give a tenth of your income to your church. Tithes are generally given throughout the entire year. Tithes are meant to be given in an automatic sense of obedience after you receive your income, whatever the source.

A first fruits offering is something different. First fruit offerings are typically an annual gift to the church done at "harvest time." Because we're not actually harvesting crops, the harvest can mean different things to different people. Perhaps you just got a bonus at work. Maybe you just received a huge tax refund check. Maybe you saved 15% or more on car insurance. All these, are harvest time moments when your hard work paid off. These are also great opportunities to turn back to God in gratitude for the blessings.

Whenever you decide to make a first fruit offering, the important thing is that you do it freely, with no guilt or obligation. This is supposed to be a celebration of all that God has done for you. It's a kind of worship that you can use to support the work of others. A first fruit offering is our opportunity to give above and beyond just a regular tithe.

The importance of the first fruits is recounted in the story of Abel and Cain. "In the course of time Cain brought some of the fruits of the soil as an offering to the Lord. And Abel also brought an offering—fat portions from some of the firstborn of his flock. The Lord looked with favor on Abel and his offering, but on Cain and his offering he did not look with favor. So, Cain was very angry, and his face was downcast" (Genesis 4:3-5). The story of course, begins when the two brothers making an offering to God. Cain brings some of his crops before the Lord, and Abel brings an offering of slaughtered animals. But there is a distinct difference between these two gifts.

Cain brings some fruit and vegetables—probably something he had left over after he had fed himself and his family. But Abel brought the best of what he had to God - the firstborn of the flock, the healthiest of his animals. God noticed this difference in these sacrifices, and he had a clear preference between the two.

Disregarding what famously happens in the rest of the story, the sacrifices of Cain and Abel teaches us a valuable lesson. Giving our first fruits means *giving our best to God with a good attitude*. It means *sacrificing something that costs us*. It means *putting God first*, even before ourselves, or our family. Making a first fruit offering opens us up to allow God to work in our life. When we approach God with open hands - rather than clenched fists - it makes it easier for him to give us more to work with.

Giving of our first fruits reminds us that God is our ultimate priority. It shows God that we are obedient to him and we can be trusted with more. Perhaps most importantly, being generous in this way shows that we are grateful for all God has given to us. So, if the first fruits giving principle is so important, how do we give this offering? "*If the part of the dough offered as first fruits is holy, then the whole batch is holy; if the root is holy, so are the branches"* (Romans 11:16). What is Paul telling us here? I believe that he is trying to show us what practicality is all about. So, how do we determine how, when, and how much you should give as a first fruit offering? This is obviously different for every person and each season. But here are a few steps (we addressed them earlier, but it is worth summarizing again). You can take the following steps to help you get started in the right direction:

- **Pray**: If your goal is obedience to God, it only makes sense that you would first go to him in prayer. Ask him what you should do with your money and resources. Listen to what he says.
- **Prepare**: God calls us to be good stewards of the blessings he gives us. That means knowing what we're able to give and when. Have a plan in place for your offering. Approach each harvest time with an open mind and a generous heart.
- **Prioritize**: The whole idea behind a first fruit gift is to put God first. That may be donating your first paycheck of the year to the church. It may mean that you put this donation first in your budget. Just make sure that you're prioritizing God in your finances.
- **Give**: Know where you are going to give the money. Is there a specific fund at the church you want to contribute to? Is there another nonprofit you want to support? It also helps to know the amount you'll give.
- **Repeat:** How often do you want to give a first fruit offering? This was traditionally an annual practice, but you can give as often as you'd like. Making it a part of your routine will help keep it a priority, not something you do spontaneously or sporadically.

However, you give, the key thing is that *you're giving with an open-heart, cheerful spirit and open mind.* The process of giving above your normal tithe can help prepare you for God to make a difference in your life. Making a first fruit offering demonstrates obedience to God, rather than your money.

Understanding the full significance of God's "first fruits" command

"Of his own will begat he us with the word of truth, that we should be a kind of first fruits of his creatures" (James 1:18, KJV). The Old Testament patterns of giving first fruits are not so much about giving the first fruits of our financial increase, before we give our monetary tithes and offerings, which prosperity teachers maintain, but rather the patterns of giving first fruits have to do with the first fruits of the spiritual harvests that are devoted unto God. Indeed, the Old Testament's shadows and types of the barley harvest, which happens in Israel during the first month of Abib (Nisan), symbolizes that this first harvest of the year not only is an agricultural event but also a spiritual event that is connected to each of the seven commanded Jewish annual feasts.

For sure, the Feast of "First fruits" has a mutual relation with the Feast of Passover, Feast of Unleavened Bread, and the Day of Pentecost (the Feast of Weeks), as well as a shared relation with the second harvest's wheat. During the Feast of Weeks in the third month of Sivan, the first fruits of wheat begin the wheat harvest, which finally culminates in the month of Tishri, during the End Harvest around the time of the Feast of Tabernacles. This shared relation means that the Spring Feast of First fruits also is connected to ALL three of the Fall Feasts: The Feast of Trumpets, the Day of Atonement, and the Feast of Tabernacles.

In the Old Testament, after the Israelites entered the land which God had promised to them, God commanded the children of Israel to mark a special day for the purpose of acknowledging that God had provided them fertile land on which to grow their crops. God told Moses to "Speak unto the children of Israel, and say unto them, When ye be come into the land which I give unto you, and shall reap the harvest thereof, then ye shall bring a sheaf of the first fruits of your harvest unto the priest:" (Leviticus 23:10, KJV, cf. Leviticus 2:12 and 14; Leviticus 23:17 and 20).

Now, not only were the Israelites commanded to keep the Feast of First Fruits but also God says: Three times thou shalt keep a feast unto me in the year. Thou shalt keep the feast of unleavened bread: (thou shalt eat unleavened bread seven days, as I commanded thee, in the time appointed of the month Abib; for in it thou camest out from Egypt: and none shall appear before me empty) And the feast of harvest, the first fruits of thy labors, which thou hast sown in the field: and the feast of ingathering, which is in the end of the year, when thou hast gathered in thy labors out of the field. …The first of the first fruits of thy land thou shalt bring into the house of the LORD thy God. (Exodus 23:14-16 and 19a, KJV; cf. Exodus 34:22 and 26a)

For sure, the Feast of First Fruits is very significant because this feast falls on the day following the first day of Unleavened Bread, which follows Passover (one of the three mandated feasts that Jewish men had to travel to the Jerusalem Temple before they could celebrate God's mandated feasts according to God's instructions [see Exodus 23:17]). Now, sometimes people get confused about which day is really the Feast of First fruits, as the Day of Pentecost Feast also is called the Feast of First fruits. That's why knowing what God wanted His chosen people to do on the specific day that has been established for them to offer the "devoted things" to God will help in understanding the difference between the Day of First Fruits and the Day of Pentecost.

The specific day that the Israelites were to establish for the purpose of offering their sanctified "first fruits" to God would be the Feast of First Fruits (see Leviticus 23:9-14), and on this specific day, the Israelites were to offer to God the first grain (typically barley) of the first spring harvest. This first fruit offering was to take place during the week of the Feast of Unleavened Bread on the day after the regular weekly Sabbath (cf. Leviticus 23:11b). Therefore, this first fruits offering always would occur on the first day of the week (on the Jewish Sabbath, which is from sunset Saturday to sunset Sunday). The Jewish people call this Feast of First Fruits day *Reishit Katzir*, which means the "beginning of the harvest."

In biblical times, on the day after the first day of Unleavened Bread, a sheaf (*Omer*) of barley (the first grain crop to ripen) was waved before the LORD in a prescribed ceremony that marked the start of the counting of the Omer (cf. Deuteronomy 16:9-12 and Leviticus 23:15-16). The Israelites would begin a forty-nine-day countdown (the counting of the Omer) plus one extra day. This countdown started from the moment when they put the first sickle to the barley and ended with the harvest festival of *Shavu'ot* (Pentecost). The Hebrews call this period of time *Sefirat HaOmer*, which means, "counting the sheaves." Thus, the first harvest season (spring harvest) begins on the Day of First Fruits, which happens seven weeks plus one day before the Feast of Weeks/First fruits/Pentecost.

On the day of the Feast of First Fruits, the Hebrews were commanded to give God, ***without delay***, their first fruits (the very first of their sons, as well as their flocks, vines, fields and trees that appear before their whole flocks, fields, vines, and trees became ripe). The Old Testament Scriptures reveal this divine truth, thusly: "And the LORD spake unto

Moses, saying, sanctify unto me all the firstborn, whatsoever openeth the womb among the children of Israel, both of man and of beast: it is mine. …Thou shalt not delay to offer the first of thy ripe fruits, and of thy liquors: the firstborn of thy sons shalt thou give unto me. Likewise, shalt thou do with thine oxen, and with thy sheep: seven days it shall be with his dam; on the eighth day thou shalt give it me. (Exodus 13:1-2; Exodus 22:29-30, KJV)

Without a doubt, the Feast of First Fruits' spiritual implications were fulfilled through Jesus the Christ, who was the first person to return to life who would never die again. Our Lord was crucified and buried on Passover (*Pesach*), the day before the first day of Unleavened Bread (*Chag HaMatzot*).

Now, Passover begins at evening time on Abib (or Nisan) 14, which also is when the eating of Unleavened Bread first begins. What is important to note about the Jewish evening is that it falls between 3:00 pm and sundown, which makes sundown both the time when one day ends and the time when a new day starts. Because Passover continues through Nisan 15 (the first day of the Feast of Unleavened Bread), this is the reason why the celebration of the Feast of Unleavened Bread often is shown on most calendars as beginning on Abib (Nisan) 15 and ending on Abib (Nisan) 22, while on other calendars the Feast of Unleavened Bread is shown as starting from Abib (Nisan) 14 and ending on Abib (Nisan) 21. Whichever way someone denotes the day when the Feast of Unleavened Bread begins, this Feast (also called *Chag HaMatzot*) represents a holy week spent without having any leaven in our lives.

What is more important is that, in Jesus's day, Passover was on Wednesday the 14th, and the Feast of Unleavened Bread started on Thursday the 15th. Abib (Nisan) 15th, or day one of the Feast of Unleavened Bread, is also the "High" Sabbath, a special Sabbath day that, in Jesus the Christ's day, was not a Saturday Sabbath! This fact would mean that the wave offering (called *tenufat HaOmer*), which the priest is supposed to wave "…on the morrow after the sabbath" (Leviticus 23:11b, KJV) is the God-commanded first fruit wave offering that must take place on Sunday morning after the weekly Saturday Sabbath. In Jesus's case, this weekly Sabbath was on Abib (Nisan) 17th, two days after the "High" Sabbath of the first day of Unleavened Bread. Once again, a "High" Sabbath is a day of *shabbaton* (rest) that could occur on any day of the week besides the weekly Sabbath day of Saturday.

Thus, on Abib (Nisan) 14th, Wednesday at evening, which is the beginning of that day, Jesus eats His early seder (Passover) supper, as this day also is called the Lord's Passover day (cf. Leviticus 23:5). On Abib (Nisan) 14th, during the daytime, is the Preparation day mentioned in Luke 23:54 and Mark 15:42. Jesus the Christ then dies, gives up the Spirit, in the afternoon of the 14th, and His death happens at the same time that the *korban Pesach* (Passover Lamb) is sacrificed in the Temple. Jesus the Christ then is buried before the evening (before the official Passover dinner starts). [Here we must make sure that we address the leaven and unleavened issue. For the Orthodox Christians this is a very clear-cut answer. The answer comes from Jesus Himself and recorded in the gospel of Matthew 26:26 with the words: "While they were eating, **Jesus took bread**, and when he had given thanks, he broke it and gave it to his disciples, saying, "Take and eat; this is my body (NIV) - Ἐσθιόντων δὲ αὐτῶν **λαβὼν ὁ Ἰησοῦς τὸν ἄρτον** καὶ εὐχαριστήσας ἔκλασε καὶ ἐδίδου τοῖς μαθηταῖς καὶ εἶπε· λάβετε φάγετε· τοῦτό ἐστι τὸ σῶμά μου." It is imperative to recognize that Jesus uses the Greek word "*ἄρτον*" which is by definition **bread made with leaven**." You can also see the same in: Mark 14:12–25; Luke 22:7–38; and I Corin. 11:23–25). They all use the same word. Therefore, on the Mystical (Last) Supper leavened Bread was used.

On Abib (Nisan) 15th, at evening, "High" Sabbath (the actual Seder night) begins. On Abib (Nisan) 15th, during the daytime, "High" Sabbath, a time of rest, is observed.

On Abib (Nisan) 17th, at evening, Weekly Sabbath begins, and on Abib (Nisan) 17th, during the daytime, Weekly Sabbath continues. During the daytime on this day is when the priest's waving of the Omer takes place, initiating the 49-day countdown to Pentecost (or *Shavu'ot*).

On Abib (Nisan) 18th, at sundown or the start of this new day, Jesus the Christ is raised from the dead at or after Havdalah, which is the Jewish ritual of using wine, multi-wick candle, and spices for the purpose of marking the end of the Shabbat (and/or holidays) and the beginning of the rest of the week. Remember now that sundown is both the end and start of a day (in this case sundown on the 17th is both the end of day 17 and the start of day 18)! Thus, what's for certain about when Jesus arose from the grave is that He at least arose before sunrise on the 18th.

The good news (Gospel) for the believers is that, on the day after the Feast of First Fruits is celebrated by the priest waving the first sheaf of barley before the Lord our God, Jesus is raised from the dead. His resurrection makes Him the first fruit of all who, subsequently, would arise from the dead, never to die again. Moreover, Jesus's resurrection, when compared to the "wave offering" the Temple priest presented before the Father as the "first fruits" of the full harvest yet to come, explains how the biblical shadows and types that pertain to Jesus the Christ being the firstborn of the first fruits are also why our Lord represents the firstborn of man (and beast) who belongs to God. Indeed, Jesus the Christ is the firstborn of all creatures!

The "firstborn" and "first fruits" shadows and types that are seen in the agricultural former and latter rain seasons are parallel to the birth and ripening of believers. Just as the first or early ripening of the grain crops is offered on First Fruits, or the "beginning of the harvest," the same First Fruits' process takes place in the Body of Christ, except this process is a spiritual ripening of believers.

Jesus physically arises from the grave, and is literally born again as the first fruit of the brethren and the firstborn of all creatures. Then, by the Day of Pentecost, the 120 Upper Room disciples (Acts 1:15) become the first fruit of the CHURCH who later will become spiritually born again by the Holy Spirit, and the first of those who later will become physically resurrected like Jesus the Christ. For these reasons, the cutting of the *sheaf* (Omer) of the new barley that culminates in the celebration of *Shavu'ot* (Pentecost) is an important first fruit/firstborn principle, because it relates to the spiritual birth and the glorification of the CHURCH.

The Apostle Paul agrees, and in the following Scriptural quotation he declares that: But now is Christ risen from the dead, and become the first fruits of them that slept. For since by man came death, by man came also the resurrection of the dead. For as in Adam all die, even so in Christ shall all be made alive. But every man in his own order: Christ the first fruits; afterward they that are Christ's at his coming (1 Corinthians 15:20-23, KJV; cf. John 11:25; Romans 5:12; 1 Thessalonians 4:15-17).

Thus, after the counting of the Omer begins, early in the morning on the third day of Unleavened Bread, Jesus appears as the first fruit of the dead, first to Mary Magdalene. At that time, He immediately says to her: "Don't cling to me" … "for I haven't yet ascended to the Father. But go find my brothers and tell them that I am ascending to my Father and your Father, my God and your God" (John 20:17, NLT). From the Scriptures, we know that on the same day that the arisen Christ spoke to Mary Magdalene that in the evening of this day He also supernaturally appeared before His disciples, minus Thomas, who for some reason wasn't in this assembly, and minus Judas, who already had committed suicide. Then "eight days later the disciples were together again, and this time Thomas was with them. The doors were locked; but suddenly, as before, Jesus was standing among them. He said, 'Peace be with you.' Then he said to Thomas, 'Put your finger here and see my hands. Put your hand into the wound in my side. Don't be faithless any longer. Believe'" (John 20:26-27, NLT). [In the Orthodox Church we believe that the first appearance of Jesus was to His Mother during the earthquake. St. Gregory Palamas has written about this event. In fact, during the 50 days after the resurrection we sing the hymn: "The Angel spake to her that is full of grace, saying, O pure Virgin, rejoice; and I say also, rejoice; for thy Son is risen from the tomb on the third day." After the appearance of the Angel, Christ appeared to Mary Magdalen and then to the Apostles minus Thomas and Judas].

Since Jesus has told Mary that He is ascending to His Father, and then He isn't seen again by anyone after He first appears before His assembled disciples until He appears before them the second time, the logical conclusion is that during the counting of the Omer's first eight days (sometime during the fourth through the eighth day of the celebration of Unleavened Bread) Jesus not only descended into Hell to preach the Gospel to the centuries of lost sinners and the saints in Paradise, but also He ascended up to Heaven where He would present to God Himself, the other first fruits who arose out of the graves with Him, and the ones from Hell who accepted Him as their Lord and Savior. These are the sanctified "devoted" unto God first fruits who have been redeemed.

Once this work is done, Jesus is able to return back to Earth in His glorified body! How do we know this? The writer of the book of Matthew declares that the "...tombs opened. The bodies of many godly men and women who had died were raised from the dead after Jesus' resurrection. They left the cemetery, went into the holy city of Jerusalem, and appeared to many people" (Matthew 27:52-53, NLT).

Thus, once again, the logical conclusion is that Jesus had to have ascended up to Heaven sometime between the fourth and eighth day of Omer to offer to His Father the first installment on the "early crops" of what would be an overwhelming harvest by the end of the Age (by the end of the world as we know it), for it is not recorded in the Scriptures that any of these other resurrected people were seen after Jesus met again with His assembled disciples.

Keeping with the idea of first fruits installments, Jesus's *second first fruits'* installment will be the time of His return for His Church (cf. 1 Corinthians 15:51-52; 1 Thessalonians 4:15-17). For this reason, the day of the Feast of First Fruits (the beginning of the first harvest) spiritually is connected to the Day of Pentecost or the Feast of Weeks that happens 49 days later. In other words, the Day of Pentecost/Feast of Weeks is a shadow and type of the birth of the CHURCH. The apostles and their first century Hebrew converts, then, also represent the first fruits and/or the firstborn of Christians who have been devoted (sanctified) unto God—the first fruits of the Day of Pentecost's Holy Spirit pouring.

The *third and last first fruits'* installment will be the 144,000 martyred saints. The Apostle John supplies the scriptural evidence for this claim. John writes: "And they sung as it were a new song before the throne, and before the four beasts, and the elders: and no man could learn that song but the hundred and forty and four thousand, which were redeemed from the earth. These are they which were not defiled with women; for they are virgins. These are they which follow the Lamb whithersoever he goeth. These were redeemed from among men, being the first fruits unto God and to the Lamb" (Revelation 14:3-4, KJV).

Returning back to Jesus's first ascension, it is apparent that Jesus makes His first ascension during the first eight days of the counting of the Omer. At this time, He takes with Him to Heaven ALL of the ones who were resurrected from their graves when He arose, plus the Old Testament saints whom He preached to in Paradise, John the Baptist, and the New Testament repentant thief from the cross cf Psalms 67(68):18, Ephesians 4:8-10,). As a result, in Acts 1:9, Jesus now is speaking about His second ascension, which happens a few days before the Feast of Pentecost, as the Scriptures tell us that He is still on the Earth some 40 days after His resurrection (see Acts 1:3).

Thus, based on God's appointed Feasts, the fifty days between First Fruits and Pentecost are significant in that these days mark the time between the Festival of *"Physical Redemption" (Passover)* and the Festival of *"Spiritual Redemption" (Pentecost)*. For this reason, the Day of Pentecost is viewed as the climax of God's plan for believers' deliverance through Jesus, who is the true Lamb of God. The counting of the Omer, or the seven weeks plus one day from First Fruits until the Day of Pentecost, represents *the giving of the anticipated New Covenant to mankind, and the giving of the gift of the Holy Spirit through whom the Body of Christ is formed.*

Likewise, just as Jesus's first fruit resurrection from the dead and the Day of Pentecost's outpouring of the Holy Spirit are literal fulfillments of the ancient agriculturally repeated first harvest's Firstborn, First fruit, and Former Rain shadows and types, the second outpouring of the Holy Spirit and the reunion of the Groom (Jesus the Christ) and His Bride (the CHURCH from whom Jesus has been separated for over 2000 years) also will be literal fulfillments of the agriculturally repeated second harvest's "end of the year harvest" and Latter Rain shadows and types.

Besides the symbolic Old Testament's repeated agricultural Spring and Fall harvests' patterns that point to the seizure of all of us in the clouds (ἔπειτα ἡμεῖς οἱ ζῶντες οἱ περιλειπόμενοι ἅμα σὺν αὐτοῖς *ἁρπαγησόμεθα* ἐν νεφέλαις εἰς ἀπάντησιν τοῦ Κυρίου εἰς ἀέρα, καὶ οὕτω πάντοτε σὺν Κυρίῳ ἐσόμεθα (1 Thes. 4:17), there are other Old Testament shadows and types that represent the seizure. For example, in the Old Testament, the seizure - *ἁρπαγησόμεθα* - is symbolized through imagery, expressly, the Voice of God (or Trumpet of God) calling out of the mountain to Moses, beckoning him to come up to the top of Mount Sinai (cf. Exodus 19:3), which is similar to Apostle John's New Testament precursory seizure which begins with the Alpha and Omega God's voice sounding like a trumpet (Revelation 1:10-11); in Prophet Hosea's metaphorical prophesies about Israel being revived in 2 days, and raised up on the third day (Hosea 6:2); in Enoch's bodily translation (Genesis 5:24, and Hebrews11:5) - symbolizing the New Testament's twinkling of an eye catching up of alive Body of Christ members who will not be found after the seizure - ἐν ἀτόμῳ, ἐν *ῥιπῇ ὀφθαλμοῦ*, ἐν τῇ ἐσχάτῃ σάλπιγγι· σαλπίσει γάρ, καὶ οἱ νεκροὶ ἐγερθήσονται ἄφθαρτοι, καὶ ἡμεῖς ἀλλαγησόμεθα. (1 Corinthians 15:51-52); 1 Thessalonians 4:15-17); in Elisha's witness of the supernatural appearance of the chariot and horses of fire that were followed by Elijah's whirlwind (storm cloud) disappearance (IV Kings, LXX, 2 Kings 2:11-13) - symbolizing the middle of the Tribulation's left behind people who will witness both the life and death of two Old Testament witnesses and then see these two witnesses raptured, also these left behind people will witness the disappearance (seizure) of the 144,000 Messianic Jews (Revelation 11:3-

12 and Revelation 14:3-4); and finally the disappearance of Moses' gravesite (Deuteronomy 34:6), which symbolizes the dead without Jesus nonbelievers who, once resurrected, will leave behind no earthly gravesites where those who inherit the Earth can find the wicked ones' bodies!

Now, just like it is in the natural concerning the harvesting of a field of wheat, so will it be with the harvesting of the world (the field in which the Lord plants His Gospel seed). After the world has been judged during the seven-year Tribulation, near the end of that time, Jesus the Christ will come on the clouds with a host of angels, and He will oversee the angels' reaping (cutting with a sickle) and harvesting of Jesus the Christ's Wheat—the angels will separate (winnow) the figuratively speaking mature grains of wheat (believers) from the chaff (unbelievers and nonbelievers or tares) - the spiritual souls and spirits which, like the literal inedible waste of the wheat's chaff, will be thrown away. In the tares' case, they will be thrown into the Lake of Fire (Matthew 13:37-43), while the genuine Wheat is saved/delivered from the Lake of Fire.

This Wheat, then, is the overwhelming harvest that will happen after God determines that He is finished dealing with mankind; this Wheat Harvest will be the harvest that comes about all because Jesus first became the literal and figurative firstborn and first-fruit wave offering. Lastly, this end of the Age Wheat harvest also will be the fulfillment of the shadows and types found in the Fall or second harvest that the Hebrews have practiced for years in their end of the year harvest-feast celebrations. For this reason, this Wheat harvest also will be the finale to the Great Commission.

The current countdown from the birth of the CHURCH to the full ripening of believers, which includes the Wheat being separated from the tares at the end of the Age, also will bring about a clearer focus on the true meanings of the Fall Feasts and the second harvest's principle of three main yields from the Grain. These three main yields are:

1. *First Fruits Harvest* (cf. Leviticus 23:10; Matthew 27:52-53; Acts 26:23; and 1 Corinthians 15:20) - the Sheaf (Omer), which is a Bundle of Grain. This sheaf is made from the first few ripened heads of grain;
2. *New Grain Harvest* (cf. Exodus 23:16, 34:22a; Leviticus 23:16; 1 Corinthians 15:51-54a and 1 Thessalonians 4:13-17) - the field's new grain growth - no matter if the grain is barley, wheat,

      and so forth. This grain, minus the four corners, is picked, gathered, processed;
3. Remnant (cf. Leviticus 19:9; 23:22; Deuteronomy 24:19; Matthew 13:24-30, 37-42; Joel 3:13; and Revelation 14:15 and 17-20; Revelation 20:7-9) - the grain harvested from the field's corner edges that originally was food left for the poor, the widowed, the orphaned, and the strangers.

The first fruits (the few heads of ripened grain), the new grain (the whole field except for the corners), and the remnant (that which is left after the rest of the field has been harvested) are shadows and types of the SECOND ADVENT—the END-TIME period when JESUS the CHRIST returns back to EARTH, in phases. Once again, the very "first-fruits" of the barley and wheat fields are Jesus, the Old Testament Saints, John the Baptist, the repentant thief from the cross, and the Body of Christ (the CHURCH) first-fruits who spiritually were born on the Day of Pentecost and thereafter - in essence, all of the dead in Christ and the living believers who are around when Christ seizes (αρπάζει) His CHURCH (Bride). [The Roman Catholics, using the Jerome's translation (Vulgate) of the word *αρπάζει* has been rendered as ***rapture***. For Protestant's rapture has been a key theme of their proselytizing and continuous to be a topic of many of their denominational ministries worldwide].

The "new grain" refers to: (1) the 144,00 martyred Tribulation evangelists; (2) the 2 Tribulation witnesses; and (3) the Tribulation believers (Wheat) who are evangelized by the 144,000 Messianic Jews. These Tribulation believers (or Wheat), though a great number, will be those individuals from all tongues and nations who are NOT glorified.

Lastly, where the end of the Age is concerned, the "remnant" grain now refers to those people from the Lord's 1,000-year Kingdom who side with the recently released Dragon - Satan who has been set free from the bottomless pit. They, however, will not have a chance to attack the Lord and His true remnant, because God rains fire down upon them and consumes them. As for Satan, who deceives this remnant of people who are born during Jesus' reign, convincing them to march on God's holy city to war against the Lord and His saints, this Satan/Devil is thrown into the Lake of Fire (Rev. 21:8).

In a nutshell, all of the aforesaid shadows and types and literal and figurative grain yields are found in the repeated agricultural patterns that run through the seven mandated Hebrew feasts. Four of these feasts are celebrated in the spring of each new ceremonial/festival year, and each one of these four spring feasts relates to Christ's first coming. Moreover, all four of these spring feasts have been fulfilled!

The four spring feasts are: (1) *Passover Feast*, which symbolizes our salvation and our deliverance that are made possible by the Lamb of God's atoning sacrifice, as Passover represents our Lord's explicit, sinless, and substitutionary death; (2) the *Feast of Unleavened Bread*, which testifies to the reality that, as the Lamb of God, Jesus's body could not decay in the grave, the Unleavened Bread, then, also represents our sanctification process - the Holy Spirit's work related to getting rid of the old leaven in our lives that is symbolized by our carnal nature/desires; finally, the Feast of Unleavened Bread symbolizes Jesus the Christ's death and burial and our identification with His humiliation and the cruel and brutal way that He died; (3) the *Feast of First fruits*, which illustrates that death could not hold Jesus the Christ prisoner, because His body could not remain in the grave; therefore, the Feast of First fruits also represents Jesus the Christ's resurrection and our future glorious state that will happen at the end of the CHURCH age in conjunction with the *snatching* of the CHURCH; additionally, the Feast of First fruits represents the first fruits of the 144,000 who are raptured near the end of time, as we know it; lastly, (4) the *Feast of Weeks* (Day of Pentecost), which commemorates the gift of the Holy Spirit and the birthday of the CHURCH.

There are also three fall feasts, but none of these feasts have been fulfilled! Moreover, the three fall feasts portray the events associated with Jesus's Second Coming. These three fall feasts are:

1. *The Feast of Trumpets*, which depicts Jesus the Christ's second phase of the first fruits' ascensions (*i.e.,* the seizure). The first phase dealt with Jesus the Christ's initial ascension, when He takes those who rose from the grave after Him, and the redeemed Old Testament saints, John the Baptist, and the repentant thief from the cross from Paradise to Heaven, to offer them to God as the first fruits of the dead. Lastly, the third phase will deal with the Tribulation's martyred saints, or the 144,000;
2. *The Day of Atonement*, which points to the wrath of God against the great host of surviving tribulation people, Jews and Gentiles, who take the mark of the Beast (This first beast is initially mentioned in Revelation 11:7 as coming out of the abyss. His

appearance is described in detail in Revelation 13:1-10, and some of the mystery behind his appearance is revealed in Revelation 17:7-18; The two beasts are aligned with the dragon in opposition to God. They persecute the "saints" and those who do "not worship the image of the beast [of the sea]" and influence the kings of the earth to gather for the battle of Armageddon. The two beasts are defeated by Christ and are thrown into the lake of fire mentioned in Revelation 19:18-20. See also Rev. 13:16-17 - Antichrist).

When the Lord returns (when He appears in the clouds with His host of angels to reap the world's harvest—to separate the Wheat from the Tares), He will destroy these individuals by metaphorically trampling them under His feet and then squeezing the grapes' juice out with the metaphorical winepress (Himself);

3. *The Feast of Tabernacles*, which speaks of the day when the Messiah Himself will tabernacle or dwell with His Kingdom people forever. Today, our first fruits are our gods of fortune, power, beauty, talent, and intelligence. No longer are we more concerned about the souls of mankind, but rather we are more concerned about our money; our material possessions; our position in life, and the power behind that position; our outer facial and bodily appearances; our abilities, skills, and gifts; and our mental capacity. Furthermore, the first fruits that have become our gods are also the things we worship, instead of letting them serve us! That is why it is so easy for prosperity teachers to encourage so many people to become FINANCIAL partners with their ministries. [This is especially true with many Protestant Televangelist preachers. If any one of you has ever watched their TV or listened to their radio programs, it becomes quite obvious, that most of these prosperity teachers do not consistently stress that the people watching and/or listening to their ministries should be doing their own God-appointed share of the Great Commission work, which is over and above making a donation to their church or ministry by writing a check, or by using a credit card, in excess of buying their self-help books, sermon on cassettes or CDs, Christian movies on DVDs, and so on]!

Once again, the Old Testament patterns of giving first fruits are not about giving the first fruits of our financial increase, before we give our monetary tithes and offerings, which prosperity teachers maintain. The Old Testament patterns of giving first fruits have to do with the first fruits of our spiritual harvests that are devoted unto God—our spiritual lives, our spiritual resources that God "freely" has given to us, our passionate commitment to evangelism and discipleship (to be zealous about reaching lost souls), and our desire to ALWAYS be about doing our Father's business of building up the Kingdom of Heaven on Earth.

Jesus is coming back for the rest of His first fruits - for the rest of His soul winning CHURCH and His soul winning martyred Tribulation saints. He also is coming back for His end of the Age abundant harvest - His Wheat. For these reasons, being counted as the spiritual first fruits in the next event on the prophetic timetable, the seizure (αρπαγή), should be the goal of every orthodox believer living today!

The harvest indeed is plentiful, but the laborers are few! That is why every person who has eyes and ears should understand and apply what he or she has read here or heard about the full significance of God's first fruit commands. Once again, God's first fruits' commands pertain to us making sure that we are cooperating with His Holy Spirit's sanctification process - that we not only are filled with but also are growing in His Holy Spirit. Secondly, God's first fruits' commands pertain to us making sure that we are using *Everything* God has blessed us with (spiritual gifts, talents, abilities, skills, character, money, possessions, and so on) so that, we can be productive field workers – and we can be laborers who actively are involved with evangelism and discipleship. Finally, God's first fruits' commands pertain to us being spiritually discerning Christians who *Always* promote rather than suppress the divine truth found in God's *Word* and in the *Holy Tradition* of the CHURCH!

We are living in the generation from which the largest harvest will come. Therefore, this is the time to get busy working with today's lost souls, realizing that God's saving Grace, mighty workings of the Holy Spirit, Holy Scriptures, and the faith that God gives us will help us value the Kingdom of God above everyone and everything else in this world! In other words, ***we have the supernatural resources that make it possible for us to consistently be about our Father's business!***

The holy Scriptures tell us that there will be signs of Jesus's Second Coming and that these signs are available for true Christians. Therefore, if we intend to meet our Lord in the air when He returns (if we plan to be the first-fruits of the Holy Spirit's second outpouring, to be those who are taken before the Tribulation Period starts), then we must be prepared, now, for our Lord's imminent Second Coming. We get prepared by obeying God's first fruits' commands for His New Testament saints!

First fruits and best fruits

The message so far has been a relentless attempt to demonstrate that ALL giving is performed to create relations. Those relations may be in family matters, royal and governmental, political, business and of course, between us and God.

In all cases, ALL giving must be enthusiastically perceived, and cheerful. However, it must be understood that there is no expected return. In other words, the adage of *quid pro quo* is Not allowed in this transaction – especially giving to God. All giving to God must be in appreciation of His benevolence, care, interest and for His unconditional love for us.

In our discussion of giving we have talked about first fruits and best fruits. I hope, the difference has been understood. In any case, just to make sure: when we give from our harvest the **first fruits – it pleases us.** That is because we feel good that we do our obligation. On the other hand, when we give from our harvest the **best fruits - it pleases GOD.**

So, the question now is: should we give the first or the best? The answer is simple: *We must give to God the first and the best at the same time.* Remember our gift to Him must NOT be blemished in any form. Therefore, *we may offer the first fruit but if that fruit has a blemish of any kind it is not a gift appropriate for our Lord, God.* It must be without any blemish. That is why all *our gifts to Him must be the First and Best fruits.*

So, let us see the first giving as it is written in Genesis 4:4: "And Abel also brought an offering - fat portions from some of the firstborn of his flock. The LORD looked with favor on Abel and his offering, NIV". But what does this mean?

Cain and Abel both have a relationship with the God who made their parents with His own hands. Both are bringing offerings to him. The previous verse tells us that Cain, the farmer, brought crops to the Lord: the fruit of the ground. Abel, the keeper of sheep, brought fat portions from a firstborn lamb from his flock.

Details are scarce in this part of Scripture. Only the most basic information is being given. So, we don't know if God required some particular form of sacrifice, sacrifice at certain times, or of some quantity. As far as we know from this text, God may or may not have expressed His will about the kinds of offerings He would accept.

Later, under the Law of Moses, God will require Israel to bring very similar offerings as part of their worship of Him and to receive atonement for their sin. Those details are not mentioned in this passage, and we have no way of knowing if God gave such a requirement to Cain and Abel. That being said, it seems Abel's offering (Genesis 4:4); Exodus 13:12 more closely matches the requirements of this future law than Cain's (Genesis 4:3; Leviticus 2:12; Numbers 18:12). This may help to explain why the Lord approved of Abel's offering and looked on Abel with favor, above his older brother.

The first example of sacrifice in the Bible is found in the account of Cain and Abel. When Cain and Abel, the first two sons of Adam and Eve, presented their sacrifices before the Lord Abel's sacrifice was accepted while Cain's was rejected. Why was Abel's sacrifice better? And in the process of time it came to pass that Cain brought an offering of the fruit of the ground to the Lord. Abel also brought of the firstlings of his flock and of their fat. And the Lord respected Abel and his offering but He did not respect Cain and his offering. And Cain was very angry, and his countenance fell (Genesis 4:4-5).

Why did God accept the sacrifice of Abel and reject the sacrifice of Cain? No one knows for sure. However, speculation abounds. A review of theological writings shows us at least seven main views. They are:
1. *God's sovereign choice*: The first view sees the acceptance of one offering and the rejection of the other as the sovereign choice of God. God merely chose to accept Abel's offering and reject Cain's with no explanation given. Some have argued that the reason for Abel's acceptance and Cain's rejection is based solely upon the sovereign choice of God. There was nothing different about either of the offerings. God, rather chose to accept one and reject the other without providing us any reason as to why. Therefore, it is fruitless to try to discover the reason for God's decisions for they are His and His alone.

2. *Non-Blood sacrifice*: A second view believes that the offering was rejected because Cain did not present a blood sacrifice. Blood sacrifice is the only acceptable offering God would receive. There are many who believe that Cain's offering was not accepted because it was not a blood sacrifice like Abel's. Instead, Cain brought the fruit of the cursed ground, the work of his hands. Many see in this episode the contrast between the God-revealed doctrine of blood sacrifice versus humanity trying to please God with their own self-efforts. Cain's offering is reminiscent of Adam and Eve covering themselves with fig leaves after their sin in the Garden. It is humanity attempting to work their way into a relationship with God instead of leaning on God's grace.
3. *Poor Quality:* The third view sees that Abel brought the best of what he had while Cain brought a poor-quality offering.
4. *Attitude problem*: The fourth view interprets the rejection as a problem with Cain's attitude rather than the specific offering that he brought.
5. *Occupations*: The occupations chosen by Cain and Abel were the natural results of the curse of the Fall. Since both the ground and the animal kingdom had been affected by the Fall, the sheep needed to be tended and the ground needed to be worked for food. Contrary to what some have contended, there is nothing inherently better about tending sheep than working the ground. Scripture gives no indication that one occupation was superior to another. Therefore, we should not look for the answer to the acceptance and rejection of the offerings in the various occupations the two practiced.
6. *The occasion*: It seems that there was a special occasion for this offering. The text says the offering was brought in the process of time or at the end of days. This may refer to some type of festival that the Lord established which was similar to the later rituals in the law of Moses. Some believe it was the first time that God had commanded that offerings be brought, but there is no indication of this in the text. Possibly there was some sort of primitive sanctuary where the offering was to be brought. This act of bringing the offering for sin was foreshadowing the coming of the Redeemer, Jesus Christ, Who would eventually offer Himself for the sins of the world.
7. *Fruit not flock*: Cain brought the fruit of the ground to offer to the Lord while Abel's offering was the first of the flock and of the fat.

This would have been the richest and best portion of the animal, demonstrating that Abel brought his best to the Lord.

So, the question of why Cain's offering was rejected will never be known with certainty. However, we are free to speculate based on what we read in the *OT* and *NT*. That is: Abel's offering was accepted while Cain's was rejected. This is a definite fact about the situation. We also know that animal sacrifices had been instituted before this time. Everything else is our speculation, because there is no reason given as to why. How do we know about the prior sacrifices?

For Adam and his wife, the Lord God made tunics of skin, and clothed them Genesis 3:21. To make animal skins for Adam and Eve after they had sinned, it stands to "human" reason that "killing of animals" or sacrifices would have been made. In the New Testament, the Book of Hebrews stresses the fact that Abel offered a more excellent sacrifice than Cain (by faith Abel offered unto God *a more excellent sacrifice than Cain*, by which he obtained witness that he was righteous, God testifying of his gifts: and by it he being dead yet speaketh - *Πίστει πλείονα θυσίαν Ἄβελ παρὰ Κάϊν προσήνεγκε τῷ Θεῷ, δι' ἧς ἐμαρτυρήθη εἶναι δίκαιος, μαρτυροῦντος ἐπὶ τοῖς δώροις αὐτοῦ τοῦ Θεοῦ, καὶ δι' αὐτῆς ἀποθανὼν ἔτι λαλεῖται*). By faith Abel offered to God a more excellent sacrifice than Cain, through which he obtained witness that he was righteous. God testifying of his gifts; and through it he being dead still speaks Hebrews 11:4. This version of facts leads many of us to conclude that the reason the sacrifice was rejected was because of the nature of it.

Yet another possibility of the rejection is the notion that Cain did not offer his best. Cain's fruit offering was not the best the land had produced. It is emphasized that Abel brought the first fruits of his flock- the best that he had. Cain, on the other hand, merely brought ordinary fruit to the Lord-possibly of a poor quality. Therefore, the difference between the two offerings is that Abel brought the best of what he had while Cain did not make an effort to bring his best to the Lord. *Cain's offering showed indifference or carelessness*. The heart attitude of Cain was sinful and this led to his bringing an inferior offering. Cain did not offer his best to the Lord because there was a problem with sin in his life. The Bible says, the sacrifice of the wicked is an abomination (Proverbs 21:27).

I believe that Cain's human spirit misinterpreted the offering. After all, the problem was not with the offering itself, but rather the wrong motivation. One may argue with this statement and contend that the dissatisfaction was not so much concerned with the type of sacrifice or the quality of the offering. As a result, the contention of the debate is that His main concern was with the attitude of Cain. Cain's offering was rejected because of his impure heart, not because it was the fruit of the land rather than a blood sacrifice. He may have brought the very best that he had, but he did so reluctantly and with entirely the wrong attitude. This would be comparable to somebody giving a large sum of money to the church with a grudging attitude or for human recognition. [Examples of the human recognition were shown in Chapter 2 – plaques, trees and bricks with individual names].

Yet one more perspective from the NT. In the letter to the Hebrews, Paul tells us in translating the word offering (*προσήνεγκε* τῷ Θεῷ; The implication here is a gift) is not the usual word for blood sacrifice (but Cain and his *sacrifices* he regarded not, - ἐπὶ δὲ Κάϊν καὶ ἐπὶ ταῖς *θυσίαις* αὐτοῦ οὐ προσέσχε. καὶ ἐλυπήθη Κάϊν λίαν, καὶ συνέπεσε τῷ προσώπῳ αὐτοῦ - Gen. 4:5 LXX).

Therefore, both offerings were proper for the two brothers who were at worship. In later texts, to bring an offering to the Lord suggests building an altar and placing that offering on or before that altar. Yet altar is nowhere used in Genesis 4, and we must remain uncertain as to how the brothers brought to the Lord their respective sacrifices.

Each brought an offering (*minha*) appropriate to his occupation. One would expect a farmer to bring an offering from the vintage of the ground and a shepherd to bring the best of his flock. Outside of ritual codes *minha* could refer to any offering of grain, but animals might also be included here. Here we must make the distinction that an offering IS NOT a sacrifice.

Both Cain and Abel brought proper offerings and there is nothing in the text to suggest the type of offering is the reason for God's rejection or acceptance. On the contrary, the text is clear they brought offerings (gifts) to the Lord and not sacrifices. The text is silent regarding anything wrong with the quality or type of Cain's offering. God showed acceptance to Abel, rather than Cain, because Abel made his offering to the Lord in faith.

On the other hand, Cain's response apparently was a public event. This made Cain angry and he did not repent. Rather he responded in anger against the Lord. The Lord said to Cain: If you do well, will you not be accepted? And if you do not do well, sin lies at your door. And its desire is for you, but you should rule over it (Hast thou not sinned if thou hast brought it rightly, but not rightly divided it? be still, to thee shall be his submission, and thou shalt rule over him - οὐκ ἐὰν ὀρθῶς προσενέγκῃς, ὀρθῶς δὲ μὴ διέλῃς, ἥμαρτες; ἡσύχασον· πρὸς σὲ ἡ ἀποστροφὴ αὐτοῦ, καὶ σὺ ἄρξεις αὐτοῦ (Genesis 4:7LXX).

This is one of the most difficult verses in Scripture. Its exact translation and meaning have been the subject of much debate (the original text is quoted in the previous paragraph). As it is translated here, the problem with Cain's offering lies with his attitude. Sin is depicted as a crouching animal waiting to pounce upon its prey. If the person does not resist the sin, then greater ruin can occur in his life. God tells Cain that he has the ability to fix the situation by mastering the sin that is controlling him. Unfortunately, Cain did not learn his lesson and it led him to committing a greater sin. Upset at both God and his brother, Cain then went out and killed Abel (Genesis 4:8). This clearly showed that he did not learn the lesson that God tried to teach him.

So, what can we learn from the Cain and Abel story? The character of Cain and Abel are contrasted in the rest of Scripture. Cain is spoken of in Scripture as wicked while Abel is called righteous. Jesus called him "righteous Abel" (Matthew 23:35). The Apostle John wrote "not as Cain who was of the wicked one and murdered his brother. And why did he murder him? Because his works were evil and his brother's righteous (1 John 3:12).

Jude in his letter said: "Woe to them! For they have gone in the way of Cain, have run greedily in the error of Balaam for profit, and perished in the rebellion of Korah (Jude 11). To be sure, Cain's judgment for killing his brother was definite and severe as we read Genesis 4:11-12): "So now you are cursed from the earth, which has opened its mouth to receive your brother's blood from your hand. When you till the ground, it shall no longer yield its strength to you. A fugitive and a vagabond you shall be on the earth." Therefore, Cain's judgment was banishment from God's presence and a further cursing of the ground. The earth, having been already cursed by Adam's sin, was further cursed with respect to Cain. The implication here is that Cain will never be settled. He will be a fugitive and vagabond wherever he goes. This speaks of the nature of the sinner apart from the Lord. There is never any permanent rest or peace unless a person is in God's presence.

So, it is important for all of us to recognize that the Almighty – our God – did not act arbitrarily or that He had some secrete reasons for His behavior. He acted the way He did only because Abel offered a "more acceptable sacrifice" in faith. And what makes Abel's sacrifice better? "Abel brought of the firstlings of his flock and of their fat portions" (Gen. 4:4a). That is, he offered the first-borns, the very best of what he has. But Cain *doesn't* offer God the first fruits of his harvest. Instead, he simply gives him "an offering of the fruit of the ground" (Gen. 4:3). If Abel is giving God the equivalent of filet mignon, Cain is giving him ground beef. This is a difference in both faith and works. By faith, Abel gives God everything. Cain phones it in.

The early Christians understood this. For example, St. John Chrysostom observed that Abel's piety is demonstrated by "the fact that he did not casually offer any one of his sheep but 'one of the firstborn,' that is, from the valuable and special ones," whereas in Cain's case, "nothing of the kind is suggested;" Genesis 4:3's description of Cain bringing "an offering of the fruit of the ground" suggests a lack of zeal or care.

Didymus the Blind's exegesis is virtually identical: Abel's sincerity is demonstrated by his choice of the firstborn, and "Cain should have done so as well by offering some of the first-fruits," since what is due to God ought to "be apportioned before everything else." Instead, Cain procrastinates, bringing his offering "in the course of time" (Gen. 4:3), "as if remembering God only on second thoughts."

We see something similar in the New Testament with Ananias and Sapphira, who "sold a piece of property, and . . . kept back some of the proceeds, and brought only a part and laid it at the apostles' feet," pretending that it was the entire value of the sale (Acts 5:1-2). The issue isn't that they offer God nothing but that they offer him less than everything. For their deception, and for their holding back from God, they're struck dead (Acts 5:5, 10).

To Ananias and Sapphira, as to Cain, the message is the same as Christ's message to Laodicea: "I know your works: you are neither cold nor hot. Would that you were cold or hot! So, because you are lukewarm, and neither cold nor hot, I will spew you out of my mouth" (Rev. 3:15-16).

It's worth remembering that, just as in the trials of the Israelites in the desert, "these things happened to them as a warning, but they were written down for our instruction, upon whom the end of the ages has come" (1 Cor. 10:11). For we are each faced with the same choice: do we want to give God *everything* or try to settle for less?

In a world encouraging us to settle for being "basically good people," *Christ repeatedly warns us that isn't good enough.* He says anyone who "does not hate his own father and mother and wife and children and brothers and sisters, yes, and even his own life, he cannot be my disciple. Whoever does not bear his own cross and come after me, cannot be my disciple" (Luke 14:26-27). Immediately after this, he compares discipleship to building a tower or going to war. Undertaking either of these endeavors halfheartedly is a surefire way to lose a battle or build half a tower (Luke 14:28-32). And so "whoever of you does not renounce all that he has cannot be my disciple" (Luke 14:33).

Scripture tells us *not just to give God whatever fruit we have left over and lying around. Instead, "the first of the first fruits of your ground you shall bring into the house of the Lord your God"* (Exod. 23:19, 34:26). In other words, don't wait until you're comfortable to tithe, don't wait until you feel like you have the time to start making time for prayer. Give to God *immediately*, give from your necessity, give to Him (in time, in money, in trust, and so on) when it seems like you can't.

This is why Christ praises the widow who put two mites into the treasury as having given more than the others, because "they all contributed out of their abundance; but she out of her poverty has put in everything she had, her whole living" (Mark 12:44). She doesn't just give one coin out of her poverty but two. Be generous with God in your poverty, and he'll be generous with you in his limitless abundance. "Honor the Lord with your substance and with the first fruits of all your produce; then your barns will be filled with plenty, and your vats will be bursting with wine" (Prov. 3:9-10).

The world encourages us to be Cain, "good enough" moralistic Christians who pay lip service to God. Christ calls us instead to be Abel.

So, if we ask a number of Christian leaders and theologians whether or not Christians are still required to tithe, you'll get a variety of responses. Some will tell you that Christians need to give God a tenth of their first fruits right off the top; others will tell you that Jesus released us from the law's obligation to tithe and we should give freely. This isn't a new debate by any means. The Church has been struggling with the question of tithing on generosity for a long time.

As for the Orthodox Church, we believe in the principle of giving as *much as you can*. This means: from very little to all you have. This is based on the NT writers and the sayings of many Fathers of the Church. What we all must remember is not how much we give but what attitude we have towards giving.

Chapter 9
What do the Scriptures say about Giving?

We have both implied and said in no uncertain terms that Jesus is the most generous person who ever lived. He left the comforts of heaven, took on human flesh, and gave his life on the cross so that we might live in him. In response to Jesus' generosity, we are also called to be generous. We are called to be generous with our money. We are called to steward our possessions. We are called to volunteer our time. No one argues over whether Christians should be generous - it's a hallmark of the Christian faith. Eastern Orthodox are not exempted from being generous. There is plenty of proof of this. So, in this chapter we will address some of these truths.

However, whether we admit to it or not, the fact is that discussing money as it relates to "faith" is a serious discussion and all of us should participate in a fruitful discussion. So, let us review some of the key issues that should concern us. A good starting point for that discussion is a review of God's word as it is written in the Bible. Therefore, let us examine some key topics about tithing directly from the Bible itself. Specifically, let us look at:

- An overview of giving as found in the Scriptures
- Specific Old Testament scriptures on tithing
- Specific New Testament scriptures on tithing
- Living a generous life

An overview of giving as found in the Scriptures

What is tithing in the Bible? First, let's start by answering the question **"what is a tithe**?" The definition comes from Hebrew and means "a tenth." Therefore, **tithing in the Bible** refers to giving 10 percent of your annual earnings, productions, or possessions. In the Old Testament, we observe Abraham and Jacob offering a tithe to God in Genesis 14 and 28. The Israelites were also commanded to tithe from what they earned (Lev. 27:30; Num. 18:25–28; Deut. 14:22–24; 2 Chron. 31:5–6).

Obviously, the Bible is crystal clear – especially in Leviticus 27:30 where it proclaims: "A tenth of the produce of the land, whether grain or fruit, is the Lord's, and is holy." And Proverbs 3:9 (NIV) says, "Honor the Lord with your wealth, with the first fruits of all your crops." It's critical to recognize that tithing was central to God's law, and as such all Israelites didn't wait to feel inspired to tithe, it was expected. And so, it was done.

Where was tithing first mentioned in the Bible? The first tithe made in the Bible happened in Genesis14: 19-20. **The first person to do so in the bible was Abram**. Abram (more well known as Abraham) returned from battle and was met by Melchizedek. During their encounter Melchizedek attributes Abram's victory to God and he blesses Abram. Abram responds to the blessing in gratitude and gives Melchizedek a tenth (that is a tithe) of all his possessions. So, we read: *"And he blessed him and said, "Blessed be Abram by God Most High, Possessor of heaven and earth; and blessed be God Most High, who has delivered your enemies into your hand!" And Abram **gave him a tenth of everything**.* For more on Melchizedek see Appendix A.

Jacob offers the second tithe as recorded in the Bible. Over in Genesis 28:20–22 Jacob responds to a dream he received from God by building an altar and vowing that, in exchange for God's care and provision, he would give a tenth of his belongings. Jacob made a vow, saying, "If God will be with me and will keep me in this way that I go, and will give me bread to eat and clothing to wear, so that I come again to my father's house in peace, then the Lord shall be my God, and this stone, which I have set up for a pillar, shall be God's house. And of all that you give me I will give a full tenth to you."

Are Christians required to participate in tithing? To be sure, tithing is a Hebrew tradition and a directive for them by God. But is it also a requirement for the Christians to follow? Many opinions are available as to what is the correct answer. However, two basic views are the predominant ones. They are:

1. Christians are commanded to tithe: Tithing in the Bible began in the Old Testament, and it's still commanded today. This position stands on three pillars.
   a. First, is that the requirement to tithe was made before the Mosaic covenant (Gen. 14; 28; Heb. 7:1). If this is true, then this means the tithe was not abolished in Christ and is still in force today.
   b. Second, this position argues that Jesus affirmed the continuation of the tithe (Matt. 23:23). Since Jesus upheld the tithe, then Christians are commanded to tithe today.

    c. Third, in Matthew 5:17, Jesus is very emphatic that he came to "fulfill the law and not to abolish it" with the words "Do not think that I have come to abolish the Law or the Prophets; I have not come to abolish them but to fulfill them – ESV." And in Matthew 23:23 we read again the confirmation of Matthew 5:17 with the words: "Woe to you, scribes and Pharisees, hypocrites! For you tithe mint and dill and cumin, and have neglected the weightier matters of the law: justice and mercy and faithfulness. These you ought to have done, without neglecting the others-ESV."

2. Christians are commanded to be generous: Christians are called to give generously, but they're not commanded to tithe. This position stands on three main points.
    a. First, the offerings that were tithed by Abraham (Gen. 14) and Jacob (Gen. 28) are descriptions—not prescriptions. In other words, there's no evidence that Abraham and Jacob continued to tithe or that their actions were binding for others then or today.
    b. Second, the tithing required by the Israelites was a part of the Mosaic Law. When Jesus fulfilled the requirements of the Mosaic Law (Matt. 5:17), the obligation to tithe was also abolished. What is more, when Jesus talked about tithing and offering sacrifices (Matt. 5:23–24; 23:23; Luke 11:42), He did so before He started the New Covenant, which means it's not binding today.
    c. Finally, the New Testament (NT) does not command Christians to tithe. When giving is referenced in the NT, followers of Christ are commanded to give generously (2 Cor. 8–9) - not to give strict 10 percent.

What does all this mean for us? This is followed by should I give? There are no definite answers to these two questions other than to say. They are personal questions and everyone has to decide by themselves as to what to do. What is key here is: a) study the Holy Scriptures for guidance b) serve God with a sincere conscience and 3) follow your Church's guidance.

What are offerings in the Bible? The Bible tells us "offerings" are a bit more nuanced than "tithing." Actually, what you think about "offerings" is largely based on what you believe about "tithing." An offering is a financial gift you make to your church that is more than your tithe (10%). For example, if you give 10 percent of your annual income to your local church, then an offering is any money you donate that exceeds this amount.

If you believe that Christians are called to give generously, then an offering is a financial gift you make to your local church - regardless of the amount you give. For most of us we think of "offering" as what we call giving to our church.

In addition, for most of us we think of "giving" as "give some amount of money." This obviously is a very narrow definition as God wants us to offer ourselves as a living sacrifice to him. How do we know this? The Apostle Paul tells us so: "Therefore, I urge you, brothers and sisters, in view of God's mercy, to offer your bodies as a living sacrifice, holy and pleasing to God - this is your true and proper worship" (Rom. 12:1, NIV).

To offer yourself as a living sacrifice to God is to offer yourself entirely to him. Offering your life to God is not something you do one time or on the days you feel good. Living sacrificially for God is something he calls everyone to do every day. Paul clarifies this sacrifice in the next verse by writing: *"Do not conform to the pattern of this world, but be transformed by the renewing of your mind. Then you will be able to test and approve what God's will is - his good, pleasing and perfect will"* (Rom. 12:2). So, what is the message here? Paul is telling us to: a) Don't be conformed to this world (Remember the words in John 17:16) and b) Renew your mind. This means:

- Living the Christian life is more than just saying no to anything.
- Living the Christian life is more about living for God.
- When it comes to offering yourself to Christ, we are called to renew our minds. Practically speaking, we renew our mind by studying the Bible, meditating upon the scriptures, and reading the lives of the saints. Renewing our mind is one way we can learn how to live for God. At least one more way to do this renewal is through our finances.

What percentage of Christians participate in tithing? Today, most Christians don't tithe. Consider these statistics. Bradley (2018) summarizing the survey data from *State of the Plate*, only 10–25 percent of church member's tithe. Only 5 percent of the United States population participates in tithing. On average, Christians give 2.5 percent of their income, which is down from the 3.3 percent given during the Great Depression.

There are more stats I can share, but I think you get the point. Giving in the Church is on a downward trend regardless of what we might think about tithing in the Bible. However, as the news seem discouraging, one thing is for certain. That is: When one places their faith in Christ, one will - in time - be transformed into a giver. This does not mean that one magically will be in a position to give 10 percent or some other amount. Rather, it means that through faith in Christ, you will be empowered to be generous with what you have.

Why one may not want to give? There are many reasons, some of which are: a) Going through a difficult financial season b) Have too much debt c) Be growing in your faith in Christ d) Not know why you should give, e) suspect malfeasance by the steward of the church and f) Not be sure how to give to your church. So, regardless of what the situation is or what one believes about giving or tithing, the fact remains that Christ is calling us to a generous life.

As one offers their life as a living sacrifice to Christ, it is worth taking the time to: study, meditate and review the many verses in the Bible regarding giving and generosity. The following verses are typical and they are only a few of what one can find in Scriptures.

Specific Old Testament scriptures on tithing

- **Genesis 28:20–22**: (Jacob offers a tithe) Jacob made a vow (to God), "If God will be with me and will watch over me…all that You give me I will give You a tenth."
- **Exodus 35:21**: Everyone who was willing and whose heart moved him came and brought an offering to the LORD for the work.
- **Exodus 35:22**: All who were willing, men and women alike, came and brought gold jewelry of all kinds: brooches, earrings, rings and ornaments. They all presented their gold as a wave offering to the LORD.
- **Leviticus 27:30**: (The tithe is introduced into law) A tithe of everything from the land, whether grain from the soil or fruit from the trees, belongs to the LORD; it is holy to the LORD.

- **Leviticus 27:32**: The entire tithe of the herd and flock-- every tenth animal that passes under the shepherd's rod-- will be holy to the LORD.
- **Numbers 18:21**: I give to the Levites (priests/ministers) all the tithes…in return for the work they do while serving (the Lord).
- **Numbers 18:26**: (The Levites tithe) Moreover, you shall speak and say to the Levites, "When you take from the people of Israel the tithe that I have given you from them for your inheritance, then you shall present a contribution from it to the Lord, a tithe of the tithe."
- **Deuteronomy 14:22–23**: You shall tithe all the yield of your seed that comes from the field year by year. And before the Lord your God, in the place that he will choose, to make his name dwell there, you shall eat the tithe of your grain, of your wine, and of your oil, and the firstborn of your herd and flock, that you may learn to fear the Lord your God always.
- **Deuteronomy 14:27–29**: At the end of every three years you shall bring out all the tithe of your produce in the same year and lay it up within your towns. And the Levite, because he has no portion or inheritance with you, and the sojourner, the fatherless, and the widow, who are within your towns, shall come and eat and be filled, that the Lord your God may bless you in all the work of your hands that you do.
- **Amos 4:4–5**: (God requires more than the tithe) "Come to Bethel, and transgress; to Gilgal, and multiply transgression; bring your sacrifices every morning, your tithes every three days; offer a sacrifice of thanksgiving of that which is leavened, and proclaim freewill offerings, publish them; for so you love to do, O people of Israel!" declares the Lord God.
- **2 Chronicles 31:4–5**: And he commanded the people who lived in Jerusalem to give the portion due to the priests and the Levites, that they might give themselves to the Law of the Lord. As soon as the command was spread abroad, the people of Israel gave in abundance the first fruits of grain, wine, oil, honey, and of all the produce of the field. And they brought in abundantly the tithe of everything.
- **2 Chronicles 31:12**: God's people faithfully brought in the contributions, tithes and dedicated gifts.

- **Nehemiah 12:43–44**: (God's people) offered great sacrifices, rejoicing because God had given them great joy. The women and children also rejoiced. The sound of rejoicing…could be heard far away. Men were appointed to be in charge of the storerooms for the contributions, first fruits and tithes.
- **Nehemiah 12:47**: All (of God's people) contributed the daily portions for the singers, gatekeepers…Levites (ministers).
- **Nehemiah 13:11–12**: I rebuked the officials and asked them, "Why is the house of God neglected?" Then I called them together and stationed them at their posts. All (God's people) brought the tithes…into the storerooms.
- **Malachi 3:7–9**: Return to me, and I will return to you," says the LORD Almighty. "But you ask, 'How are we to return?' "Will a man rob God? Yet you rob me. "But you ask, 'How do we rob you?' "In tithes and offerings. You are under a curse-- the whole nation of you-- because you are robbing me.
- **Malachi 3:11–12**: (God says to those who bring him tithes and offerings) "I will prevent pests from devouring your crops, and the vines in your fields will not cast their fruit," says the LORD Almighty. "Then all the nations will call you blessed, for yours will be a delightful land."
- **1 Kings 17:13, 8–16**: Elijah said to (the starving widow woman), "Don't be afraid…first make a small cake of bread for me from what you have and bring it to me, and then make something for yourself and your son. For this is what the LORD says: 'The jar of flour will not be used up and the jug of oil will not run dry'…She went away and did as Elijah had told her. So, there was food every day for Elijah and for the woman and her family.
- **Exodus 36:3–6**: The people continued to bring freewill offerings morning after morning. So, all the skilled craftsmen who were doing all the work on the sanctuary left their work and said to Moses, "The people are bringing more than enough for doing the work the LORD commanded to be done." Then Moses gave an order…"No man or woman is to make anything else as an offering for the sanctuary." And so the people were restrained from bringing more.
- **Malachi 1:6–7**: "A son honors his father; a servant honors his master. I am your Father and Master, yet you don't honor

me…you despise my name." "Who? Us?" you say. "When did we ever despise your name?" "When you offer polluted sacrifices on my altar." "Polluted sacrifices? When have we ever done a thing like that?" "Every time you say, 'Don't bother bringing anything very valuable to offer to God!'"
- **Malachi 1:8–10**: (God's ministers tell people) 'Lame animals are all right to offer on the altar of the Lord-- yes, even the sick and the blind ones.' And you claim this isn't evil? Try it on your governor sometime-- give him gifts like that-- and see how pleased he is! … I have no pleasure in you," says the Lord Almighty, "and I will not accept your offerings."
- **Malachi 1:11**: "My name will be honored…from morning till night. All around the world people will offer…pure offerings in honor of my name. For my name shall be great among the nations," says the Lord Almighty.
- **Malachi 1:12–13**: (Ministers dishonor God by telling people) God's altar is not important and encouraging people to bring cheap, sick animals to offer to God. "You say, 'Oh, it's too difficult to serve the Lord and do what he asks.' And you turn up your noses at the rules he has given you to obey. Think of it! Stolen animals, lame and sick-- as offerings to God! Should I accept such offerings as these?" asks the Lord.
- **Malachi 1:14**: "Cursed is that man who promises a fine ram from his flock and substitutes a sick one to sacrifice to God. For I am a Great King," says the Lord Almighty, "and my name is to be mightily revered among the people of the world."
- **Haggai 1:4**: "Is it a time for you yourselves to be living in your paneled houses, while (God's) house remains a ruin?"
- **Haggai 1:5–8**: This is what the LORD Almighty says: "Give careful thought to your ways. You have planted much, but have harvested little. You eat, but never have enough. You drink, but never have your fill. You put on clothes, but are not warm. You earn wages, only to put them in a purse with holes in it." This is what the LORD Almighty says: "Give careful thought to your ways…build (My) house…so that I may take pleasure in it and be honored."
- **Haggai 1:9–11**: "You expected much, but see, It turned out to be little. What you brought home; I blew away. Why?" declares the LORD Almighty. "Because of my house, which

remains a ruin, while each of you is busy with his own house. Therefore, because of you the heavens have withheld their dew and the earth its crops. I called for a drought on the fields and the mountains, on the grain, the new wine, the oil and whatever the ground produces, on men and cattle, and on the labor of your hands."
- **Proverbs 3:9–10**: Honor the LORD with your wealth, with the first fruits of all your crops; then your barns will be filled to overflowing, and your vats will brim over with new wine.
- **Proverbs 18:9**: One who is slack in his work is brother to one who destroys.
- **Proverbs 28:22**: A stingy man is eager to get rich and is unaware that poverty awaits him.
- **Proverbs 28:27**: He who gives to the poor will lack nothing, but he who closes his eyes to them receives many curses.
- **1 Chronicles 29:2–3**: (King David said to God's people) "With all my resources I have provided for the temple of my God - gold… silver… bronze… iron… wood… onyx… turquoise… all kinds of fine stone and marble - all of these in large quantities. In my devotion to the temple of my God I now give my personal treasures of gold and silver for the temple of my God, over and above everything I have provided.
- **1 Chronicles 29:5–8**: (King David said to the leaders) "Who is willing to consecrate himself today to the LORD?" Then the leaders of families…officers…commanders of thousands and commanders of hundreds…and the officials…gave willingly. They gave toward the work on the temple of God gold…silver…bronze…iron. Any who had precious stones gave them to the treasury of the temple of the LORD.
- **1 Chronicles 29:9**: The people rejoiced at the willing response of their leaders, for they had given freely and wholeheartedly to the LORD. David the king also rejoiced greatly.
- **1 Chronicles 29:11–12**: Everything in heaven and earth is Yours, O LORD. Wealth and honor come from you; you are the ruler of all things. In your hands are strength and power to exalt and give strength to all.
- **1 Chronicles 29:13–14**: (David prayed to God) "God, we give you thanks, and praise your glorious name. "But who

am I, and who are my people, that we should be able to give as generously as this? Everything comes from you, and we have given you only what comes from your hand."
- **1 Chronicles 29:16**: LORD our God, as for all this abundance that we have provided for building you a temple for your Holy Name, it comes from your hand, and all of it belongs to you.
- **I Chronicles 29:17**: (David prayed to God) "I know, my God, that you test the heart and are pleased with integrity. All these (offerings) I have given willingly and with honest intent. And now I have seen with joy how willingly your people who are here have given to you."
- **Ezra 2:68–69**: Families gave freewill offerings toward the rebuilding of the house of God. According to their ability they gave to the treasury for this work.
- **Deuteronomy 28:12**: The LORD will open the heavens, the storehouse of his bounty, to send rain on your land in season and to bless all the work of your hands. You will lend to many nations but will borrow from none.
- **Psalm 49(50):10**: Every animal of the forest is mine, and the cattle on a thousand hills…the creatures of the field are mine… the world is mine, and all that is in it.
- **Deuteronomy 8:18**: Remember the LORD your God, for it is he who gives you the ability to produce wealth.
- **Deuteronomy 16:10**: Celebrate the Feast of Weeks to the LORD your God by giving a freewill offering in proportion to the blessings the LORD your God has given you.
- **Deuteronomy 16:16**: No man should appear before the LORD empty-handed.
- **Deuteronomy 16:17**: Each of you must bring a gift in proportion to the way the LORD your God has blessed you.
- **Isaiah 32:8**: The noble man makes noble plans, and by noble deeds he stands.

Specific New Testament scriptures on tithing

- **Matthew 23:23**: "Woe to you, teachers of the law…You give a tenth…But you have neglected the more important matters - justice, mercy and faithfulness. You should have practiced the latter, without neglecting the former.

- **Luke 6:38**: If you give, you will get! Your gift will return to you in full and overflowing measure, pressed down, shaken together to make room for more, and running over. Whatever measure you use to give - large or small - will be used to measure what is given back to you.
- **Luke 6:38**: Give, and it will be given to you. A good measure, pressed down, shaken together and running over, will be poured into your lap. For with the measure you use, it will be measured to you."
- **Luke 18:9–14**: He also told this parable to some who trusted in themselves that they were righteous, and treated others with contempt: "Two men went up into the temple to pray, one a Pharisee and the other a tax collector. The Pharisee, standing by himself, prayed thus: 'God, I thank you that I am not like other men, extortioners, unjust, adulterers, or even like this tax collector. I fast twice a week; I give tithes of all that I get.' But the tax collector, standing far off, would not even lift up his eyes to heaven, but beat his breast, saying, 'God, be merciful to me, a sinner!' I tell you, this man went down to his house justified, rather than the other. For everyone who exalts himself will be humbled, but the one who humbles himself will be exalted."
- **Matthew 6:1–4**: Beware of practicing your righteousness before other people in order to be seen by them, for then you will have no reward from your Father who is in heaven. Thus, when you give to the needy, sound no trumpet before you, as the hypocrites do in the synagogues and in the streets, that they may be praised by others. Truly, I say to you, they have received their reward. But when you give to the needy, do not let your left hand know what your right hand is doing, so that your giving may be in secret. And your Father who sees in secret will reward you.
- **2 Corinthians 8:2–2**: Out of the most severe trial, their overflowing joy and their extreme poverty welled up in rich generosity. For I testify that they gave as much as they were able, and even beyond their ability. Entirely on their own, they urgently pleaded with us for the privilege of sharing in this service to the saints.
- **2 Corinthians 8:5**: They gave themselves first to the Lord and then to us in keeping with God's will.

- **2 Corinthians 8:7**: Just as you excel in everything-- in faith, in speech, in knowledge, in complete earnestness and in your love for us-- see that you also excel in this grace of giving.
- **2 Corinthians 8:10–11**: Last year you were the first not only to give but also to have the desire to do so. Now finish the work, so that your eager willingness to do it may be matched by your completion of it, according to your means.
- **2 Corinthians 8:12**: If the willingness is there, the gift is acceptable according to what one has, not according to what he does not have.
- **2 Corinthians 8:20–21**: We want to avoid any criticism of the way we administer this liberal gift. For we are taking pains to do what is right, not only in the eyes of the Lord but also in the eyes of men.
- **2 Corinthians 9:5**: I thought it necessary to urge the brothers to visit you in advance and finish the arrangements for the generous gift you had promised. Then it will be ready as a generous gift, not as one grudgingly given.
- **2 Corinthians 9:6**: Remember this: Whoever sows sparingly will also reap sparingly, and whoever sows generously will also reap generously.
- **2 Corinthians 9:7**: Each man should give what he has decided in his heart to give, not reluctantly or under compulsion, for God loves a cheerful giver.
- **2 Corinthians 9:8**: God is able to make all grace abound to you, so that in all things at all times, having all that you need, you will abound in every good work.
- **2 Corinthians 9:10**: Now he who supplies seed to the sower and bread for food will also supply and increase your store of seed and will enlarge the harvest of your righteousness.
- **2 Corinthians 9:11**: You will be made rich in every way so that you can be generous on every occasion, and through us your generosity will result in thanksgiving to God.
- **2 Corinthians 9:12**: This service that you perform is not only supplying the needs of God's people but is also overflowing in many expressions of thanks to God.
- **2 Corinthians 9:13**: Men will praise God for the obedience that accompanies your confession of the gospel of Christ, and for your generosity in sharing with them and with everyone else.

- **Matthew 6:26**: Look at the birds of the air; they do not sow or reap or store away in barns, and yet your heavenly Father feeds them. Are you not much more valuable than they?
- **Matthew 6:27–31**: Who of you by worrying can add a single hour to his life? So do not worry, saying, 'What shall we eat?' or 'What shall we drink?' or 'What shall we wear?' For the pagans run after all these things, and your heavenly Father knows that you need them.
- **Matthew 6:33–34**: Seek first his kingdom and his righteousness, and all these things (food, clothing, drink) will be given to you as well. Therefore, do not worry about tomorrow, for tomorrow will worry about itself. Each day has enough trouble of its own.
- **Mark 12:41–44**: Jesus sat down opposite the place where the offerings were put and watched the crowd putting their money into the temple treasury. Many rich people threw in large amounts. But a poor widow came and put in two very small copper coins, worth only a fraction of a penny. Calling his disciples to him, Jesus said, "I tell you the truth, this poor widow has put more into the treasury than all the others. They all gave out of their wealth; but she, out of her poverty, put in everything-- all she had to live on."
- **1 Corinthians 16:2**: On every Lord's Day each of you should put aside something from what you have earned during the week, and use it for this offering. The amount depends on how much the Lord has helped you earn.
- **1 Timothy 6:6–8**: Godliness with contentment is great gain. For we brought nothing into the world, and we can take nothing out of it. But if we have food and clothing, we will be content with that.
- **1 Timothy 6:9**: People who want to get rich fall into temptation and a trap and into many foolish and harmful desires that plunge men into ruin and destruction.
- **1 Timothy 6:17–19**: Command those who are rich in this present world not to be arrogant nor to put their hope in wealth, which is so uncertain, but to put their hope in God, who richly provides us with everything for our enjoyment. Command them to do good, to be rich in good deeds, and to be generous and willing to share. In this way they will lay up treasure for themselves as a firm foundation

for the coming age, so that they may take hold of the life that is truly life.
- **Matthew 6:19–21**: (Jesus said) "Do not store up for yourselves treasures on earth, where moth and rust destroy, and where thieves break in and steal. But store up for yourselves treasures in heaven, where moth and rust do not destroy, and where thieves do not break in and steal. For where your treasure is, there your heart will be also.
- **Hebrews 6:10**: God is not unjust; he will not forget your work and the love you have shown him as you have helped his people and continue to help them.
- **Acts 2:44–45**: All the believers were together and had everything in common. Selling their possessions and goods, they gave to anyone as he had need.
- **Romans 12:13**: Share with God's people who are in need. Practice hospitality.
- **Hebrews 13:16**: Do not forget to do good and to share with others, for with such sacrifices God is pleased.
- **Hebrews 7:1–2**: For this Melchizedek, king of Salem, priest of the Most High God, met Abraham returning from the slaughter of the kings and blessed him, and to him Abraham apportioned a tenth part of everything. He is first, by translation of his name, king of righteousness, and then he is also king of Salem, that is, king of peace.
- **I John 3:17**: If anyone has material possessions and sees his brother in need but has no pity on him, how can the love of God be in him?
- **Luke 18:22–25**: When Jesus heard this, He said to the rich young ruler, "You still lack one thing. Sell everything you have and give to the poor, and you will have treasure in heaven. Then come, follow me." When he heard this, he became very sad, because he was a man of great wealth. Jesus looked at him and said, "How hard it is for the rich to enter the kingdom of God! Indeed, it is easier for a camel to go through the eye of a needle than for a rich man to enter the kingdom of God."
- **Luke 11:42**: But woe to you Pharisees! For you tithe mint and rue and every herb, and neglect justice and the love of God. These you ought to have done, without neglecting the others.

- **Galatians 6:6**: Those who are taught the Word of God should help their teachers by paying them.
- **Galatians 6:6**: Anyone who receives instruction in the word must share all good things with his instructor.
- **Matthew 25:35–40**: I was hungry and you gave me something to eat, I was thirsty and you gave me something to drink, I was a stranger and you invited me in, I needed clothes and you clothed me, I was sick and you looked after me, I was in prison and you came to visit me.' "Then the righteous will answer him, 'Lord, when did we see you hungry and feed you, or thirsty and give you something to drink?'..."The King will reply, 'I tell you the truth, whatever you did for one of the least of these brothers of mine, you did for me.'
- **Acts 20:35**: (Remember Jesus' words when he said) "It is more blessed to give than to receive.

Living a generous life

So, it is a definite fact that *tithing* was used by God in the Old Testament to take care of His people. Today, Christ works through our offerings to advance His kingdom and bless others. To participate in Christ's work, it is essential to live a generous life. A generous life includes serving with one's time and talents. To live for Christ, one has to know what Christ asks of that person. To do this, one has to study the Bible and the lives of the Saints. By studying both, one establishes the rock foundation of living a generous life for Christ. However, the next step is to **pray about one's situation**. Praying through what one has studied is one of the best ways one can receive guidance in one's life from Christ. He will guide you through His Word, and give you the grace you need to live a generous life. In this area, studying and meditating on the lives of the saints, will prove very beneficial, since they were humans like all of us and yet they conquered the essence of Christ's wishes and lived a righteous life. If it was possible for them to be winners, it is possible for us as well.

Even though one has to take personal responsibility for their life, Christ doesn't call us to do it alone. He invites us to **seek counsel** in our life. When it comes to our finances and our thoughts around tithing in the Bible, getting advice from a friend, priest, or financial advisor can make a significant difference. Someone looking at our situation from the outside can provide new insight or confirm what we are already thinking. These three principles work best together, and as one strives to live a generous life; they will point one in the right direction.

Over to you! What have you learned about tithing in the Bible? Let me leave you with this parting word: Be generous like Jesus was generous. Regardless of what you decide to believe about tithing, my hope is that you'll model Jesus' generosity - and not get hung up on the theological minutia. As Orthodox Christians, our goal is to be like Jesus. Jesus modeled a generous life, and he calls us to reflect his generosity. In the words of the Apostle John: *"Whoever says he abides in him ought to walk in the same way in which [Jesus] walked"* (1 John 2:6). Today, I encourage you to follow in the footsteps of our Savior and live a generous life. Why? So that we may become "imitators of God" (Ephes. 5: 1).

Chapter 10
Offering versus Tithing

We read that the first *offering* to God is from Cain and Abel in Genesis 4. That OFFERING was indeed an act of Thanksgiving. In the Orthodox Church, we emphasize this thanksgiving every time we conduct our Holy Liturgy every Sunday or holiday. However, because of its significance, we call it *Eucharist*, which is the same but with a more distinguished name.

Throughout all of the Eucharistic prayers, we are constantly referring to this giving of thanks. The priest says, "Let us give thanks unto the Lord." Everyone replies, "We lift them up to the Lord." and "It is proper and right." Those moments embody the central theme of *why we all exist*…to lift up every part of our lives to the Lord in continual acts of worshipful-thanksgiving.

Saint Paisios of the Holy Mountain talks about a Greek word, φιλότιμο *"philótimo"* – sense of honor." Holy-Philótimo is having so much gratitude, that we feel a great and humble indebtedness to God…and even to the created-image-of-God in our neighbor. It turns out that this is at the heart of Orthodox Worship. When we feel this holy-philótimo, we're so filled with joy in offering, that the only thing we regret is that we can't offer more. Our deepest need is to become so aware and grateful for what God is doing in our lives, that we see God's image in our neighbor and feel indebted even to them.

At the very beginning of every Orthodox Christian's life (at our baptism), God gives us a brilliant symbol of Orthodox life and worship—we're tonsured. Little pieces of our hair are cut from our head [in the form of the cross], while the priest recites from the baptismal service, "The first *offering* of the hairs of your head." It is an odd ritual in that it begs the question, "Why does God need an offering of your hair?" The answer is, "God doesn't *need* anything." And likewise, God doesn't need our money any more than He needs our hair, or anything else for that matter, because He created it all and thus, it all belongs to Him anyway.

As Orthodox Christians, He has simply given us responsibility over the things in our possession to use it *all* in worship. So why do we offer this hair at our baptism? Because for babies, it's practically all they have to offer. In their first act, as someone newly baptized and chrismated, they make an offering to God. Thus, it demonstrates to the Godparents and the parents that this is central to what they should be teaching the child as they train them up in the Lord. Being an offeror is vital to a right relationship with God and to worshipping Him. Why? Because, Christ is the ultimate offeror of Himself—self-sacrificially pouring Himself out as an act of love for His Father, for us, and for our neighbor. Each of us who were baptized, were united to Christ in that baptism. And every Christian is called to grow in His likeness…to be Christ-like (see Galat. 3:27). So self-sacrificial offering simply becomes an essential part of worshipping and being united to God.

On the other hand, we come across tithing for the first time in Genesis 14:20. The tithe, which means 10% of one's entire income should be given to God. In the *OT* since they were a farming society, this included ten percent of their fruit and grain harvests and ten percent of their flocks each year, but it wasn't just any ten percent. They were supposed to tithe *the first and best ten percent*—the first fruits—as sacred and set apart to the Lord. In other words, they were supposed to offer to God first, before they took any for themselves and before they paid any of the rest of their debts. For the ancient Israelites, it wasn't an option. It was a part of Jewish Law, because God was trying to teach them that they could trust Him to care for them, even when they gave this significantly.

So, what is more interesting is that for Israel this was not the only tithe. In fact, there were actually three tithes that they were commanded to give. The first was *the sacred tithe to the Lord*, that went to the care and ministry of their place of worship (Numbers 18: 21, 24). The second tithe went toward a kind of yearly, shared Thanksgiving feast, *praising God in gratitude for His blessings* (Deuteronomy 14:22-27). It was a sort of family recreation/renewal and festal savings system. And then there was a third tithe (given every third year), which *went to the poor* (Deuteronomy 14:28-29) - a community project for the sake of widows, orphans and to offer hospitality to poor visiting travelers.

For the *NT* and modern Christians, these tithes present several objections. Perhaps, the most interesting and powerful is the one that claims that tithing is an OT practice. They have nothing to do with the NT, since we are not under the Law but rather under Grace. These individuals forget that even Christ did not avoid the responsibility of tithes when He said: "Do not think that I have come to abolish the Law or the Prophets; I have not come to abolish them but to fulfill them" (Matthew 5:17). This is a profound statement and supports the continuation of tithing. Obviously, for Jesus to have said those words, He did not want to place unbearable burdens, but rather for our own spiritual and mental health and for the blessing of the world. As people who are united with Christ, we're called to be obedient to the Law of Christ, which is merely a Law of Love. Christ voluntarily, lovingly, and self-sacrificially gave Himself for us. He took the form of a servant, even though He was God by nature. So, God gives us this gift of choosing with our finances whether we actually want to be united to Him - to faithfully choose to participate with Him in His way of offering.

Thus, if we want to be united to Christ, we can't give God our leftovers: We have to give Him our first-fruits. That's the only way to really acknowledge, and teach ourselves (and our children) that everything we have belongs to God. When we partake in *active offering* it affects our salvation, because it reflects the degree to which we have become united to Christ. The message of tithing is loud and clear: trust God (not your money) to take care of your needs.

This is important to emphasize. Our offering to God was never supposed to be about paying the Church's bills and budget (even if the Church does use it for the care of its ministries and place of worship). Reflect on the poor widow's story, who offered only two small copper coins to the Lord (Luke 21:1-4). It was all she had, yet she offered them anyway. Jesus said that her offering was far greater than the impressive gifts given by the rich people around her because what she gave was self-sacrificially substantial for her, exercising an enormous amount of faith—trusting that God was the one taking care of her.

A rich person might give a large sum of money, but if it's not really a self-sacrificially generous amount of money for them, then it's not given with any trust in God and thus, *it's not transformative* for them. Sure, the money might be put to good use, paying the Church's bills, but that's not why we offer*!* ***The best way to offer, is to offer the way God taught us to give: proportionally***. This way our offering will be significant enough to really teach us that everything we have belongs to God and that we really do trust Him to care for us, because *our money is not God.* ***He is***.

Let us remember the holy-philotimo of Saint Paisios (as mentioned earlier) and ask: Can you imagine what would happen in the life of any parish, if the kind of holy-philótimo that Saint Paisios talks about became our central, most recognizable virtue? Our witness of having such transformed lives of holy philótimo is the number one evangelical tool that we have. When we become very faithfully and seriously focused about our transformation in Christ (offering every part of ourselves to Him), that will become the best means for spreading His Good News.

Membership

A parishioner (ενορίτης) is one who belongs to a particular parish church (ενορια); is known unto the spiritual father, that is the priest; and is a registered member, committed to the parish community and supporting it in the stewardship of time, talent and tithe.

As an active member of the community (parish -ενορια), the parishioner (ενορίτης) is responsible to support their parish through the usage of offering *AND* tithing, year around. The act of "supporting" **the** church needs to be understood in the context of making offerings to God. This we do at every Divine Liturgy. Here, we offer ourselves - our hearts, minds and wills to Jesus Christ. Jesus Christ takes us - washing us in His Blood and offers us with Himself as a gift to God the Father. We proclaim it during the Holy Anaphora with: "Thine own of Thine own we offer unto Thee, in behalf of all and for all – Τα σα εκ των σων σοι προσφερομεν κατά παντα και δια παντα," which means "for everyone and for everything."

We give (offer as a gift) ourselves over to the Lord. This giving of ourselves is expressed in a symbolic manner - the tithe, candles, prosphora, flowers, incense, monetary gifts, *etc*. They express in a "partial" way the "full" offering of our lives to God.

Aside from the aspect of "offering," there is that of "fulfilling the salvific work» of the church - that is the offerings and support we give the church enables the church to pay bills and provide for missions, education, outreach and fellowship – unfortunately not all these are undertaken by many parishes. It is however, essential that we understand that the offering of our lives and what we are gifted with - time, talent and treasure - is transformed into the work of serving the Mission of Jesus Christ.

Fr. J. Matusiak (2007, pp 5-6) addresses the issue of the need for tithing as: "Even though tithing is from the Old Testament, it should not be seen as something that should not be practiced, such as stoning. Would one also recommend that Christians ignore the Ten Commandments because they are found in the Old rather than New Testament? Jesus Christ came to fulfill the law, not to abolish it. That which was worth saving from the Old Covenant was incorporated into the New."

Therefore, all of us should make an effort to learn about stewardship, as it involves our Christian way of life which touches everything: birth, growth, eating, learning, time, marriage, family, vocation and even death, burial and resurrection. The fundamental issue is: how do we handle everything that God has entrusted us with! To help in this meditation, take the time to read and meditate on the following verses: Psalm 115:3 LXX (116):12 "What shall I render to the Lord for all the things wherein he has rewarded me?" (See also: 1 Corinthians 16:2; Matthew 16:26).

Appendix A
Melchizedek – The High Priest and King of Salem

The Righteous Melchizedek, King of Salem is commemorated on May 22 and again among all the Old Testament righteous on two Sundays (about the 11th of December) before the Nativity. Who was he and why should we care? Actually, you need to know about Melchizedek because he's an Old Testament image of the Lord Jesus Christ, and you desperately need to grow in knowing who Jesus is, because we're supposed to grow in unity with Him. Saint Paul feels so strongly about this, that in Hebrews 7:3, he gives an imperative command that we should intensely observe and discern this Melchizedek.

We first come across Him in the Old Testament. There's a thrilling story from Genesis 14, where several kings combined their armies to attack and kidnap a very wealthy businessman named Lot, also abducting all his family and stealing everything he owned. As these kings and their soldiers absconded across the countryside with Lot, Lot's uncle, the great Patriarch Abraham, set out with his own armies on a rescue mission to liberate his nephew. When Abraham's army caught up with these evil kings, he attacked their forces at night for maximum confusion, and came at them from several directions at once, thoroughly crushing them. Abraham was able to save his nephew Lot, together with the rest of Lot's family, recovering all their possessions.

The next morning, all the defeated kings collected their dead and wounded, assessed their situation, and then gathered together in the area of Salem (in what's called the "King's Valley") so that terms of surrender and the spoils of war could be negotiated with Abraham. Suddenly, a new King came upon the scene, someone named Melchizedek.

Melchizedek was the King of "*Salem*" (which means "Right-relationship; Wholeness and Peace"). Not only was he a King, but the Bible tells us that he was also a Priest of the Most-High God. His name, "Melchizedek," means, "King of Righteousness." Thus, remarkably, he was King AND Priest of Right-relationship and Righteousness. Does that sound familiar? Melchizedek had nothing to do with the kidnapping or any part of the battle the night before. However, while those other wicked kings gathered to extract as much plunder as possible from the other kings, Melchizedek by contrast, instead came offering hospitality, bringing bread and wine - food and refreshment for everyone there - a meal with the goal of rebuilding fellowship among these soldiers and kings and the families present.

This priestly king, Melchizedek, then gave Abraham a blessing, saying, *"Blessed be Abraham by God Most-High, Creator of heaven and earth. And blessed be God Most-High, who delivered your enemies into your hand."* This generous act of blessing and hospitality from the "Priest and King of Right-relationship and Righteousness," so thoroughly impressed Abraham that, **in an act of gratitude and worship to the Most-High God**, he refused to take any of the spoils of war, realizing that he didn't need them, because God was the true source of his blessings. Abraham is transformed in seeing this powerful act of love. So, *in Eucharistic gratitude to God for His many blessings, and in a generously tangible act of faith, Abraham offered God's High-Priest, Melchizedek, one tenth of everything he owned.*

So, who was this life-transforming King and Priest of Salem, Melchizedek? Where did He come from, and where did He then go? Well that's the mysteriously delightful thing about him. We don't quite know the answer to either of those questions. In his Epistle to the Hebrews, Saint Paul, writing about Melchizedek (mostly in chapter 7), pulls some fascinating details from Melchizedek's life-story, to talk about Jesus as "High Priest." In Hebrews 7:3-7, St. Paul says, *"Melchizedek had no father or mother and there is no record of any of His ancestors. He was never born and He never died but His life is like that of the Son of God - a priest forever. See then how great this Melchizedek is: Even Abraham, the first and most honored of all God's chosen people, gave a tithe of his possessions to Melchizedek. One could understand why Abraham would do this if Melchizedek had been a Jewish priest, since, later on, God's people were required by law to give gifts to help their priests because the priests were their relatives. But Melchizedek was not a relative, and yet Abraham paid him. Melchizedek placed a blessing upon mighty Abraham, and as everyone knows, a person who has the power to bless is always greater than the person he blesses.*" Paul goes on to point out that Melchizedek was a different kind of priest - actually greater than all the priests that would ever follow, the greatest of great high-priests, part of a different plan of God. He says that Christ as High Priest, in the way of Melchizedek, became a priest in a new way, on the basis of power flowing from a life that's timeless and enduring. Because of this, Christ forever guarantees the success of this new and better arrangement. Therefore, He's able to wholly save those who come to God through Him, because He lives to ceaselessly intercede on their behalf.

Some Church Fathers, like Cyprian of Carthage, lean towards Melchizedek being purely some mysterious person who was merely prefiguring or foreshadowing Jesus Christ. Other Church Fathers, like St John Chrysostom, go a little further, talking about Melchizedek as though he's a Theophany - a pre-incarnate appearance of Jesus Christ Himself. Given the way Saint Paul draws so many parallels between Melchizedek and Christ, it seems wise to lean in carefully towards Chrysostom's inference. There's a kind of Theophany in Melchizedek's presence on the scene in Genesis 14.

There are three vitally important things that can be learned from Melchizedek as a pre-incarnate Theophany of Jesus, and what we're supposed to become under his high-priesthood:

1. Notice, in Genesis 14, that Melchizedek lived with the sinful city of Sodom on one side and the pagan Canaanites on the other, and yet He remained there to serve the community. Our Lord, in His love, is committed to having godly witnesses for Himself in the midst of the worst of communities to bless and transform them. [By comparison, most Orthodox parishes move to new locations when their neighborhood becomes poor and many minorities move to close proximity of the church rather than stay and preach the Gospel to the destitute and less fortunate].
2. Also notice that Melchizedek and Jesus are, both, King and Priest in one person. Likewise, when every Christian is chrismated at their baptism, the prayers within the service connect this anointing with the Prophet Samuel's anointing of David as king. Every Christian is anointed at their Chrismation to become royalty - sons and daughters (princes and princesses) of God, to become *kingly* after the manner of

Christ's way of humble kingship - in self-offering servanthood, in offering a blessing for an insult, and in self-sacrificially offering our lives for the sake of God's Kingdom. Yet also, at our baptism, every Orthodox Christian also becomes a part of what St. Peter calls "the royal, *priesthood*" (what is also known as "the priesthood of believers"). From baptism on, every Christian is supposed to live and operate through life as the priest does with the gifts at the altar - taking everything we encounter and essentially lifting it up to God in praise and thanksgiving, for Him to transform into a blessing for all of creation.

3. Pay attention to the fact that Melchizedek shows up in loving contrast to a very negative situation (where kings are selfishly trying to take advantage of each other). There instead, Melchizedek offers gifts of refreshment, offering hospitality—with the goal of rebuilding fellowship among everyone present. He is truly the King and Priest of Salem (Shalom), of restoring peaceful, right-relationship between people who have gotten off track. Thus, a key part of his ministry is to move them back toward the Father, Son and Holy Spirit's way of offering of love as community, always seeking the wellbeing of the other. That's the image in whom and for what we were created. As He constantly intercedes for us that we become unified with God in this way, transformed into that for which we were created. Jesus, our Great High-priest is able to wholly save those who come to God through Him.

Portions of this text are adopted and used with permission from Fr. Gabriel-Allan Boyd. And found in the internet site: "Melchizedek." https://www.stbasil.com/news/2019/5/22/the-old-testament-melchizedek-showing-us-jesus. Retrieved on September 11, 2020.

Appendix B
A Classic Example of Giving: The Samaritan Story

Every year we hear the Gospel lesson of the Good Samaritan (Luke 10: 25-37). However, not too many of us contemplate God's love for us. In fact, in all honesty, I doubt very much if we consider His Love for us in an unconditional way, with all our heart, soul, mind and strength and our neighbor as us. Therefore, let us examine the story with His Love in mind.

The setting of the story is approximately in the Fall of 29 A.D. It begins with a lawyer (an expert in the Mosaic Law, not civil law) trying to justify himself with Jesus (Luke 10:29). He first asked Jesus, "What shall I do to inherit eternal life?" (Luke 10:25) Jesus replied, "What is written in the Law?" (Luke 10:26) The lawyer replied by quoting the Greatest Commandment, "You shall love the Lord your God with all your heart, with all your soul, with all your strength and with all your mind, and your neighbor as yourself" (Luke 10:27). The lawyer did not come up with this completely on his own. His statement was part of a creed used in the synagogue worship that was learned and memorized by school children. This is also a quote from Deuteronomy 6:5 and Leviticus 19:18.

The same issue came up again in the Spring of 30 A.D. during Holy Week, where the Pharisees and Scribes also asked Jesus which is the Greatest Commandment (Matthew 22:34-40, Mark 12:28-34). Jesus replied that all the (Mosaic) Law and the Prophets hang on this same statement that the lawyer made; that is, the Greatest Commandment (Matthew 22:40). One scribe replied to Jesus, "to love Him with all the understanding, with all the soul, and with all the strength and to love one's neighbor as oneself is more than all the whole burnt offerings and sacrifices" (Mark 12:33). Jesus remarked then that he had answered wisely; so, Jesus, said to him, "You are not far from the Kingdom of God" (Mark 12:34). This is to say: you know what to do; all you need now is to go do it (Kern 2007). [Scribes were experts in the Mosaic Law and could be called lawyers].

When the lawyer quoted the Greatest Commandment, Jesus replied, "You have answered rightly; do this and you will live" (Luke 10:28). Thus, the opinion of the experts on the Mosaic Law (Scribes, Pharisees, lawyers) concur that the Greatest Commandment is the answer for obtaining eternal life, and the Lord agreed with them.

Clement of Alexandria (*The Instructor*, III, 12) discussed why Christ first asked the lawyer if he had kept the Commandments. Keeping them leads to eternal life in that the Commandments define sin and what God requires. Good deeds and the keeping of the Commandments are an acceptable prayer to God. "God dispenses many treasures; some disclosed by the Law, others by the prophets; some by the mouth of God, and others by the Spirit singing accordingly. And the Lord is the same instructor by all these. Here is then a comprehensive precept, and an exhortation of life, all embracing, 'As you wish that men should do to you, do likewise to them' (Luke 6:31). We may comprehend the Commandments in two parts, 'You shall love the Lord your God with all your heart, with all your soul, and with all your strength; and your neighbor as yourself'. From these He infers, 'on this hang the Law and the prophets' (Matthew 22:37-40).

Further, to him that asked, 'What good thing shall I do, that I may inherit eternal life?', He answered, 'Do you know the Commandments?' And on him replying, Yes, He said, 'This do (here Clement has added a few of the expressions from Luke 10:25-28), and you shall be saved' (Matthew 19:16-20). Especially conspicuous is the love of our instructor set forth in various Commandments. We have the Ten Commandments given by Moses, an elementary principle, defining the designation of sins in a way conducive to salvation. These things are to be observed, and whatever else is commanded in reading the Bible. And He directs us, 'Wash yourselves, make yourselves clean; put away the evil of your doings from before My eyes. Learn to do good; seek justice, rebuke the oppressor; defend the fatherless, plead for the widow. Come now, and let us reason together, says the Lord' (Isaiah 1:16-18). We find many examples in other places, as, for instance, respecting prayer, where good works are an acceptable prayer to the Lord (see the example of the Judgment of Works (Matthew 25:31-46, where people are saved by virtue of their dedication to serving the Lord's brethren). And the manner of prayer is described: 'If you see the naked, cover him; and you shall not overlook those who belong to your seed. Then shall your light spring forth early, and your healing shall spring up quickly; and your righteousness shall go before you, and the glory of God shall encompass you'. What, then, is the fruit of such prayer? 'Then shall you call, and God will hear you; while you are yet speaking, He will say, I am here'" (Isaiah 58:7-9).

Irenaeus of Lyon stated (*Against Heresies*, IV, xii, 5 p 222) that when Jesus asked the lawyer if he had kept the Commandments, this was in keeping with what He had imposed on mankind from the beginning; but the lawyer hadn't kept them, even though he said that he had. Jesus offered the lawyer the reward of an Apostle if he would diligently pursue his question, but the lawyer turned Him down. "The Law beforehand taught mankind the necessity of following Christ, and He made this clear, when He replied to him who asked Him what he should do that he might inherit eternal life. 'If you want to enter into life, keep the Commandments.' When the lawyer asked 'Which?', again the Lord replied, 'Do not commit adultery, kill, steal, or lie; honor your father and mother, and love your neighbor as yourself' (Matthew 19:16-19). He set this as an ascending series of precepts before those who wished to follow Him, where the precepts of the Law are the entrance into life. What He said to this lawyer, He says to everyone. The former said, 'All these have I done', and most likely he had not kept them, for if he had, the Lord would not have said to him, 'Keep the Commandments' (Matthew 19:17). The Lord, exposing his covetousness, said to him, 'If you wish to be perfect, sell all that you have, and distribute to the poor; and come, follow me' (Matthew 19:21). He promised to those, who would act thus, the portion of the Apostles. [This is not an unusual request. It is exactly what the Twelve Apostles did; they left everything (Matthew 19:29), and so did the entire Early Church after Pentecost (Acts 2:44-45)]. He did not preach to His followers another God the Father, besides Him, who was proclaimed by the Law from the beginning, nor the fables invented by the heretics. But He taught that they should obey the Commandments, which God imposed from the beginning, and do away with their former covetousness by good works, and follow after Christ. That possessions distributed to the poor annul former covetousness, Zacchaeus made clear, when he said, 'Half of my goods I give to the poor; and if I have defrauded anyone, I restore fourfold'" (Luke 19:8).

The Temptation of the Lawyer in the Gospel tells us that the lawyer wanted to justify himself and sought clarification on the word "neighbor"

(Luke 10:29). The implication was that he was only interested in tempting Jesus (Luke 10:25), not in inheriting eternal life.

Cyril of Alexandria (*Commentary on the Gospel of Luke, Homily 68*, Studion Publishers, 1983, pp 287-290,) comes out smoking against the lawyer, saying that he had no intention of learning from Him, but merely sought to tempt Him. Thus, Jesus rightly returned his focus to that part of the Mosaic Law that might lead to his understanding and repentance. "For a man to make a pretense of pleasant-spoken words, with a tongue anointed with the *honey of deception*, with *a heart full of bitterness is double-dealing and hypocrisy in action and conduct*. 'Their tongue is a piercing arrow; the words of their mouth are deceitful; he speaks peacefully to his neighbor, and enmity is in his heart' (Jeremiah 9:8 LXX). And again, 'Their words are smoother than oil, yet they are arrows' (Psalm 54:21 LXX); by which is meant that their words have the force of arrows shot from bows and striking violently." "As proof of my assertion let us examine the lawyer's words. 'A certain lawyer stood up, and tempted Him, saying, Teacher, what shall I do to inherit eternal life?' (Luke 10:25)

A lawyer, according to the custom of the Jews, was one acquainted with the Law, or at least having the reputation for knowing it; but in this case, he really didn't know it. This man imagined that he could trap Christ! Many people had accused Christ, saying that He taught that the commandments given by Moses were of no value, while He introduced new teachings, which were not in accordance with the Law.

The lawyer, expecting to be able to trap Christ, and get Him to say something against Moses, tempted Him, saying, 'What shall I do to inherit eternal life?'" "But he didn't know Who he was dealing with! How could he have ventured to tempt God, Who tries the hearts and reins (Psalm 7:9 LXX), and to Whom nothing in us is hid? He might have said, 'What shall I do to be saved, or to please God, and receive reward from Him?' But he passed by this, and used rather Christ's expressions, trying to pour ridicule upon His head. Since Jesus spoke constantly of eternal life to as many as drew near to Him, the haughty lawyer, to ridicule Him, made use of His own expressions." "Now had he been truly desirous of learning, he would have heard from Him the things that lead on to eternal life; but as he wickedly tempted Him, he heard nothing more than those commands, which were given by Moses. Jesus said, 'What is written in the Law? How do you read it?' (Luke 10:26) And on the lawyer's repeating what is enacted in the Law, as if to punish his wickedness, and reprove his malicious purpose, Christ, as knowing all things, said, 'You have answered rightly; do this, and you shall live' (Luke 10:28). At this point, the lawyer had missed his prey; his wickedness was unsuccessful, the net of deceit was torn apart. He was 'found and caught, because he contended against the Lord'" (Jeremiah 50:24). "Having missed his prey, he fell headlong into vanity; hurried from one pitfall to another, he fell from deceit to pride.

One kind of wickedness, as soon as it has seized him, thrusts him on to another, making him wander from destruction to destruction. He does not ask in order that he may learn, but wishing to justify himself. For observe how from self-love as well as pride he shamelessly called out, 'And who is my neighbor?' (Luke 10:29) There is no one like you, O lawyer? Do you raise yourself above everyone? Those who are able to judge themselves are wise (Proverbs 13:10 LXX). As he exalted himself and boasted in vain imaginations, he learned from Christ, that he was destitute of love towards his neighbors; the profession of being learned in the Law didn't profit him in any way whatever." "Very skillfully Jesus weaved the parable of him who fell into the hands of thieves, saying, that when he was lying half dead, a priest passed by, and in like manner a Levite, without feeling towards him any sentiment of humanity, or dropping upon him the oil of compassionate love. But rather, their mind was unsympathetic and cruel towards him. But one of another race, a Samaritan, fulfilled the law of love. Justly He asked, which of these three, he thinks, was the sufferer's neighbor. He said, 'He that showed mercy to him'. And to this Christ added, 'Go also, and act in like manner' (Luke 10:37). You have seen, O lawyer, and it has been proved by the parable, that it is of no avail whatever to any man, to be set up by empty names, and to pride yourself with meaningless titles, so long as the excellence of deeds does not accompany them. The dignity of the priesthood is useless to its owners, and equally so being called learned in the Law, unless they excel also in deeds.

For a crown of love is being made for him who loves his neighbor; and he proves to be a Samaritan. As Peter testified, 'I perceive that God shows no partiality. But in every nation whoever fears Him and works righteousness is accepted by Him' (Acts 10:34-35). For Christ, Who loves our virtues, accepts all who are diligent in good pursuits." Loving Our Neighbor as Ourselves The command in the Mosaic Law to love one's neighbor (Leviticus 19:18) uses the Hebrew word "rea" meaning friend or companion and thus implies a very close neighbor. But the Mosaic Law also says to treat the stranger among you as the native and to love the stranger as yourself, remembering that you were once strangers in Egypt (Leviticus 19:33-34).

The Hebrew word for stranger is "ger" meaning sojourner; in the Greek Septuagint, the corresponding word is "προσήλυτος - proselytos" meaning one who draws near; that is, a proselyte. So how far should loving one's neighbor extend? Should it extend just to one's friends and companions, to the members of one's own tribe or people, as far as to Gentile proselytes or to any sojourner passing through? For a Mosaic Law scholar knowledgeable about minute details of the Law, this was a thought-provoking question that might be used to trap Jesus into saying something against Moses.

Jesus proceeded with the Parable of the Good Samaritan to clarity this. In the Parable the victim is:

- Robbed, stripped and wounded
- Ignored by a priest and a Levite
- Given first aid by a Samaritan
- Transported to the nearest inn and treated further by the Samaritan
- Given 1 to 2 weeks further paid medical care by the Samaritan.

In the context, it is implied that the victim was a Jew. [Remember that in the 1st Century Jews and Samaritans generally despised each other (John 4:8, 20). If the Samaritan had helped another foreigner, it would be no big deal. But for him to stop to help a Jew was remarkable]. Being left half dead, he was likely bleeding to death from puncture wounds. By the time the Samaritan reached him, he had probably lost enough blood to make him very weak. Pouring wine on his wounds served as an antiseptic due to the alcohol in the wine. Pouring oil on his wounds also served as an ointment to further prevent infection. The priest and Levite passing by had good excuses for not getting involved. They were probably either going to or coming from serving in the Temple in Jerusalem. Priests and Levities were divided up into 24 lots (1 Chronicles 24) where those in one lot served in the Temple in Jerusalem for one week, then went home. Twenty-three weeks later they served one week again. That way, service in the Temple was divided up among all the priests and Levities.

The homes of the priests and Levities were confined to the "Levitical Cities" prescribed in the Mosaic Law (Numbers 35:1-8, Joshua 21:1-42). This lasted until the kingdom was divided after the death of Solomon and most Levites abandoned the Northern cities and returned to Judah. After the Babylonian captivity, Levitical cities were not distinct anymore and priests and Levites 1st Century Jews and Samaritans generally despised each other (John 4:8, 20). If the Samaritan had helped another foreigner, it would be no big deal. But for him to stop to help a Jew was remarkable, grouped together into what were called "Priestly Centers." From these "Priestly Centers", they traveled together to and from Jerusalem. One such "Priestly Center" was Nazareth (Edersheim, 1995 pp 36-37). From the viewpoint of the priest or Levite, it was easy to rationalize not getting involved. The man was bleeding, and therefore he was unclean and so would they be if they touched him (Leviticus 15:2-13). And they couldn't serve in the Temple if they were unclean (Leviticus 22:2- 6). But yet, the Lord cut through this religiosity excuse by saying, "I desire mercy, not sacrifice" (Matthew 9:13, 2:7, both of which quote Hosea 6:6). Even the scribe understood this, saying that loving one's neighbor is more important than sacrifice (Mark 12:33). God can raise up from stones children to Abraham who can offer sacrifices (Matthew 3:9, Luke 3:8, 19:40).

What God really wants is someone who will be like Him and show mercy. For the Samaritan to transport the wounded man to an inn was not a small task either. If the man was unconscious or drifting in and out, he couldn't ride. Somehow, the Samaritan "set him on his own animal" (Luke 20:34).

Finally, after taking care of the wounded man overnight, the Samaritan gave the innkeeper two denarii (this represented two days' wages for a laborer!) to continue his medical care and promised more if more was needed. Jesus concluded the story by asking the lawyer which of the three was a neighbor to him who fell among thieves (Luke 10:36). The lawyer got the message, "He who showed mercy on him" (Luke 10:37). Then Jesus said to him (and to us) "Go and do likewise."

Ambrose of Milan (*Duties of the Clergy*, I, xi, 36-39) stated that there are "ordinary duties" and "perfect duties". "Ordinary duties" are keeping the Commandments; everyone should do this without even thinking about it. "Perfect duties" refer to loving our enemies and showing mercy to the poor, whereby we receive more than we give. The righteous Job is a good example of this. "Every duty is either 'ordinary' or 'perfect,' a fact which we can also confirm by the authority of the Scriptures. For the Lord said, 'If you will enter into life, keep the Commandments. The lawyer said, 'Which?' Jesus said to him, 'Do not murder, commit adultery, steal, or bear false witness; honor your father and your mother, and love your neighbor as yourself' (Matthew 19:17-19). These are ordinary duties, to which something is lacking." "Upon this the young man said to Him, 'All these things have I kept from my youth, what do I still lack? Jesus said to him, 'If you will be perfect, go and sell all your goods and give to the poor, and you shall have treasure in heaven; and come and follow Me' (Matthew 19:20-21).

Earlier the same is written, where the Lord said that we must love our enemies, and pray for those that falsely accuse and persecute us, and bless those that curse us. This we are bound to do, if we want to be perfect as our Father Who is in heaven. He directs the sun to shed his rays over the evil and the good, and makes the lands of the whole earth fertile with rain and dew without any distinction (Matthew 5:45). This, then, is a perfect duty, whereby all things are put right, which could have any failings in them." "Mercy is a good thing, for it makes men perfect, in that it imitates the perfect Father. Nothing graces the Christian soul so much as mercy; mercy as shown chiefly towards the poor, that you may treat them as sharers in common with you in the produce of nature, which brings forth the fruits of the earth for use to all. Thus, you may freely give to a poor man what you have, and in this way help him who is your brother and companion. You give silver; he receives life. You give money; he considers it his fortune. Your coin makes up all his property."

"Further, he bestows more on you than you on him, since he is your debtor in regard to your salvation. How? If you clothe the naked, you clothe yourself with righteousness; if you bring the stranger under your roof, if you support the needy, he procures for you the friendship of the saints and eternal habitations. That is no small recompense. *You sow earthly things and receive heavenly.* Do you wonder at the judgment of God in the case of holy Job? Wonder rather at his virtue, in that he could say, 'I was an eye to the blind, and a foot to the lame. I was a father to the poor, and I searched out the case that I did not know' (Job 29:15-16). Their shoulders were made warm with the skins of my lambs.

The stranger dwelt not at my gates, but my door was open to everyone that came. Clearly blessed is he from whose house a poor man has never gone with empty hand. Nor again is anyone more blessed than he who is sensible to the needs of the poor, and the hardships of the weak and helpless. In the Day of Judgment, he will receive salvation from the Lord, Whom he will have as his debtor for the mercy he has shown." John Chrysostom (*Homilies on Romans*, XXIII, vv. 9-10) looked very carefully at Paul's words, "All the Commandments are summed up in this saying, namely, 'You shall love your neighbor as yourself'. Love does no harm to a neighbor; therefore, love is the fulfillment of the law" (Romans 13:9-10). God puts love for our brethren on a par with love for God Himself; that is, one Commandment "is like" the other. There are two parts: abstinence from evil and doing good deeds. He considers us worthy to share His love, and He has been saying this even from ancient times. "He does not say merely it is fulfilled, but 'it is summed up', that is, the whole work of the Commandments is concisely and, in a few words, completed. For the beginning and the end of virtue is love. This it has for its root and its groundwork, this for its summit. If then it is both beginning and fulfillment, what is there equal to it? But he does not seek love merely, but intense love. He does not say merely 'love your neighbor' but, 'as yourself.'

Christ also said that 'the Law and the Prophets hang on it.' And in making two kinds of love, see how He has raised this! For after saying that the first commandment is, 'You shall love the Lord your God', He added a second; and He did not stop there, but added, 'like it; You shall love your neighbor as yourself' (Matthew 22:37-40). What can be equal to this love for man, or this gentleness? When we were at infinite distance from Him, He brought the love for us into comparison with that toward Himself, and said that it 'is like this'. He puts the measures of either as nearly the same, of the one He says, 'with all your heart, and with all your soul', but of the love towards one's neighbor, He says, 'as yourself'. When we are fond of anyone, we say, if you love him, then you love me. So, He also showed this and said, 'is like it'; to Peter, He said, 'If you love Me, feed My sheep'" (John 21:16). "Observe how the Law has two virtues: (1) abstinence from evils, for it 'works no harm', and (2) the working of good deeds. 'For it is,' he says, 'the fulfilling (or filling up) of the Law' (Matthew 5:18). It does not bring before us instruction only on moral duties in a concise form, but makes the accomplishment of them easy also.

He was not just careful that we should become acquainted with things that are profitable to us, but also the doing of them was a great assistance to us. He did not just accomplish some part of the Commandments, but the whole sum of virtue in us. Let us then love one another, since in this way we shall also love God, Who loves us. He considers you worthy to share His love, and hates you when you don't share it. For man's love is full of envy and grudging; but God's love is free from all passion; therefore, He seeks for those to share His love. For He says, love with Me, and then I will love you the more. These are the words of a vehement lover! If you love My brethren, then I will also reckon Myself to be greatly beloved of you. For He vehemently desires our salvation, and this He showed from ancient times. Hear what He said when He was forming man, 'Let Us make man in Our Image', and again, 'Let Us make a helper for him. It is not good for him to be alone' (Genesis 2:18). And when man had transgressed, He rebuked him, but observe how gently. He did not say, 'Wretch! After receiving so great benefits, have you trusted the devil, and left your Benefactor, to take up with the evil spirit?' But what did He say? 'Who told you that you were naked, unless you have eaten of the Tree, which is the only one I commanded you not to eat of?' (Genesis 3:11).

This is as if a father were to say to a child, who was ordered not to touch a sword, and then disobeyed and got wounded, 'How did you come to be wounded? You came so by not listening to me.' You see they are the words of a friend rather than a master, of a friend despised, and not even then forsaking. Let us then imitate Him, and when we need to rebuke, let us preserve this moderation." Tertullian (*An Answer to the Jews*, I, vii, 2. P. 152-153) stated that Adam, in the Garden, knew the Law given to Moses in a condensed form, and he gives evidence for this from the Scriptures. This condensed form certainly included loving God and neighbor. "Why should people believe that God, the founder of the universe, the Governor of the whole world (Jeremiah 31:27 LXX (37:27), Hosea 2:23, Zechariah 10:9, Matthew 13:31-43), had given a Law through Moses to one people, and not to all nations? Unless He had given it to everyone, He would not have permitted proselytes out of the nations to have access to it. He gave to all nations the same Law, which at definite times He directed should be observed, when He willed, through whom He willed, and as He willed.

In the beginning of the world, He gave to Adam and Eve a Law, that they were not to eat of the fruit of the tree planted in the middle of Paradise; if they did otherwise, they were to die (Genesis 2:16-17, 3:2-3). In this Law given to Adam, we recognize in embryo all the precepts, which afterwards sprouted when given through Moses. If they had loved the Lord their God, they would not have disobeyed His precept (Genesis 3:6). If they had loved their neighbor (here it is worth comparing the following: Leviticus 19:18, Matthew 22:34-40, Matthew 19:19, Mark 12:28-34, Luke 10 :25-28, Romans 13:9, Galatians 5:14, James 2:8, Deuteronomy 6:4-5, Exodus 20:12-17, Deuteronomy 5:16-21), that is, themselves, they would not have believed the persuasion of the serpent, and thus would not have committed murder upon themselves, falling from immortality, by disobeying God's precept. They also would have abstained from theft, stealthily tasting the fruit of the tree (Genesis 3:12-13); they would not have been anxious to hide beneath a tree to escape the view of the Lord their God (Genesis 3:8-9).

Further, they would not have made themselves partners with the lies of the devil, by believing him that they would be 'like God' (Genesis 3:4-5). And thus, they would not have offended God either, as their Father, if they had not coveted another's, they would not have tasted of the unlawful fruit." "Therefore, in this general and primordial Law of God, we recognize all the precepts of the Mosaic Law, which germinated when disclosed at their proper times.

For the subsequent addition of a Law is the work of the same Being who had before given a precept; it is His function subsequently to train those, whom He had formed as righteous creatures. Before the Law of Moses, I contend that there was a Law unwritten, which was habitually understood naturally, and by the fathers was habitually kept. How was Noah 'found righteous' (Genesis 6:9, 7:1, Hebrews 11:7), if in his case the righteousness of a natural Law had not preceded him? How was Abraham accounted 'a friend of God' (Isaiah 41:8, James 2:23), if not on the ground of righteousness, in the observance of a natural Law? How was Melchizedek named 'priest (See Genesis 14:18; Psalm 109(110):4; Hebrews 5:10, 7:1-3, 10, 15, 17) of the Most High God,' if before the Levitical priesthood, there were no Levites who offered sacrifices to God? It was after the above-mentioned patriarchs that the Law was given to Moses, 430 years after Abraham at their Exodus from Egypt (Genesis 15:13, Exodus 12:40-42, Acts 7:6).

From this we understand that God's Law preceded Moses, and was not first given at Sinai but existed in Paradise. It was updated for the patriarchs, and again for the Jews, at definite periods and even set forth to the Gentiles. We Are Like the Man Fallen Among Thieves. Of course, there are many ways where we are like the man who fell among thieves. Sin, the passions, covetousness have wounded us and the devil has beaten us up.

As we get mired in sin, we feel like we are half dead. Christ, who was even called a Samaritan by His enemies (John 8:48), doesn't pass us by, but comes to help us. He pours wine and oil on our wounds: the wine is an antiseptic, like discipline, that may cause temporary pain as it does its work. The oil is soothing, like compassion, and seals the wounds to prevent further infection. After carrying us to a place, the Church, where we can be taken care of, our Good Samaritan gives us two denarii, which is like the servant who received two talents from his master. If we need more, He will provide more later.

Clement of Alexandria (*Salvation of the Rich* Man, 27-30) stated that true love, such as shown by the Samaritan, buds into well-doing, since "a man is justified by works, and not by faith only" (James 2:24). Our love is directed first to God, then to our neighbor.

Love shown to our neighbor, God accepts as if done to Himself. On another level, we are like the wounded man lying on the road, and Christ is the Good Samaritan "The Master accordingly, when asked, 'Which is the greatest of the Commandments?', said, 'You shall love the Lord your God with all your soul, and with all your strength' (Matthew 22:36-38). That no commandment is greater than this, He says, with good reason; it commands us regarding the Greatest God Himself. Being loved by Him beforehand, it is impious for us to regard anything else older or more excellent." "The second in order, and not any less than this, He says, is, 'You shall love your neighbor as yourself' (Matthew 22:39); that is, God above yourself. When the lawyer inquired, 'Who is my neighbor?' (Luke 10:29), He did not specify the blood relation, the fellow-citizen, the proselyte, him that had been circumcised, or the man who uses the same Law.

But He introduces one on his way down from Jerusalem to Jericho, and represents Him stabbed by robbers, thrown half-dead on the road, passed by the priest, looked sideways at by the Levite, but pitied by the vilified and excommunicated Samaritan. He did not, like those, pass casually, but provided such things as the man in danger required, such as oil, bandages, a beast of burden, money for the inn-keeper (part given now, and part promised). 'Which of them was neighbor to him that suffered these things?' On his answering, 'He that showed mercy to him' (Luke 10:36-37), He replied, 'Go, therefore, and do likewise', since love buds into well-doing."

"In both the Commandments, then, He introduces love; but distinguishes it in order. *He assigns to God the first part of love, and allots the second to our neighbor.* He has pitied us most of all, we who were all but put to death with many wounds, fears, lusts, passions, pains, deceits, and pleasures by the rulers of darkness? Of these wounds the only physician is Jesus, who cuts out the passions thoroughly by the root. He does not do as the Law does, with bare effects [notice here: He does not just say, "Thou shall not" to a stiff-necked people, but calls to those who have a willing heart. another place, 'He that receives you; receives Me; and he that doesn't receive you, rejects Me'" (Matthew 10:40; Luke 10:16)], but applies His ax to the roots of wickedness. He it is that poured wine on our wounded souls that brought the oil, which flows from the compassions of the Father, and gave it abundantly. He it is that produced the bindings of health and salvation that cannot be undone, Faith, Hope, Love. He it is that subjected angels, and principalities, and powers to serve us. They also shall be delivered from the vanity of the world through the revelation of the glory of the sons of God. We are therefore to love Him equally with God. And he who loves Christ, Jesus does His will and keeps His Commandments. 'For not everyone that said to Me, Lord, Lord, shall enter the kingdom of heaven; but he that does the will of My Father' (Matthew 7:21). And 'Why call Me Lord, Lord, and not do the things which I say?' (Luke 6:46) 'And blessed are you who see and hear what neither righteous men nor prophets' have seen or heard (Matthew 13:16-17), if you do what I say." "He then is first who loves Christ; and second, he who loves and cares for those who have believed on Him.

For whatever is done to a disciple, the Lord accepts as done to Himself, and reckons the whole as His. 'Come, you blessed of My Father, inherit the kingdom prepared for you from the foundation of the world. For I was hungry, and you gave Me to eat' (Matthew 25:35 *etc.*). And in another place, 'He that receives you; receives Me; and he that doesn't receive Me, rejects Me'" (Matthew 10:40; Luke 10:16).

Ambrose of Milan (*Two Books Concerning Repentance*, I, xi, 50-52) applied the imagery of the wounded man, who was helped by the Samaritan, to those who have lapsed (denied the Faith) under persecution and succumbed to the pleasures and comforts of this life. In this way, he is wounded and half dead, and he needs both the comfort of the oil and the discipline or disinfectant of the wine. "It is a twofold grace that everyone who believes might, in addition, suffer for the Lord Jesus. He who believes receives His grace, but he receives a second, if his faith is crowned by suffering. Peter received grace before he suffered, but when he suffered, he received a second gift. And many who have not had the grace to suffer for Christ have nevertheless had the grace of believing on Him." "Therefore, 'everyone that believes in Him should not perish' (John 3:15-16). Let no one, whatever his condition, fear that he will perish, even after a fall. It may come to pass that the Good Samaritan may find someone going down from Jerusalem to Jericho; that is, falling back from the martyr's conflict to the pleasures of this life and the comforts of the world.

We may be wounded by robbers, that is, by persecutors, and left half dead. That Good Samaritan, Who is the Guardian of our souls - for the word 'Samaritan' means Guardian - won't pass him by, but tend and heal him." "He doesn't pass him by, because He sees in him some signs of life, so that there is hope that he may recover. Doesn't it seem to you that he who has fallen is half alive if faith sustains any breath of life? He is dead who completely casts God out of his heart. He who does not completely cast Him out, but under pressure from torments has denied Him for a time, is half dead. If he is dead, you cannot ask him to repent, seeing he cannot be healed? If he is half dead, pour in oil and wine, not wine without oil, oil for comforting and wine for the sting of disinfectant. Place him on your beast, give him over to the host, lay out two denarii for his cure, be a neighbor to him. You cannot be a neighbor unless you have compassion on him; for no one can be called a neighbor unless he has healed, not killed, another.

If you wish to be called a neighbor, Christ says to you, 'Go and do likewise'" (Luke 10:37). Gregory the Great, Pope of Rome, wrote (*Book of Pastoral Rule*, II, 6) to shepherds in the Church regarding the balance between compassion and discipline, where both are necessary. One extreme is the High Priest Eli, who was unable to discipline his sons out of excess compassion and lost everything.

On the other hand, *harsh discipline without compassion represents a lack of love*. The Good Samaritan exhibits a balance in that he poured wine on the man's wounds as an antiseptic (discipline) but also poured oil on the wounds to soothe them (compassion). "Eli, overcome by false affection, would not punish his delinquent sons, and smote himself along with his sons before the strict Judge (1 Samuel 4:17-18). God said to him, 'You have honored your sons more than Me' (1 Samuel 2:29). The Lord also criticized the shepherds of Israel saying, 'That which was broken you have not bound up, and that which was cast away you have not brought back' (Ezekiel 34:4). One who has fallen away is brought back when anyone who has fallen into sin is recalled to a state of righteousness by pastoral diligence. For binding a fracture is similar to discipline subduing a sin; if not done, the injured might bleed to death for lack of the wound being compressed and constrained adequately. But often a fracture is made worse, when it is bound too tight, so that the cut is more severely felt from being constrained improperly.

Wounds of sin in subordinates should be done with great carefulness, so that it exercises discipline against delinquents, but retains loving-kindness. Care should be taken that a ruler shows himself to his subjects as a mother in loving-kindness, and as a father in discipline. It should be done with anxious overview, so that neither discipline is rigid nor loving-kindness is lax. There is much lacking both to discipline and to compassion, if one is used without the other. Rulers ought to exercise both compassions justly considerate, and discipline affectionately severe towards their subjects. For the Truth teaches, the man is brought by the care of the Samaritan half dead into the inn, and both wine and oil are applied to his wounds (Luke 10:34); the wine to make them smart, the oil to soothe them. For whoever superintends the healing of wounds needs to administer the wine to the smart of pain, and in oil the softness of loving-kindness.

Through wine *what is festering may be purged, and through oil what is curable may be soothed*. Gentleness must be mingled with severity; a sort of compound must be made of both, so that subjects are neither overcome by too much severity, nor relaxed by too great kindness. This is well signified by that ark of the tabernacle, in which, together with the tablets, there was a rod and manna (Hebrews 9:4). With knowledge of sacred Scripture in the good ruler's heart there is the rod of constraint, there should be also the manna of sweetness. David said, 'Your rod and Your staff, they have comforted me' (Psalm 22(23):4). For *with a rod we are disciplined, with a staff we are supported*. If, then, there is the constraint of the rod for striking, there should be also the comfort of the staff for supporting.

Therefore, let there be love, but not weakness; let there be vigor, but not aggravation; *let there be zeal, but not senseless burning*; let there be pity; but not sparing more than is expedient. Justice and mercy blend themselves together in the best rule. Irenaeus of Lyon (*Against Heresies*, III, xvii, 3.) likened the dew on the fleece for Gideon to the Holy Spirit diffusing throughout the world. We are the ones who had fallen among thieves that the Holy Spirit cares for; we receive the two denarii for our care to make us fruitful and bring an increase to our Master "Gideon, foreseeing the gracious gift of God, changed his request, and prophesied that there would be dryness upon the fleece of wool (a type of the people), on which alone at first there had been dew (Judges 6:36-40). This indicates that those people should no longer have the Holy Spirit from God, as Isaiah said, 'I will also command the clouds, that they rain no rain upon it' (Isaiah 5:6). But that the dew, which is the Spirit of God, who descended upon the Lord, should be diffused throughout the earth. This is 'the spirit of wisdom and understanding, the spirit of counsel and might, the spirit of knowledge and piety, the spirit of the fear of God' (Isaiah 11:2).

This Spirit He conferred on the Church, sending the Comforter from heaven throughout the entire world. The Lord also told us that the devil, like lightning, was thrown down from heaven. We need the dew of God, that we might not be consumed by fire, nor rendered unfruitful. Where we have an accuser, there we need an Advocate, the Lord commending to the Holy Spirit His own man, who had fallen among thieves. He Himself had compassion, and bound up his wounds, giving two royal denarii. We, receiving by the Spirit the image and superscription of the Father and the Son, might *cause the denarius entrusted to us to be fruitful, counting out the increase to the Lord.*"

John Chrysostom (*Homilies on Hebrews,* X, 7-8.) stated that we should not be overly curious about the spiritual condition of those that we give help to. The Samaritan didn't do this to the wounded man, but gave him help immediately. *Being overly curious and selective can take away the greater part of charity.* Even if we are dealing with an unbeliever, he may be sanctified by someone else. "I beseech you, brethren, to minister to the saints. For every believer is a saint in that he is a believer. Though he is a person living in the world, he is a saint. 'The unbelieving husband is sanctified by the wife, and the unbelieving wife by the husband' (1 Corinthians 7:14).

See how the faith makes the saint? If then we see even a secular person in misfortune, let us stretch out a hand to him. Let us not be zealous for those only who dwell in the mountains; they are indeed saints both in manner of life and in faith; these others however are saints by their faith, and some of them also in manner of life. Let us not, if we see a monk thrown into prison, in that case go in to visit; but if it is a secular person, refuse to go in. He also is a saint and a brother." "What then, you say, if he is unclean and polluted? Listen to Christ saying, 'Judge not that you be not judged' (Matthew 7:1). Help him for God's sake! Even if we see a heathen in misfortune, we ought to show kindness to him, and to every man without exception who is in misfortunes, and much more to a believer who is in the world. Listen to Paul, saying, 'Do good to all men, but especially to those who are of the household of faith' (Galatians 6:10). I don't know why this notion has been introduced, or where this custom has prevailed. For he that only helps monks, and with others is over-curious in his inquiries, and says, 'unless he be worthy, unless he be righteous, unless he works miracles, I won't stretch out my hand'; such a one has taken away the greater part of charity. In time he will destroy the act of charity itself. And yet that is charity, which is shown towards sinners, towards the guilty.

This is charity, not the pitying those who have done well, but those who have done wrong." "Listen to the Parable! 'A certain man went down from Jerusalem to Jericho, and fell among thieves' (Luke 10:30-37). When they had beaten him, they left him next to the road, having badly bruised him. A certain Levite came, and when he saw him, he passed by; a priest came, and when he saw him, he hurried past. A certain Samaritan came, and showed great care for him. He 'bandaged his wounds' (Luke 10:34), dropped oil on them, set him upon his donkey, 'brought him to the inn, said to the host, Take care of him' (Luke 10:35). Observe his great liberality, 'I will give you whatever you shall spend'. Who then is his neighbor? 'He that showed mercy on him! Go then also and do likewise' (Luke 10:37). What a parable He spoke! He didn't say that a Jew did this to a Samaritan, but that a Samaritan showed all that liberality.

Having then heard these things, let us not care only for 'those that are of the household of faith' (Galatians 6:10), and neglect others. If you see any one in affliction, do not be curious to inquire further. His being in affliction involves a just claim to your aid. For if you see a donkey choking, you raise him up, and do not curiously inquire whose he is. Much more about a man, one ought not to be over-curious in inquiring whose he is. He is God's, whether he is heathen or Jew; since even if he is an unbeliever, still he needs help. If it had been committed to you to inquire and to judge, you would have had something to say. But, as it is, his misfortune does not allow you to search out these things. Even about men in good health, it is not right to be over-curious, or to be a busybody in other men's matters; much less about those that are in affliction.

Appendix C
Close the Loop on Tithes, Festivals and Alms

In Old Testament Tithing Under Mosaic Law, there were three types of tithes, often referred to by scholars today as the first, second and third tithe. The righteous Tobin described these three tithes and his almsgiving (Tobit 1:5-8 LXX). In the Old Testament, they are referred to as the tithe, festival offerings, and alms. Since the Mosaic Law was given to Moses in the wilderness, no central city had yet been established where one might bring one's tithes. Later this would be Jerusalem where the Temple was located. At the place that the Lord will choose (this is, Jerusalem, Deuteronomy 12:5-7) everyone was to gather and bring their:

- Burnt offerings
- Sacrifices
- Tithes
- Alms or gifts
- Vows or promises
- Free will offerings

The firstborn of everything - Tithes: The first tithe was used for the support of the Levites, who had no land for an inheritance (Numbers 18:20-24). The way this worked in an agricultural economy was that every 10th sheep (for example) coming into the sheepfold went to the Lord (Leviticus 27:30-33) and was received by the Levites. The Levites, in turn, contributed a tithe of what they received to the high priest, which was Aaron and his descendants (Numbers 18:26-28). Following their model, most Orthodox jurisdictions in the United States contribute a percentage to their bishop (metropolitan) who in turn gives to the archdiocese and who in turn gives to the patriarch (Kern, 2007).

Festivals: The tithes and other vows, alms and freewill offerings were to be brought to Jerusalem three times per year at *Passover, Pentecost and Tabernacles* where everyone rejoiced before the Lord. The first tithe belonged to the Levites; the tithe used at the festivals was actually a second tithe, since everyone used it, not just the Levites (Deuteronomy 12:12-19).

Alms: Every third year, an additional portion was set aside for the aliens, the orphans, the widows and the Levites (Deuteronomy 14:28-29, 26:12-

13). Josephus wrote (*Antiquities of the Jews*. IV, viii, 22, 240) that this was a third tithe and it had been set up that way from the days of Moses. Following the giving of this third tithe, the people were to say "before the Lord" that they have not withheld any and to ask the Lord for a blessing that they might continue to have a land flowing with milk and honey (Deuteronomy 26:12-15). This third tithe was all that the widow of Nain could expect if the people were faithful to follow the Mosaic Law. Since Jesus criticized the Scribes and Pharisees for devouring widows' houses (Matthew 23:14), the widow of Nain could probably expect nothing and was probably in dire straits with the death of her son.

The harvest of the land was dependent on the peoples' observing the Lord's statutes. For example, every seventh year, the land was to lie fallow with no planting or reaping (Leviticus 25:2-5). If the people observed the Lord's statues, the sixth year's crops would be extensive enough to carry them for three years, or until the eighth-year crop was in (Leviticus 25:18-22). The same was true with the tithe; the more they gave, the more they had.

The same applied to helping the poor. They were to freely open their hand to him and generously lend him sufficient for his needs (Deuteronomy 15:7-8). To not do so was a sin and the poor man may cry to the Lord against his rich neighbors. In being generous to him, however, "the Lord will bless them in all their work and in everything they do" (Deuteronomy 15:9-11).

The Firstborn: The firstborn of both man and beast was devoted to the Lord (Exodus 13:2). The Lord intended the firstborn of man to be devoted to Him as priests. However, when all the people sinned by worshipping the golden calf, it was only the Levites who responded to Moses' call to return to the Lord (Exodus 32:26). Therefore, the Lord dedicated the Levites instead of the firstborn to serve in the Tabernacle (Numbers 3:12-13). All the firstborn of non-Levites and all the firstborn of unclean animals were to be redeemed (Numbers 28:15-16). All the firstborn of clean animals were to be offered as a sacrifice, where the priests received the meat of the animals after it was offered (Numbers 18:17-19). The dedication of the firstborn was in addition to the tithes. At the time of Joshua, the Canaanites and the surrounding nations took this one step further and offered the firstborn of man as a human sacrifice. This was heresy and implied that man could redeem himself by himself.

Where Did Tithes Originate? The practice of tithing was well established at the time of Abraham when Abraham (Abram) gave a tithe to Melchizedek (Hebrews 7:1-6). Two generations later Jacob made a vow or promise to give the Lord a tithe upon his safe return home (Genesis 28:20-22). Vows or votive offerings were well established then also. [In the Orthodox Church we have a similar tradition with the *tamata*. A *tama* is a vow to a saint or Jesus or the Theotoko for a favorable outcome of a specific need. Quite often, the *tamata* are silver pictures of the need (for example an eye or a leg, having a special service – liturgy in a remote ecclesia named after the specific saint, *etc.* and they are hung in front of the intercessor saint's icon].

Sacrifice had already been established before Cain killed Abel, and it was jealousy over the Lord's acceptance of Abel's offering that led Cain to kill Abel (Genesis 4:2-5). Had Cain and Abel been instructed to give tithes? The Lord taught them to make clothes out of animal skins (Genesis 3:21); yet people before the flood weren't meat-eaters (Genesis 9:2-4). The meat of the animals must have been used for sacrifices and the skin for clothing, just as the priests later received the skin of the animal that they helped to sacrifice (Leviticus 7:8). [There is no direct linkage to animal sacrifice in the Bible in the verses mentioned. However, with the human knowledge and logic we can project that animal sacrifice must have been a practice due to the results of having animal clothing and so on].

New Testament Tithe: One might contend that tithing is Old Testament Law and is not applicable to life in the New Testament. But in a discussion with the Scribes and Pharisees who paid a strict tithe of everything they received, Jesus criticized them for neglecting weightier matters of the Law (justice, mercy and faith). He said, "These you ought to have done without leaving the others (*i.e.* tithing) undone" (Matthew 23:23).

Under the Old Testament Law, the Prophet Malachi spoke to the people of his day about robbing God by refusing to contribute their tithes: "But you say, 'How have we robbed Thee?' In tithes and offerings! You are cursed with a curse, for you are robbing Me, the whole nation of you. Bring the whole tithe into the storehouse, so that there may be food in My house. Test Me now in this, says the Lord of Hosts, if I will not open for you the windows of heaven and pour out for you a blessing until it overflows" (Malachi 3:8-10: compare Deuteronomy 26:12-15).

In the Early Church, people gave not just a Tithe, but they sold everything they had and laid the proceeds at the Apostles' feet for the Apostles to do as they pleased (Acts 2:45, 4:36-37). This demonstrates a singular detachment from worldly possessions among members of the Early Church.

New Testament Alms: The Apostle Paul was involved in bringing alms to the Church in Jerusalem on at least two occasions. One occurred during a famine in 45 A.D. where Paul and Barnabas brought relief from Antioch to the churches in Judea (Acts 11:27-30). On another occasion in 57 A.D. at the end of Paul's 3rd Missionary Journey, Paul collected alms from the Churches in Achaia (Corinth and Athens), Macedonia, (Berea, Philippi, Thessalonica) and Galatia (Iconium, Lystra, Derbe) to bring to Jerusalem (Acts 24:17). Paul felt it was the duty of the Gentile churches to help out materially since they benefited spiritually from Jerusalem (Romans 15:25-27). The collection of these alms was systematic and well planned (1 Corinthians 16:1-4). Even though the churches in Macedonia were mired in deep poverty, they still managed to give alms well beyond their ability (2 Corinthians 8:1-4).

Paul's References to Tithing: 2 Corinthians 9:6-11: In the Epistle of the 18th Sunday after Pentecost we read two specific references from the OT (Psalm 112:9 and Isaiah 55:10). Psalm 112 begins with "How Blessed is the man who fears the Lord, who greatly delights in His commandments" (Psalm 112:1). This man has descendants who are mighty (Psalm 112:2), has wealth in his house (Psalm 112:3) and does not fear evil tidings (Psalm 112:7). He is light arising in the darkness (Psalm 112:4); he is gracious and lends his money (Psalm 112:5); and he freely gives to the poor (Psalm 112:9, quoted in 2 Corinthians 9:9). The implication is that the reason he is strong and wealthy is because he gives and lends. That is, he is not attached to his worldly possessions, and there is a great deal of wisdom in this.

In Isaiah 55:10, the prophet spoke about how the Lord's ways and thoughts are higher than our ways and thoughts as much as the heavens are higher than the earth (Isaiah 55:8-12). In the context of the epistle lesson, the implication is that the Lord has the foresight to see the long-term fruit of one's generosity, very much like a crop that can be harvested. The imagery Isaiah used were rain and snow as compared to the Word of God. The rain and snow come down from heaven, water the earth and make it sprout with seed and thus bread before returning to heaven (as evaporation). So, also the Word does not return empty without accomplishing what He desires and succeeding in that which He sent.

A Cheerful Giver: Paul used this reference to Isaiah in connection with giving alms and tithes. The seed that we sow, like rain and the Word of God, will return. If we sow sparingly, we will reap sparingly; if we sow bountifully, we will reap bountifully (2 Corinthians 9:6). There is an analogy here to the 6th year crop (Leviticus 25:18-22). The Lord will see to it that "all grace abounds toward us that we may have an abundance for every good work" (2 Corinthians 9:8), and that we "are enriched in everything for all liberality" (2 Corinthians 9:11).

However, God is not a tax collector; we are not forced to do this. In the Early Church, people were not forced to sell all that they had. God loves a cheerful giver, not one doing so "grudgingly or of necessity" (2 Corinthians 9:7). A cheerful giver is like the camel that passes through the eye of the needle easily because his pack or burden comes off easily (Matthew 19:22-26). To understand what this means, we need to understand how ancient cities were constructed.

The main gates of most cities in ancient times were huge wooden structures set in an archway and often overlaid with brass for strength and flame proofing. At night, the gates were closed and locked with a bar on the inside and not opened until morning. Travelers that arrived late in the day after the gates were closed were forced to spend the night outside the city unless there was some provision for them to get into the city. Outside the city, law and order did not exist at night and travelers were at the mercy of outlaws. This is still the case today in some third world countries.

To deal with this situation, many ancient cities had a "needle's eye gate" which was a small, low door beside the main gate. Such a feature existed on at least one of the gates of Jerusalem and Damascus (Weiss, 1972 pp 24-25). A man could fit easily through the "needle's eye gate," but a camel, being a large animal, could not fit easily. If the camel's pack (which could weight up to 1,000 pounds) were removed and the camel were made to kneel, the camel could just barely crawl through the "needle's eye gate." The statement Jesus made, that it is easier for a camel to go through the needle's eye gate than for a rich man to enter the Kingdom of God, made use of the above imagery. Like the camel, the rich man first needs to unload his pack or burden.

The parable of the sower refers to this pack as "the cares of this world, the deceit of riches, the desire for other things" (Mark 4:19) and the pleasures of life (Luke 8:14). These are things that appeal to our flesh and which can lead us away from God. Some of the early disciples, like Barnabas (one of the Seventy) sold a large amount of property and brought the entire proceeds to the Twelve (Acts 4:34-37). Ananias and Sapphira on the other hand, were caught in the deceit of riches and held back part of the proceeds – and paid dearly (Acts 5:1-10).

A cheerful giver, then, is one whose pack or burden comes off easily (Matthew 19:22- 26). This aspect of the Christian life has been little understood in our generation in the West. *To be a cheerful giver takes faith.* As John Chrysostom said (Chrysostom Homilies on 2 Corinthians XIX, v. 8 p 369), "Many persons are afraid to give alms, saying, 'In case I become poor; in case I need aid from others.'" To give when one expects a return is an investment; even tax collectors do that! To give without expecting a return is being God-like (Luke 6:31-36). As Chrysostom said (Homilies on 2 Corinthians XIX v. 7 pp 369), "If one is doing work of virtue, and yet all that is done is of necessity, it is shorn of its reward; with reason also Paul labors at this point."

John Chrysostom noted (*Commentary on Acts* VII v 46) that when, "All that believed were together, and had all things in common" (Acts 2:44), this early Christian community was a collection of cheerful givers. The result was very beneficial not just to them but also to the community. They immediately obtained a reward, that is, the 'hundredfold' that Jesus spoke of (Mark 10:29-30), for having left everything for Christ's sake. In this case, the reward was 'the favor with all the people' (Acts 2:47).

"They had become angels all of a sudden, all of them; continuing in prayer and hearing, they saw that spiritual things are common, no one there had more than another, and they speedily came together, to the same thing in common. This does not mean that they were together in one place, but that this was an angelic commonwealth, not to call anything of theirs their own. The root of evils was cut out; by what they did, they showed what they had heard. This was what he said, 'Save yourselves from this perverse generation' (Acts 2:40), and 'daily continuing with one accord in the temple' (Acts 2:46). Daily they went up as to a sacred place, and frequently we find Peter and John doing this; for at present they disturbed none of the Jewish observances (See note 1).

Observe the increase of piety; they abandoned their riches, rejoiced and had great gladness, for greater were the riches they received without labor. None reproached, none envied, none grudged; no pride, no contempt was there. As children they accounted themselves to be under teaching; as newborn babies, such was their disposition. No talk of 'mine' and 'yours' then. Gladness waited at their table; no one seemed to eat of his own, or of another's. The poor man knew no shame, the rich no haughtiness. This is gladness! The latter deemed himself the obliged and fortunate party; the others felt themselves as honored by this, and closely were they bound together. When people increase their wealth, there are apt to be insults, pride, grudging; therefore, Paul said, 'Not grudgingly, or of necessity' (2 Corinthians 9:7). See of how many things Paul bears witness to them! Genuine faith, upright conduct, perseverance in hearing, in prayers, in singleness, in cheerfulness! Two things there were which might deject them, their abstinent living, and the loss of their property (Kern, 2005; see also Note 2). Yet on both these accounts did they rejoice, and they 'had favor with all the people' (Acts 2:47). For everyone loves men of this character, as common fathers! They conceived no malice toward each other; they committed all to the grace of God.

There was no fear even though they had taken their position in the midst of dangers. By singleness, he denotes their entire virtue, far surpassing their contempt of riches, their abstinence, and their perseverance in prayer. Thus, they offered pure praise to God! Observe here how they immediately obtain their reward by 'having favor with all the people'! They were engaging, and highly beloved. Who would not prize and admire their simplicity of character; who would not be linked to one in whom was nothing underhanded?"

Removal of Our Sins: There is a greater benefit to giving alms than most people realize. In the giving of alms there is a working of relief from our sins. Christ had said, 'He that receives a prophet in the name of a prophet, shall receive a prophet's reward' (Matthew 10:41). John Chrysostom stated (*Homilies on Philippians* I, v. 7) that there are similar rewards for giving alms; in doing so with the right motive, we receive relief from our sins. This takes some discernment, however, and it is not at all a case of purchasing indulgences by giving alms. If the Judge actually receives us into His eternal Kingdom for seeing Him hungry and feeding Him (Matthew 25:34-40), there must be a removal of our offenses involved in the proper giving of alms. However, we should not be overly curious about who it is that we give alms to and whether he is deserving of such.

Imposters and con men can sometimes appear to be more deserving than Christ Himself. "If one gives alms as if granting a favor to the receiver, it would be better for him not to give at all. For my concern is not that the saints may be supported. Even if you don't give, someone else will. What I want is that you may have a relief from your own sins. But he that gives as if it were a favor will have no relief. For it is not the giving of alms that is doing alms, but the doing it with readiness; it is the rejoicing, and the feeling grateful to him that receives. 'Not grudgingly', Paul said, 'or of necessity; for God loves a cheerful giver' (2 Corinthians 9:7).

Except one give in this manner, let him not give at all; for that would be a loss, not a giving of alms. If you know that you (the giver) will gain, not they (the receivers), be assured that your gain becomes greater. The body of those receiving your alms is fed, but your soul is approved; for them, not one of their sins is forgiven when they receive, but for you, the greater part of your offenses is removed."

John Chrysostom, *Homilies on Philippians, I, v. 7.* "Let us share with the poor in their great prizes. Adopt Christ in your almsgiving, and you shall have great security. If there is any of the rulers of the church that lives in abundance and needs nothing, though he is a saint, don't give to him, but prefer to him one that is in need, though he is not as admirable. Christ wills this, as when He said, 'If you make a dinner, don't call your friends, or your kinsmen, but call the maimed, the lame and the blind, that cannot recompense you' (Luke 14:12-14). One needs discernment in paying such attention to the poor, the hungry, the thirsty, those who need clothing, strangers, and those who from riches have been reduced to poverty. For He said not simply, 'I was fed', but 'I was hungry', for, 'You saw Me hungry and fed Me' (Matthew 25:35).

There are two parts to the claim, both that he is a saint and that he is hungry. For if he that is simply hungry ought to be fed, much more when he is a saint that is hungry. If then he is a saint, but not in need, don't give; for there is no gain for you in this. And neither did Christ ask you to do it; or rather, he is not a saint if he is in abundance and allows himself to receive. Do you see that these things have been said to you for your profit? Feed the hungry, that you may not feed the fire of hell. The hungry man, eating what is yours, sanctifies also what remains" (Luke 11:41).

"Think how the widow-maintained Elijah; she did not feed more than she was fed; she did not give more than she received. This also takes place in a much greater thing. For it is not a 'barrel of flour,' or 'a jar of oil' (III King LXX or 1 Kings 17:14); but 'a hundredfold and eternal life' (Matthew 19:21, 29) is the recompense for doing so. You become the mercy of God; the spiritual food; a pure leaven. She was a widow; famine was pressing, and nothing hindered her. She had children, and she still did not hold back (III Kings LXX or 1 Kings 17:12). This woman has become equal to her that cast in the two mites (Luke 21:1-4). She didn't say to herself, 'What shall I receive from this man? He stands in need of me. If he had any power, he would not be hungry; he would have broken the drought; he would not have been subject to this suffering. Perhaps he too offends God'. None of these things did she think of. Do you see how great a good it is to do well with simplicity, and not to be overly curious about the person who is benefited? If she had chosen to be curious, she would have doubted; she would not have believed."

"Abraham also, if he had chosen to be curious, would not have received angels. For it cannot be, that one who is exceedingly nice in these matters, should ever meet with them. Such people usually invite impostors. The pious man does not desire to appear pious, and does not clothe himself for show, and is likely to be rejected. But the impostor, as he makes a business of it, puts on a great deal of piety that is hard to see through. So that while he who does good, even to those who don't seem to be pious, will fall in with those who are pious; he who seeks out those who are thought to be pious, will often fall in with those who are not so.

Therefore, I ask you; let us do all things in simplicity. Let us even suppose that he is an impostor that comes; you are not asked to be curious about this. 'Give to everyone that asks you' (Luke 6:30); and, 'Deliver them that are led away to death, and redeem them that are appointed to be slain; be sure to help' (Proverbs 24:11 LXX). Yet most of those that are slain suffer this for some evil they are convicted of; still he said, 'Deliver them'. For in this shall we be like God, thus shall we be admired, and shall obtain those immortal blessings, which we all wish to be thought worthy of."

John Chrysostom addressed (*Homilies on I Timothy* XIV, vv. 9-10) widows in the Church and how they can help with hospitality. Be sure to do it yourself, like Abraham, not delegate it to a handmaid; otherwise you lose your reward. The stranger may feel bashful and unwilling to impose on us; we need to approach him as if we were receiving Christ, and as if we were receiving the honor of His Presence. In doing this for the poor stranger, the greater part of our sin is removed. "The hospitality here spoken of is not merely a friendly reception, but one given with zeal, cheerfulness and readiness, going about it as if one were receiving Christ Himself. The widows should perform these services themselves, not commit them to their handmaids. For Christ said, 'If I your Master and Lord have washed your feet, you ought also to wash one another's feet' (John 13:14). And though a woman may be very rich, of the highest rank, of noble birth and family, there is not the same distance between her and others, as between God and the disciples. If you receive the stranger as Christ, don't be ashamed, but rather glory. But if you can't receive him as Christ, don't receive him at all. 'He that receives you', He said, 'receives Me' (Matthew 10:40). If you do not receive him in this way, you have no reward.

Abraham was receiving men that passed as travelers, as he thought, and he did not leave it to his servants to make the preparations for their entertainment, but took the greater part of the service upon himself. He commanded his wife to mix the flour, though he had three hundred and eighteen servants born in his house (Genesis 18:6-7, 14:14), of whom there must have been many maidservants. But he wished that himself and his wife should have the reward, not of the cost only, but of the service.

Thus, we ought to exercise hospitality always by our own personal exertion that we may be sanctified, and our hands blessed. And if you give to the poor, don't hesitate to give it yourself, for it is not to the poor that it is given, but to Christ. Who is so wretched as to scornfully refuse to stretch out his own hand to Christ?" "This is hospitality; this is truly to do it for God's sake. But if you give orders with pride, though you ask the stranger to take the first place, it is not hospitality; it is not done for God's sake. The stranger requires much attendance, much encouragement, and with all this it is difficult for him not to feel bashful; for so delicate is his position, that while he receives the favor, he is ashamed.

That shame we ought to remove by the most attentive service, and to show by words and actions, that we do not think we are conferring a favor, but receiving one. So much does good will multiply the kindness! He, who considers himself a loser, and thinks that he is doing a favor, destroys all the merit of it. So, he who looks upon himself as receiving a kindness, increases the reward. 'For God loves a cheerful giver' (2 Corinthians 9:7). You are rather indebted to the poor man for receiving your kindness. If there were no poor, the greater part of your sins would not be removed. The poor are the healers of your wounds; their hands are medicinal to you. The physician, extending his hand to apply a remedy, does not exercise the healing more than the poor man, who stretches out his hand to receive your alms, and thus becomes a cure for your ills. You give your money, and with it your sins pass away.

Such were the Priests of old, of whom it was said, 'They eat up the sin of My people' (Hosea 4:8). Thus, you receive more than you give; you are benefited more than you benefit. You lend to God, not to men. You increase your wealth, rather than diminish it."

How Can We Obtain a Better Perspective? Who are some of the great examples of people who can be characterized as selfless givers? John Chrysostom gave (Homilies on 2 Corinthians XIX, v. 9 pp 369 and 371) two examples of people who excelled at generosity: the poverty-stricken woman who gave her last two mites to help the poor (Luke 21:1-4), and the woman who fed Elijah with the last handful of flour she had (III Kings LXX or1 Kings 17:10-16). "Once you have lived on what is sufficient; then if you have a mind to emulate that widow, we will lead you on to greater things than these. For you have not yet attained to the philosophy of that woman (see Luke 21: 1-4), who gave the two mites, while you are anxious about what is sufficient for your needs. She soared higher than this; for what was to have been her support; that she cast in, all of it.

Will you then still distress yourself about necessary things; and do you not blush to be outdone and left far behind by a woman? For she did not say the things we say, 'But what if when I have spent all, I am compelled to beg of another?' *In her generosity she stripped herself of all she had.* What shall we say of the widow in the time of the prophet Elijah? The risk she ran was not of poverty, but of death, and not her own only, but her children's too. She had no expectation of receiving anything from others, but she expected to die shortly. 'But,' one said, 'she saw the prophet, and that made her generous.'

But you see saints without number! You see the Lord of the prophets asking alms, and yet you do not become humane; even though you have coffers spewing one into another, you do not even give out of your excess. Was he a prophet that came to her, and did this persuade her to so great a generosity? This deserves much admiration, that she was persuaded that he was a great and wonderful person. For how was it that she, a barbarian woman and a foreigner, did not say, 'If he were a prophet, he would not have begged of me. If he were a friend of God, He would not have neglected him. If the Jews are suffering this punishment of famine because of sins, why does this man suffer?' But she entertained none of these thoughts; but opened her heart and her house to him, and set before him all she had. She put nature aside, disregarded her children, and preferred the stranger to everyone.

Consider then how great punishment will be laid up for us, if we are weaker than a foreigner, a barbarian woman, who knew nothing of the things, which we know! Just because we have strength of body, we are not automatically manly persons. Hear how Christ proclaims her! For He said, 'There were many widows in the days of Elijah, and to none of them was the prophet sent but to her'" (Luke 4:25, 26).

"Shall I say something great and startling? This woman gave more to hospitality, than our father Abraham. For she did not 'run to the herd' as he did (Genesis 18:7), but by that 'handful' (III Kings or 1 Kings 17:12) outstripped all that have been renowned for hospitality. For in this was Abraham's excellence that he entertained God; but hers, in that for the sake of the stranger she did not spare her children, even though she did not look for the things to come (Hebrews 11:9-10). But we, though a heaven exists, though a hell is threatened, though God has done such great things for us, we sink back listlessly. Let it not be so; let us 'scatter abroad', let us 'give to the poor' as we ought to give. For what is much and what little, God defines, not by the measure of what is given, but by the extent of the wealth of him that gives."

Gregory the Great, Pope of Rome, had (*The Book of Pastoral Rule*, III, 20) some encouragement and admonition to those who give compassionately to others. There are dangers such as pride, vainglory, and self-centeredness to watch out for, and there is a knowledge of and concern for those they serve to pay attention to. There are many references to this in the Scriptures that Gregory had words of illumination on. The bottom line is that *giving is a work of God and it requires the insight of the Holy Spirit regarding when and what to give.*

"Those who already give compassionately of their own should be admonished differently than those who desire to seize even what belongs to others. For those who already give are to be admonished not to lift themselves up in swelling thought above those to whom they impart earthly things. They should not think themselves better than others because they see others supported by them. Those who give should acknowledge themselves to be placed by the Lord as dispensers of temporal supplies, and to do their work all the more humbly from their understanding that the things which they dispense are not their own.

When they consider that they are appointed for the service of others, by no means let vainglory elate their minds, but let fear depress them.

"Also, it is needful for them to take anxious thought lest they distribute what has been committed to them unworthily; lest they bestow something to those on whom they ought to have spent nothing; or much to those on whom they ought to have spent little. Some dangers are that by hastiness they scatter unprofitably what they give; by tardiness they mischievously torment petitioners; or lest the thought of receiving a favor in return creep in. Other dangers are that the craving for transitory praise might extinguish the light of giving; that accompanying gloominess harass the offering of a gift; and that when they have done everything right, they give something to themselves, and so lose all the benefit they have accomplished." Gregory commented on references to giving in the Scriptures as follows:

- If any man serves as a deacon, let him do it as with the ability which God supplies (1 Peter 4:11). Donors should not attribute to themselves the virtue of their liberality.
- When you shall have done all those things, which are commanded you, say, 'We are unprofitable slaves, we have done that which was our duty to do' (Luke 17:10). Donors should not rejoice too much in benefits they bestow.
- God loves a cheerful giver (2 Corinthians 9:7). Gloominess should not spoil a donor's liberality.
- Do not let your left hand know what your right hand is doing (Matthew 6:3). Donors should not seek transitory praise for a gift bestowed. Gregory the Great, *The Book of Pastoral Rule*, III, 20. 230
- When you give a dinner, do not ask your friends, your brethren, your kinsmen, or your rich neighbors, lest they invite you back, and you are repaid. But when you give a feast, call the poor, the maimed, the lame, the blind and you shall be blessed; for they cannot repay you (Luke 14:12). Do not let the glory of the present life mix itself with the liberal giving of piety. Donors may not require a return for benefits bestowed.

- Do not say to your friend, go and come back, and tomorrow I will give it, when you have it with you (Proverbs 3:28). Donors should not supply too late what should be supplied at once.
- He that sows sparingly shall reap also sparingly (2 Corinthians 9:6). When much is necessary for donors to give, little should not be given.
- I do not mean that others should be eased and you burdened; but by an equality, that your abundance may supply their lack, and that their abundance also may supply your lack (2 Corinthians 8:13, 14). When donors ought to give little, they should not give too much, lest afterwards, badly enduring want themselves, break out into impatience.
- *Give to everyone that asks of you* (Luke 6:30). Donors should avoid giving nothing at all to those on whom they ought to bestow something.
- Give to the godly man, and do not help a sinner; do well to him that is lowly, but do not give to the ungodly (Ecclesiasticus 12:4-5 LXX). Donors should give nothing, not even something little, to those on whom they ought to bestow nothing at all.

John Chrysostom noted (*Homilies on 2 Corinthians*, XIX, v. 9 pp 369-371) that men return one favor with another; God will certainly do the same to us if we give even a little from our abundance. Some people worry that they will not have enough if they give to others. Chrysostom encouraged his people to try to live with just essentials. "A man who has received from you will not overlook the gifts, but will return the favors if he can; much more will Christ do so. If He routinely gives without receiving any return, how will He not give after receiving from you? 'What then,' said one, 'when some who have spent much come to need other men's help?' You speak of those that have spent their all; when you yourself don't give a penny. Promise to strip yourself of everything and then ask questions about such men. As long as you are stingy and give little of your substance, why throw out excuses and pretenses? I am not leading you to the lofty peak of complete poverty, but for the present I ask you to cut off your excess and to desire just sufficiency, which means using just those things, which it is impossible to live without. No one bars you from these, nor forbids you your daily food. I say food, not feasting; clothing, not ornament. If one should inquire accurately, this is in the best sense really feasting.

Consider which we should say more truly feasted, he whose diet was herbs, and who was in sound health; or he who had the table of a Sybarite (see note 3), and was full of disorders? Very plainly the former!

Therefore, let us seek nothing more than this. Let him that can be satisfied with beans and can keep in good health, seek for nothing more. Let him who is weaker and requires a diet including garden herbs, not be hindered by this. But if anyone is even weaker than this and requires the support of meat in moderation, we will not bar him either. We are not trying to injure anyone, but just trying to encourage men not to require more than they need."

The Fruits of Righteousness: Paul prayed not for riches nor for abundance, but for all sufficiency. In fleshly things, he asked for a sufficiency for them; but in spiritual things for abundance. Not in alms giving only but in all other things also, 'unto every good work' (2 Corinthians 9:8).

John Chrysostom (*Homilies on 2 Corinthians* XIX v. 9 pp 369-371) gave an example that is equally appropriate for the 4th Century and the 21st Century. Noticing what people do with their money, he said, "Do you not see how much others give to actors and harlots? Give at any rate the half to Christ as what they give to dancers. As much as they give for seeing vain shows on the stage (or screen), so much at any rate one ought to give to the hungry. For they clothe the sex kittens with untold gold; but not even with a threadbare garment the flesh of Christ, and that though beholding it naked (referring to the "lest of these my brethren; see (Matthew 25: 38-40).

What forgiveness does this deserve? How great a punishment does it not deserve, when he indeed bestows so much on her that ruins and shames him, but not the least thing on Him that saves him and makes him brighter? As long as one spends it on his belly and on drunkenness and dissipation, one never thinks of poverty. But when there is a need to relieve poverty, he becomes poorer than anybody. When feeding parasites and flatterers, he is as joyous as though he had fountains to spend from. But if he happens to see a poor man, then the fear of poverty besets him."

There are other things one can sow besides generosity (or lack of it). One can sow righteousness; doing so reaps kindness (Hosea 10:12). On the other hand, one can sow wickedness; this will reap injustice and lies (Hosea 10:13). Therefore, it behooves us to sow what we wish to receive.

As a country, the United States has been a world leader regarding charitable giving of all kinds, and this has not been limited to Christians. This fact alone has greatly helped the United States to maintain godliness, prosperity and justice because it teaches an unselfish attitude to the world. On the other hand, some surveys indicate that people in the United States spend large amounts of their income on various forms of entertainment. We can all do better by directing a little more of our income from entertainment toward feeding the poor.

Chrysostom concluded (*Homilies on 2 Corinthians* XIX v. 9 p 369), that "For this is the thing to be admired, that when they are kept, they are lost; but when dispersed abroad they abide forever. Now by 'righteousness' (2 Corinthians 9:10), here, he means love toward men. For this makes men righteous, consuming sins like a fire when it is plentifully poured out."

Cyprian of Carthage (*Treatises* VIII, 8-11) stated very strongly that there is a relationship between one's salvation and the giving of alms, and he illustrated this with the examples of Zacchaeus and Abraham. One who gives alms implicitly believes in God; he shows his faith by his giving of alms and exhibits the fruits of righteousness. Those who don't are barren and unfruitful. This may appear to Western Christians today as a works-based salvation, but perhaps they neglect to consider what is really going on in men's hearts. On the other hand, some people may fear that their estate may become exhausted if they give alms; this only shows unbelief and lack of faith. A larger concern is that we may lose our own soul out of a love for mammon if we refuse to give alms.

"Christ called those people the children of Abraham whom He sees aiding and nourishing the poor. For when Zacchaeus said, 'Behold, the half of my goods I give to the poor; and if I have done any wrong to any man, I restore fourfold.' Jesus answered and said, 'Salvation has this day come to this house, for he also is a son of Abraham' (Luke 19:8-9). For if

Abraham believed in God, and it was counted to him for righteousness (see Genesis 15:6; Rom. 4:3, 20-22; Galatians 3:6; James 2:23 for more meditation), certainly he who gives alms according to God's precept believes in God, and he who has the truth of faith maintains the fear of God. Moreover, he who maintains the fear of God considers God in showing mercy to the poor. He labors thus because he believes; he knows that what is foretold by God's word is true, that unfruitful trees, that is, unproductive men, are cut off and cast into the fire, but that the merciful are called into the Kingdom. He also, in another place, calls laboring and fruitful men faithful; but He denies faith to unfruitful and barren ones, saying, 'If you have not been faithful in the unrighteous mammon, who will commit to you that which is true? And if you have not been faithful in that which is another man's, who shall give you that which is your own?'" (Luke 16:11-12).

"If you fear that your inheritance might be exhausted by your liberal dealing, and you may be reduced to poverty, be of good courage in this respect; that cannot be exhausted where the service of Christ is supplied, where the heavenly work is celebrated. I don't speak for this on my own authority; but I promise it on the faith of the Holy Scriptures, and on the authority of the divine promise. The Holy Spirit speaks by Solomon, 'He that gives to the poor shall never lack, but he that turns away his eye shall be in great poverty' (Proverbs 28:27), showing that the merciful and those who do good works cannot lack, but rather that the sparing and barren come to be needy. Moreover, the blessed Paul says: 'He that supplies seed to the sower, shall both supply bread for your food, and shall multiply your seed sown, and shall increase the growth of the fruits of your righteousness, that in all things you may be enriched' (2 Corinthians 9:10 - 11).

And again, 'The administration of this service shall not only supply the needs of the saints, but shall be abundant also by many thanksgivings to God' (2 Corinthians 9:12). While thanks are directed to God for our almsgivings and labors by the prayer of the poor, the wealth of the doer is increased by the retribution of God. And the Lord in the Gospel, already considering the hearts of men of this kind, and with foreseeing voice denouncing faithless and unbelieving men, bears witness, and says, 'Take no thought, saying, what shall we eat? What shall we drink? How shall we be clothed? For these things the Gentiles seek. And your Father knows that you have need of all these things. Seek first the kingdom of God, and His righteousness; and all these things shall be added to you' (Matthew 6:31-33). All these things shall be added and given to them who seek the kingdom and righteousness of God. For the Lord says, that when the Day of Judgment shall come, those who have labored in His Church are admitted to receive the kingdom."

"If you are afraid that your estate should fail if you begin to donate liberally from it, there is another thing to fear. While you fear for your family property, life itself, and salvation are failing. While you are anxious about your wealth being diminished, you do not see that you yourself are being diminished, in that you are a lover of mammon more than of your own soul. You fear, for the sake of yourself, that you should lose your inheritance, you yourself are perishing for the sake of your inheritance. Therefore, the apostle well exclaims, 'We brought nothing into this world, neither can we carry anything out. Therefore, having food and clothing, let us be content. For they who will be rich fall into temptation and a snare, and into many and hurtful desires, which drown a man in perdition and in destruction. *For covetousness is a root of all evils*, which some desiring, have made shipwreck from the faith, and pierced themselves through with many sorrows'" (1 Timothy 6:7-10).

"When has it ever happened, that resources have failed the righteous man, since it is written, 'The Lord will not slay with famine the righteous soul?' (Proverbs 10:3) Ravens fed Elijah in the desert (III Kings or 1 Kings 17:4-6); and a meal from heaven was made ready for Daniel in the den (Brenton, 1990 p 138; Bel and the Dragon 1: 30-39), when shut up by the king's command for a prey to the lions (Daniel 6:7-27). Are you afraid that food should be lacking to you, laboring and deserving well of the Lord, although He Himself bears witness, for the rebuke of those whose mind is doubtful and faith small? He says, 'Behold the fowls of heaven, that they do not sow, reap, or gather into barns; and your heavenly Father feeds them; are you not of more value than they?' (Matthew 6:26). God feeds the fowls, and daily food is given to the sparrows, and to creatures, which have no sense of things divine there is no lack of drink or food. Do you think that to a Christian, a servant of the

Lord, one given up to good works, that to one that is dear to his Lord, anything will be lacking?"

John Cassian noted (*3rd Conference of Abbot Chaeremon*, II, xiii, 3) that the fruit of our righteousness is not due just to our own efforts, but it has a great deal to do with the mercy of God in many ways. Using the example of a farmer, hard work is necessary, but this is of no avail without the right amount of rain, freedom from insect damage and accidents. Even our good thoughts come from God! We need to humbly follow the mercy of God, and the fruits of our obedience will become apparent with our efforts.

- The farmer cannot ascribe the produce of the crops and the rich fruits to his own exertions. He finds that these are often in vain unless opportune rains and a quiet and calm winter aids them.
- Divine goodness does not grant these rich crops to idle farmers who do not till their fields by frequent plowing; working all night long is of no use to the workers unless the mercy of the Lord prospers it.
- Human pride should never try to put itself on a level with the grace of God, so as to fancy that its own efforts were the cause of Divine bounty, or to boast that a very plentiful crop of fruit was an answer to the merits of its own exertions. Crops sometimes fail either from too much or from too little rain.
- Even when vigor has been granted by the Lord to the oxen, and bodily health and the power to do all the work, and prosperity in undertakings, still a man must pray lest there come to him, as Scripture says, 'a heaven of brass and an earth of iron' (Deuteronomy 28:23).
- Insects can cause devastating results, such as, 'What the chewing locust left, the swarming locust has eaten; what the swarming locust left, the crawling locust has eaten; and what the crawling locust left, the consuming locust has eaten' (Joel 1:4).
- The farmer in his work needs God's help also to avoid accidents, by which the man may be deprived of what he has hoped for and actually loses the abundant fruits, which he has already gathered and stored in the barn.

We infer from this that the initiative of our actions and good thoughts comes from God, who inspires us with a good will to begin with, and supplies us with the opportunity of carrying out what we rightly desire. 'Every good gift and every perfect gift come down from above, from the Father of lights' (James 1:17), who both begins what is good, and continues it and completes it in us. 'But He who gives seed to the sower will both provide bread to eat and will multiply your seed and make the fruits of your righteousness to increase' (2 Corinthians 9:10). But it is for us, humbly to follow day by day the grace of God which is drawing us, or else if we resist with 'a stiff neck' (Exodus 32:9), and 'uncircumcised ears' (Acts 7:51), we shall deserve to hear the words, 'Shall he that falls, not rise again? And he that is turned away, shall he not turn back again? Why have my people turned away with a shameless revolting, and strengthened themselves in their willfulness, and refused to return?'" (Jeremiah 8:4-5).

Helping the Poor with "Unrighteous Mammon:" In commenting on the Parable of the Unjust Steward, Jesus made some statements about serving God versus serving mammon, where mammon generally represents the things of this world and specifically it represents all the resources of money directed to various pleasures (Clement of Alexandria, *Stromata*. VII, 12 pp 502-504). In saying thus, Jesus made a statement about making "friends by unrighteous mammon", which is a difficult statement to understand. The text of what Jesus said is: "So the master commended the unjust steward because he had dealt shrewdly. For the sons of this world are shrewder in their generation than the sons of light. And I say to you, make friends for yourselves by unrighteous mammon, that when it fails, they may receive you into an everlasting home. He who is faithful in *what is least* is faithful also in much; and he who *is unjust in what is least* is unjust also in much. If you have not been faithful with unrighteous mammon, who will commit true riches to your trust? And if you have not been faithful in what is another man's, who will give you what is your own? No servant can serve two masters; for either he will hate the one and love the other, or else he will be loyal to the one and despise the other. You cannot serve God and mammon" (Luke 16:8-13).

Christ explained that whatever is done to one of His disciples, He accepts as if done to Himself (Matthew 25:31-46). He also said, "He that receives you; receives Me; and he that doesn't receive you, rejects Me" (Matthew 10:40, Luke 10:16).

He continues, "Despise not one of these little ones; for their angels always behold the face of My Father in heaven" (Matthew 18:10). And in another place, "Fear not, little flock, for it is your Father's good pleasure to give you the kingdom of heaven" (Luke 12:32). Similarly, also He says that "the least in the kingdom of heaven", that is His own disciple, "is greater than John, the greatest among those born of women" (Matthew 11:11). And again, "He that receives a righteous man or a prophet in the name of a righteous man or a prophet, shall receive their reward; and he that gives to a disciple in the name of a disciple a cup of cold water to drink, shall not lose his reward" (Matthew 10:41- 42). This is the only reward that Christ specifies is not lost.

Clement of Alexandria commented (*Salvation of the Rich Man*, pp 591-605) on these statements by Christ to say that He wants us to seek out those to be kind to with our gifts, since we are, in effect, giving to Him. By delighting in giving to Him, we are exchanging the perishing things of this world, the unrighteous mammon, for eternal life. The poor man that we donate to ends up being a friend of God in that he receives our gifts on behalf of God. This may sound to some like it is perilously close to the selling of indulgences for forgiveness of sins, but actually it is a way of life that is 180 degrees different. The point is in considering the real value of the things of this world as compared to the Kingdom of God.

"Christ shows that by nature all property, which a man possesses in his own power, is not his own. From this unrighteousness it is permitted to work a righteous and saving thing, to refresh someone of those who have an everlasting habitation with the Father. He has not commanded you to wait to be asked, but commands you to seek those who are to be benefited and are worthy disciples of the Savior. Excellent also is Paul's saying, 'The Lord loves a cheerful giver' (2 Corinthians 9:7), who delights in giving, sparing not, sowing so that he may thus reap, without murmuring, disputing, and regret, which is pure benevolence. But better than this is the saying spoken by the Lord in another place, 'Give to everyone that asks you' (Luke 6:30). Truly such is God's delight in giving. And this saying is above all godliness, not to wait to be asked, but to inquire oneself who deserves to receive kindness."

"He appoints such a reward for liberality, an everlasting habitation! One purchases immortality for money; and, by giving the perishing things of the world, receives in exchange for these an eternal mansion in the heavens! Sail to this supermarket, if you are wise, O rich man! If need be, sail around the whole world. Do not spare peril and work, that you may purchase here the heavenly kingdom. Why do transparent stones and emeralds delight you so much, and a house that is fuel for fire, a plaything of time, the sport of the earthquake, or an occasion for a tyrant's outrage? Desire to dwell in the heavens, and to reign with God! This kingdom a man imitating God (Matthew 25:40 – emphasis on "one of the least of these My brethren") will give you. By receiving a little here, a little there, He will make you a dweller with Him. Ask that you may receive this benefit; for Christ (in the poor man) is not commanded to receive, but you to give. The Lord said to make a friend, but a friend proves himself such by long intimacy. It is not faith, love, hope, or the endurance of one day, but 'he that endures to the end shall be saved'" (Matthew 10:22).

"Who is it that is the friend of God and how then does he give these things to us as we donate to the poor? Do you judge who is worthy or who is unworthy to receive your alms? It is possible you may be mistaken in your opinion. It is better to do good to the undeserving for the sake of the deserving, than by guarding against those that are less good, you fail to give to the good. For by sparing some, it is possible for you to neglect some that are loved by God. By offering to all that need, you must find someone of those who have power with God to save. 'Judge not, then, that you be not judged. With what measure you use, it shall be measured back to you; good measure, pressed and shaken, and running over, shall be given to you' (Matthew 7:1-2, Luke 6:37-38). Open your compassion to all who are enrolled as the disciples of God; not looking contemptuously to personal appearance, nor preferring young or old. Do not fret in soul and turn away if one appears penniless, ragged, ugly, or feeble. Within may dwell the hidden Father, and His Son, who died for us and rose with us."

John Chrysostom (*Homilies on Matthew*, V, 8-9) stated that Jesus was definitely speaking of almsgiving when He spoke about "making friends by unrighteousness mammon." The "unrighteous mammon" refers generally to all kinds of ill-gotten gains, and Chrysostom addressed what to do about it once one has ceased his acquisition of the ill-gotten gains. The answer is to spend this "unrighteous mammon" by lending it to God in the form of almsgiving.

"When Christ said, 'Make friends for yourselves,' he did not stop at this only, but He added, 'by unrighteous mammon' (Luke 16:9); that the good work may be your own; for it is nothing else but almsgiving, which He has here signified. For what He said is like this: 'Do you have ill-gotten gains? Spend well! Have you gathered by unrighteousness? Scatter abroad in righteousness'. And yet, what manner of virtue is this, to give out of ill-gotten gains? God, however, being full of love to man, condescends even to this and if we do this, promises us many good things.

However, we are unfeeling, that we don't give even of our unjust gain; plundering without end, if we contribute the smallest part, we think we have fulfilled everything. Have you not heard Paul saying, 'He who sows sparingly, shall also reap sparingly?' (2 Corinthians 9:6). Why then do you spare? If you had to till a rich and deep soil, that was capable of receiving much seed, you would both spend what you had, and would borrow of other men, since withholding investment in such a case would be a loss. But when it is Heaven, which you are to cultivate, which is exposed to no variation of weather, and will surely repay your outlay with abundant increase, you are slow and backward. That is, he imitates God by being "one of the least of these My brethren" You do not consider that it is possible by withholding investment to lose, and by being generous to gain."

"Disperse therefore, that you may not lose; spend, that you may gain. If your treasures are hoarded, you will surely throw them away; entrust them to God, for then no man plunders them. When you do business, you don't know at all how to gain; lend to Him who gives an interest greater than the principal. Lend where there is no envy, accusation, evil design, or fear. Lend to Him who lacks nothing, yet has need for your sake; who feeds all men, yet is hungry, that you may not suffer famine; who is poor, that you may be rich. Lend there, where your return cannot be death, but life instead. For His interest is the herald of a kingdom, while this world's interest speaks of hell; one comes of self-denial, the other of covetousness; one comes of humanity, the other of cruelty."

Note 1: It is worth noting that the Jewish worship in the Temple did not bother the Jewish leaders, only their teaching about Jesus. This suggests that they used a liturgy similar to the OT liturgy and even participated in the on-going Temple liturgy.

Note 2: The Evangelist Mark founded a number of monasteries in Alexandria in the late 40's AD, where the lifestyle of everything in common was patterned after the early Christian community at Pentecost.

Note 3: *Sybaris* was an ancient Greek city in Southern Italy, founded in 720 BC and destroyed in 510 BC. It was famous as a center of luxurious living.

Portions of his chapter are adopted from the church bulleting of St. Athanasius on November 12, 2017.
https://www.stathanasius.org/site/assets/files/5424/study_11_12_17.pdf.
Used with permission.

Epilogue

I hope I have been able to convince the reader that giving is an obligation that all of us as Christians and especially Orthodox have. However, that giving must be with a *cheer* (2 Corin. 9: 6-7) and enthusiasm (Luk. 21: 1-4). As I keep on reading the Holy Scriptures, I am more convinced that perhaps giving is one of the most important spiritual practices a follower of Jesus can claim. I also believe that the attitude we have toward our money and finances directly influences the condition of our relationship with Jesus. How we feel about tithing and sharing our finances can also reflect the level of giving in other areas of our lives.

Generosity is contagious, as it spreads from our money to our time, our talents, our abilities and our presence. Our lack of generosity and the willingness to share is also contagious.

We know as Christians we are taught to share what has been given to us with those who have less. We share our gifts, talents, time, ourselves and, yes, even our financial resources. However, in any discussion about financial generosity, we must have as a starting point the fact that all giving in any form is **the** recognition that everything that we have comes from God. So, if we really love God, then we recognize that love gives and when love blossoms generosity follows – always (John 3:16). Furthermore, 1 John 3: 16-18 and 1 John 2: 5-6 show us the model to follow which is what Christ Himself did.

In addition, the realization and rational of giving may be found in Psalm 23(24):1 ("The earth is the Lord's and the fullness thereof; the world, and all that dwell in it" LXX). James 1:17 (NIV) echoes this truth: "Every good gift, every perfect gift, comes from above. These gifts come down from the Father."

Some time ago I heard a story about giving, especially as it relates to tithing - the practice of giving back to God what really belongs to him anyway. I like to share it. So here it is:

Once upon a time there was a man who had nothing, so God gave him 10 apples. The first three apples were for the man to eat, the second three were to trade for shelter, and the next three were to trade for clothing. The last apple (the 10th), God gave it to him so he might have something to give back to God in gratitude for the other nine.

So, the man did just that, he ate the first three and traded the others for shelter and clothes. Then he looked really hard at the 10th apple, knowing that God wanted him to give it back with a grateful heart. But this last apple seemed so much bigger and juicer than the others, and the man reasoned that God already had all the apples in the world anyway. Why would God need his apple? So, the man ate the 10th apple and gave the core to God.

We should not give because we think God needs our gifts in order to be God, or that the church needs our money to be the church. We give because of our gratitude to Him. We give back to God what is God's so that through our gifts the love of God can become a tangible reality in our world. Our giving is a reminder of the blessings God gives us and gave to us through Jesus Christ. See Acts 20:32–35. Set a generous example; 2 Corinthians 8:12–15, Giving shouldn't be a burden; 2 Corinthians 9:6–8, God doesn't want to coerce generosity; 1 Timothy 6:17–19, Being rich in good works and generosity.

We find in John 3:16 three thoughts that should be the foundation of all our giving. God's motivation for giving was love; he gave himself in the person of Jesus; and God gave in response to our need. As we use this example for the basis of our giving, we realize that the only giving God recognizes is giving wrapped in love. In 1 Corinthians 13:3, Paul writes, "If I give all I possess to the poor and surrender my body to the flames, but have not love, I gain nothing" (NIV).

The story that Luke tells us in Chapter 21 reflects Jesus' teachings about our giving as his disciples. The widow gave two coins worth a penny, but her gift came from her heart. Jesus saw the rich people throwing their pocket change into the offering plate. Jesus commented that the poor widow had outgiven them all.

Jesus defines giving not by the size of our gifts, but by the condition of the heart from which it is given. For Jesus and for us, motivation is everything when it comes to giving. A disciple of Jesus will give because of his/her gratitude for God's gifts so freely given.

So, in closing let us again be reminded of the words that we recite during every liturgy in our worship: "We offer to You these gifts from Your own gifts in all and for all – Τα σα εκ των σων σοι προσφερομεν κατά παντα και δια παντα."

GLORY BE TO GOD

References

Ambrose of Milan. (1994). NPNF2. Vol. 10. *Duties of the Clergy*, I, xi, 36-39. Pp. 7.

Ambrose of Milan. (1994). NPNF2. Vol. 10. *Two Books Concerning Repentance*, I, xi, 50-52. Pp. 337-338.

Augustine. (1999). NPNF1. Vol 8. *Exposition on the Psalms: Psalm 35 # 7, 9,16,17. Pp. 80 -85; Psalm 43 # 7 p. 140; Ps. 49 # 9 p.171; Ps. 56 # 17. P. 224; Ps. 126 # 8. P.605; Ps. 147 # 13. P. 668.*

Basil. (1994). "Basil: Letters and Select Works." Letter CCXXXVL. Trans. Blomfield Jackson. *Nicene and Post-Nicene Fathers*. Library of Christian Classics. Hendrickson Publishers. pp 178-79).

Basil the Great. (2009). *On social justice*. Trans. P. Schroeder. Crestwood/Yonkers, NY. SVS Press.

Basil the Great. PG 31, 277A, in St. Basil's homily "On the saying of the Gospel According to Luke.

Basil the Great. (October 25, 2008). *Sermon to the rich*. https://bekkos.wordpress.com/st-basils-sermon-to-the-rich/.

Basil the Great. "Sermon on the rich." J.-P. Migne's *Patrologia Graeca*, vol. 31, cols. 277C-304C.

Basil the Great. (December 5, 2018). *honor and wealth*. http://honorshame.com/honor-and-wealth-9-quotes-from-st-basil/.

Baumer, J. and J. Cortines. (2016). *God and Money*. Peabody, MA. Rose Publishing.

Bingham, J. (1855). *The Works of Joseph Bingham. Vol 2*. ed. R. Bingham, 10 vols. Oxford: Oxford University Press. 179–82.

Blue, R. (1997). *Generous leaving: Finding Contentment Through Giving*. Grand Rapids, MI. Zondervan Publishers.

Boyd, Fr. G. (2019). "Melchizedek." https://www.stbasil.com/news/2019/5/22/the -old-testament-melchizedek-showing-us-jesus. Retrieved on September 11, 2020.

Bradley, J. (July 18, 2018). Church Giving Statistics, 2019 Edition. https://pushpay.com/blog/church-giving-statistics/. Retrieved on September 14, 2020.

Brenton, L. C. L. (1990). *The Septuagint with Apocrypha*. Hendrickson Publishers. Peabody MA. 1961, 1990, p. 138. Bel and the Dragon 1:30-39.

Cassian, J. (1994). NPNF2. Vol. 11. *3rd Conference of Abbot Chaeremon*, Ch. 13. Pp. 430.

Chrysostom, Saint John. (1984). *On Wealth and Poverty* [trans. C. P. Roth]. Crestwood, NY: St. Vladimir's Seminary Press.

Chrysostom, J. *Homily IV: Homilies on Ephesians* (*NPNF*1 13:69). For some incidental references to tithing see Chrysostom, *Homilies on Genesis* 35, 54 (cited by Murray, *Beyond Tithing*, 112, n. 28) and Chrysostom, *Homilies on Hebrews* 12 (NPNF1 14:423–26). Chrysostom, *The Gospel of Matthew* 64.4 (*NPNF*1 10:395–96).

Chrysostom, Saint John. (1999 p 69). "4th Homily on Ephesians." In Trans. P. Schaff. (Ed.). *Chrysostom: Homilies on Galatians, Ephesians, Philippians, Colossians, Thessalonians, Timothy, Titus, and Philemon. Nicene and Post-Nicene Fathers.* First Series. Volume 13. Peabody, Mass. Hendrickson Publishers.

Chrysostom, J. (1999). NPNF1. Vol. 11. *Commentary on Acts*, VII, v. 46-47. Pp. 45-46 pay attention to the footnote on p. 46 indicated with an (*).

Chrysostom, J. (1999). NPNF1. Vol. 13. *Homilies on 1 Timothy*, XIV, vv. 9-10. Pp. 454-458.

Chrysostom, J. (1999). NPNF1. Vol. 12. pp 369. *Homilies on 2 Corinthians*, XIX, v. 7.

Chrysostom, J. (1999). NPNF1. Vol. 12 pp 369.*Homilies on 2 Corinthians*, XIX, v. 8.

Chrysostom, J. (1999). NPNF1. Vol. 12. pp 369-371. *Homilies on 2 Corinthians*, XIX, v. 9.

Chrysostom, J. (1999). Nicene and Post-Nicene Fathers. (NPNF1). Editor, P. Schaff. Vol. 12. 1st Series. "Chrysostom: Homilies on the Epistles of Paul to the Corinthians." Peabody, MA. Hendrickson Publishers, Inc.

Chrysostom, J. (1999). NPNF1. Vol. 14. *Homilies on Hebrews*, X, 7-8. Pp. 416-417.

Chrysostom, J. (1999). NPNF1. Vol. 10. *Homilies on Matthew*. V, 8-9. Pp. 35-36.

Chrysostom, J. (1999). NPNF1. Vol. 13. *Homilies on Philippians*. I, v. 7. Pp 186-187.

Chrysostom, J. (1999). NPNF1. Vol. 11. *Homilies on Romans*, XXIII, vv. 9-10. Pp. 514-516.

Chrysostom, J. (1999). NPNF1. Vol. 13. *Homily IV: Homilies on Ephesians*. 13:69. For some incidental references to tithing see Chrysostom, *Homilies on Genesis* 35, 54 (cited by Murray, *Beyond Tithing*, 112, n. 28) and Chrysostom, *Homilies* on Hebrews 12 (NPNF1 14:423–26). Chrysostom, *The Gospel of Matthew* 64.4 (*NPNF1* 10:395–96).

Clement of Alexandria. (1994). *Salvation of the Rich Man.* ANF. Vol. 2. 27-30.

Clement of Alexandria, *Salvation of the Rich Man*. ANF. Vol 2. pp 31-33.

Clement of Alexandria. (1994). *Sromata*. ANF. Vol 2. Ch. 9-10, pp 356-358. http://www.biblical.ie/page.php?fl=Patristic/Clement_Alex.

Clement of Alexandria. Ante-Nicene Fathers. (ANF). (1994). Fathers of the 2nd century: Hermas, Tatian, Athenagoras, Theophilus and Clement of Alexandria (entire). Vol. 2. Edited by A. Roberts and J. Donaldson. Peabody, MA. Hendrickson Publishers, Inc.

Clement of Alexandria. (1994). *Stromata*, ANF. Vol 2. Ch. 7-12. Pp. 354-360.

Clement of Alexandria. (1994). *The Instructor*. ANF. Vol 2. Ch. III, and VII. Pp. 275-281. Clement has added a few of the expressions from Luke 10:25-28.

Clement of Alexandria. (1994). *The Instructor*, VII. Pp 280-281. In ANF: Fathers of the 2nd century. Volume 2. American Edition. Trans. A. C. Coxe. Peabody, MA. Hendrickson, Publishers.

Clement of Alexandria. (1994). *The Stromata.* XV-XVI. Pp 361-363. In ANF: Fathers of the 2nd century. Volume 2. American Edition. Trans. A. C. Coxe. Peabody, MA. Hendrickson, Publishers.

Coleman, L. (1852). *Ancient Christianity Exemplified in the Private, Domestic, Social, and Civil Life of the Primitive Christians, and in the Original Institutions, Offices, Ordinances, and Rites of the Church*. Philadelphia, PA. Lippincott, Grambo & Company. P. 229.

Cyprian of Carthage. (1994). ANF. Vol. 5. *Treatises*, VIII, 8-11. Pp. 478-479.

Cyril of Alexandria. (1983). *Commentary on the Gospel of Luke, Homily 68*, Studion Publishers. pp 287-290,

Cyril of Alexandria. (2019). *The Church Fathers: Glaphyra on the Pentateuch. Exodus through Deuteronomy*. Vol 2. Trans. By N. Lunn. Washington, D. C. The Catholic University of America Press (CUP). Pp. 112,128-129, 217-218.

Edersheim, A. (1995). *Sketches of Jewish Social Life*. Peabody, MA. Hendrickson Publishers. *Sketches of Jewish Social Life.*, p. 245, 101-104.

Flavius Josephus. (1960). Josephus: *Complete works: Antiquities of the Jews*, Bk. IV, Ch. viii, item 22. Grand Rapids, MI. Kregel Publications. Pg. 98. (Pay extra attention to the second footnote indicated with the cross (+) symbol).

Florovsky, G. (1948). "The Church: Her Nature and Task" appeared in volume 1 of the *Universal Church in God's Design*. S.C.M. Press.

Gonzales, J. (1990). *Faith and Wealth*. San Francisco: Harper. P 219.

Gower, R. (2005). *New Manners and Customs of Bible Times*. Chicago, IL. Moody Publishers. p. 79.

Gregory the Great. (2007). *The Book of Pastoral Rule*, II, 6. Tran. G. Demacopoulos. Crestwood/Yonkers, NY. SVS Press.

Gregory the Great. (2007). *The Book of Pastoral Rule*, III, 20. Tran. G. Demacopoulos. Crestwood/Yonkers, NY. SVS Press.

Hermas. Ante-Nicene Fathers. (ANF). (1994). Fathers of the 2nd century: Hermas, Tatian, Athenagoras, Theophilus and Clement of Alexandria (entire). Vol. 2. Edited by A. Roberts and J. Donaldson. Peabody, MA. Hendrickson Publishers, Inc.

Hilary, of Pottiers. (2012). The Fathers of the Church: *Commentary on Matthew* 23. Washington, D.C. The Catholic University of America Press (CUP). Pp. 234-239. (Also, cited by Powers, "Historical Study of the Tithe," 42; Lansdell, *Sacred Tenth*, 192–93). See also: http://orthochristian.com/78020.html.

Irenaeus of Lyon. (1994). ANF. Vol. 1. *Against Heresies*, IV, xii, 5. Pp. 431-432. [Ch 18. "Concerning sacrifices and oblations and those who truly offer them. And for this reason they (the Jews) had indeed the tithes of their goods consecrated to Him, but those who have received liberty set aside all their possessions for the Lord's purposes, bestowing joyfully and freely not the less valuable portions of their property, since they have the hope of better things [hereafter]; as that poor widow acted who cast all her living into the treasury of God"].

Irenaeus of Lyon. (1994). ANF. Vol 1. *Against Heresies*, III, xvii, 3. P. 445

Jerome. (1994). NPNF2. Vol 6. *Letter to Nepotian* 1:91. Trans. W. H. Fremantle. (LII)." Peabody, MA. Hendrickson Publishers, Inc. pp. 89-96. Jerome also commends Christians to tithe in his *Commentary on Matthew* 2.22 (cited by Murray, *Beyond Tithing*, 117). Also, see CUP vol 117. Pp 258.

Justin Martyr. (1994). The First Apology of Justin. ANF. Vol. 1. Ch. 14. P. 167.

Kern, M. (2005). The Life of the Evangelist Mark. St Athanasius Press, The Evangelist Mark founded a number of monasteries in Alexandria in the late 40's AD, where the lifestyle of everything in common was patterned after the early Christian community at Pentecost.

Kern, M. (November, 12. 2017). "Tithes, Festivals and Alms. The Good Samaritan." https://www.stathanasius.org/site/assets/files/5424/study_11_12_17.pdf. Retrieved on September 19, 20.

Lansdell, H. (2012). *The Sacred Tenth: Or Studies in Tithe-Giving, Ancient and Modern.* London, UK. Forgotten Books. P. 187.

Lightfoot, J and J. Harmer. Ed. M. Holmes. (1992). The Apostolic Fathers. 2nd ed. Grand Rapids, MI, Baker Book House. The specific references are: *First Clement.* The letter of the Romans to Corinthians. Pp. 33, 41, 43, 47, 57 (the analogy of the Phoenix bird, 71, 73, 79, 87, 93. An Ancient Christian Sermon. (*2 Clement*). Pp 115. The letter of Polycarp to the Philippians. Pp 209-210, 213, 215. The Epistle of Barnabas. P 277. The Shepherd of Hermas. Mandate 2-3, pp 377-378; 8, p 397; 10-11, pp 403-407. Parable 2: p 423; Parable 6, pp 448-449.

Longenecker, B.W. (2010). *Remember the poor: Paul, poverty and the Greco-Roman world,* Eerdmans, Grand Rapids, MI and Cambridge, UK.

Maslow, A. (1943). "A theory of human motivation". *Psychological Review.* **50** (4): 370–96.

Matusiak, Fr. J. (March 4, 2007). "Tithing." *Weekly Bulletin.* St. Peter and Paul. Orthodox Church. Manville, NJ.

Nicola, R. (October 2005). "Changing Our Patterns of Giving: Exploring the Virtues and Wisdom of Tithing." *The Word.*

Nicola, R. (October, 2003). "Money and the Church." *The Word.*

Nicola, R. (February, 2004). "Our patterns of giving." *The Word.*

Nikodimos of the Holy Mountain. (1995). *The Philokalia.* Vol 4. Trans. G. E. H. Palmer, P. Sherrard and K. Ware. London, UK. Faber and Faber Limited. P 163.

Panagiotou, J. "Orthodox Christian stewardship: what do" Chrysostom: Jesus, the bible, and the church fathers say about tithing and giving to god?" https://www.aoiusa.org/orthodox-christian-stewardship-what-do-jesus-the-bible-and-the-church-fathers-say-about-tithing-and-giving-to-god/. Retrieved on 10/30/20.

Powers, T. (1948) *An Historical Study of the Tithe in the Christian Church to 1648*. Southern Baptist Theological Seminary.

Schaff, P. (1999). Nicene and Post-Nicene Fathers. Vol. 12. 1st Series. "Chrysostom: Homilies on the Epistles of Paul to the Corinthians." Peabody, MA. Hendrickson Publishers, Inc.

Stithatos, N. (1995). "On the inner nature of things and on the Purification of the intellect: one hundred texts." In *Philokalia*. Vol.4. Trans. G. E. H. Palmer, P. Sherrard and K. Ware. London, UK. Faber and Faber Limited.

Tertullian. (1994). ANF. I, II, III. Vol 3. The Apology. Edited by C. Coxe. Peabody, MA. Hendrickson Publishers, Inc.

Tertullian. (1994). ANF. I, II, III. Vol 3. An Answer to the Jews. Edited by C. Coxe. Peabody, MA. Hendrickson Publishers, Inc.

Vaporis, Fr. N. (1977). *An Orthodox Prayer Book – Μικρον Ευχολογιον*. Brookline, MA. Holy Cross Orthodox Press.

Wisnewski, J. (August 20, 2020). "Short guide to understand first fruits offering" in https://get.tithe.ly/blog/first-fruit.

Weiss, G. (1972) *Insight into Bible Times and Customs, Good News*. Lincoln NE. Broadcasting Association,

Wittgenstein, L. (1958). Philosophical Investigations. #43. Trans. G.E.M. Anscombe. Basil Blackwell. http://gormendizer.co.za/wp-content/uploads/2010/06/Ludwig.Wittgenstein.- Retrieved on August 30, 2020.

Zell, Fr. Thomas, Fall 2005). "The Trail of the Tithe." AGAIN MAGAZINE.

Zuckerman, A. (May 29, 2020). "39 Employee Theft Statistics: 2019/2020 Impact & Costs To Business." https://comparecamp.com/employee-theft-statistics/#:~:text=3%20out%20of%204%20employees,average%20loss%20of%20%245.4%20million. Retrieved on August 27, 2020.

Selected Bibliography

Bingham, J. (1855). *The Works of Joseph Bingham*, ed. R. Bingham, 10 vols. Oxford: Oxford University Press. V. 2:179–82.

Coleman, L. (1852). *Ancient Christianity Exemplified in the Private, Domestic, Social, and Civil Life of the Primitive Christians, and in the Original Institutions, Offices, Ordinances, and Rites of the Church.* Philadelphia: Lippincott, Grambo & Company. P 229. 229.

Cozby, D. (ND). *Tithes and Firstfruits.* https://www.dneoca.org/articles/tithesandfirstfruits0397.html.

Donougher, C. (2013). *Les Misérables.* NY. Penguin Classics. A new translation of the full work, with a detailed biographical sketch of Victor Hugo's life, a chronology, and notes.

Edersheim, A. (1995). *Sketches of Jewish Social Life.* Peabody MA. Hendrickson Publishers. pp. 36-37.

Kendall, R. (1983). *Tithing: A Call to Serious Biblical Giving.* Grand Rapids, MI. Zondervan,

Sharp, J. (2017). *The Naked Truth about Tithing and Giving to the Church.* Vol 1. CreateSpace Independent Publishing Platform

Westerberg, M.L. (ND). *The challenge of tithing.* https://www.dneoca.org/articles/tithingchallenge0493.html.

About the author

D. H. Stamatis, Ph.D. is a lifelong member of the Orthodox Church. He has taught Catechetical School for 14 years (Fifth grade to adults); was appointed to the educational committee in the Diocese of Detroit by the late Bishop Timothy for eight years; has represented his Parish (St. George, Lincoln Park in the Clergy Laity congress two different times; was elected to the Parish Council for eight years (St. George, Lincoln Park and later Southgate, MI); and he has been the Protopsaltis of the Detroit Metropolis at the Annunciation Cathedral, Detroit MI since 1996.

His formal education is in Engineering, St.atist.ics, Reliability and Management. He has taught at several universities in USA, Europe and China in both graduate and undergraduate levels. He has a diploma (Ptichio) in chanting Byzantine Music (Ιεροψαλτου) and a diploma of teaching Byzantine Music (Μουσικοδιδάσκαλου) from the Glyfada Conservatory of Music.

He has published 65 books in his academic field and 13 dealing with Orthodox issues. This work is the result of his love for Orthodoxy and its traditional practices. He believes that the church in which he was baptized and brought up *is* in truth *the Church, i.e., the true Church* and the *only* true Church that can really provide an effective and efficient road to salvation. He believes this for many reasons: by personal conviction and by the inner testimony of the Spirit which breathes in the mysteries (sacraments) of the Church and by all that he has learned from Scripture and from the universal Tradition of the Church through the Fathers of the Church. He is therefore compelled to regard all other Christian churches as deficient, and in many cases, he can identify these deficiencies accurately enough. Therefore, for him, Christian reunion is simply universal conversion to Orthodoxy. He has no confessional loyalty; his loyalty solely belongs to the *Una Sancta – Orthodoxy!*

Books by the same author

A Catechetical Handbook of the Eastern Orthodox Church. (2003). Light and Life Publishing.
Tradition: Practical Orthodoxy. Vol. 1-3. (2008). Institute of Advanced Business Learning Systems.
The Triumphant Church: A daily synaxarion of the Eastern Orthodox Church. (2009). Vol. 1. Orthodox Research Institute.
The Triumphant Church: Selected golden nuggets from the saints of the Orthodox Church. (2009). Vol 2. Orthodox Research Institute.
The Triumphant Church: Eastern Orthodox Iconography. (2009); Vol 3. Orthodox Research Institute.
An Introduction to the Eastern Orthodox Teleturgics. (2017). Bookstand Publishing.
Rediscovering Orthodoxy in the middle of heretics and ecumenists. (2018). FL. Xulon.
OXI στον Οικουμενισμο (No to Ecumenism). (2018). Athens, Greece. In Greek.
Why I am an Eastern Orthodox Christian. (2019). Bookstand Publishing.
Understanding the WAY to Salvation through Orthodoxy. (2020). Archangels Books, Publishing.
Revival in Orthodoxy. (2020). Archangels Books, Publishing.
Αναζητώντας τους ταγούς και τους καλούς ποιμενες - Looking for Good Religious and Political Leaders. (2020). Bookstand Publishing. (In Greek).

The Widow's Mite

As Orthodox Christians, the Bible is clear throughout its pages that we're called to give generously. In the *OT* Exodus chapter 35 we see the Israelites all generously giving the materials and time to build the tabernacle. If any of those people decided to withhold the materials they owned or the skills they had, the tabernacle wouldn't have come together. Furthermore, in Malachi 3:10-12, giving is the one thing God tells us to test him in.

On the other hand, in the *NT* God himself gave His only Son (John 3:16) because he loves us so much, and that Son died on a cross for us. It sets a model that generosity in God's people should be private and sacrificial. The Widow's Mite is an example of a giving behavior that is generous, cheerful and without expectations. Let us all imitate her!

CPSIA information can be obtained
at www.ICGtesting.com
Printed in the USA
LVHW010158030221
678101LV00010B/154